Reproducing Reproduction

Reproducing Reproduction

Kinship, Power, and
Technological Innovation

EDITED BY
Sarah Franklin and Helena Ragoné

PENN

University of Pennsylvania Press

Philadelphia

10 9 8 7 6 5 4 3 2 1

Published by
University of Pennsylvania Press
Philadelphia, Pennsylvania 19104-4011

Library of Congress Cataloging-in-Publication Data
Reproducing reproduction : kinship, power, and technological innovation /
edited by Sarah Franklin and Helena Ragoné.
    p.   cm.
   Includes bibliographical references and index.
   ISBN 0-8122-3352-2 (cloth : alk. paper). — ISBN 0-8122-1584-2 (pbk. : alk. paper)
1. Human reproduction—Social aspects. 2. Human reproductive technology—Social
aspects. 3. Kinship. I. Franklin, Sarah, 1960– . II. Ragoné, Helene.
GN482.1.R46 1997
306.4′61—dc21   97-36945
                                                                      CIP

Contents

Introduction

Although the analysis of reproduction was central to the origins of anthropology, it has only recently begun to reemerge as an important theoretical focus.[1] The reasons for this historical centrality and later exclusion are significant, as are those informing the recent surge of interest in such classical anthropological topics as kinship, parenthood, procreation, conception, genealogy, and consanguinity. We begin by reviewing both the importance of reproductive models to late-nineteenth- and early-twentieth-century anthropology and the narrowness of these foundational models. We then consider some of the major influences that have brought about a transformation in the way reproduction is studied by anthropologists. In the third section, we introduce the aims of *Reproducing Reproduction* along with the contributions to this anthology.

Anthropology and the "Facts of Life"

Anthropology was founded amidst what has been described by some as an "obsessive" interest in matters of kinship, procreation, and succession (Coward 1983). Nineteenth-century accounts of social organization offered by Bachofen (1861), McLennan (1865), and Westermarck (1891) centrally concerned knowledge of and beliefs about procreation, kinship, and conception, or what are colloquially described as "the facts of life." Specifically, accurate knowledge of physical paternity was seen by early anthropologists, and by nineteenth-century theorists such as Engels (1884), Morgan (1871), and Maine (1861), as an index of stages of social development towards civilization. Frazer (1910), Rivers (1910), Van Gennep (1906), and later Malinowski (1913) positioned reproductive arrangements centrally in their accounts of social structure, displaying considerable curiosity towards conception models and procreative knowledge. Even late in his career, Malinowski insisted that the question of physical paternity was no less than "the most exciting and controversial issue in the comparative science of man" (1937: xxiii). The infamous "virgin birth" debates that swept through anthropology midcentury similarly positioned detailed knowledge of the precise mechanisms of procreation and conception as central to questions of knowledge and belief, primitivism and modernity, and religion and cosmology, as well as issues of theory and method (Leach 1967; Spiro 1968). In sum, an important genealogy of modern anthropology can readily be traced through its relationship to a core set of ideas related to reproduction, or "the facts of life."

Of course, any such genealogy is both reductive and instrumental. For our purposes here, it is offered by means of illustrating an important paradox within the history of anthropological theory concerning reproduction. For, although anthropology is in some respects quite unusual among the modern human sciences in its "obsessive" attention to the details of human reproductive knowledge in cross-cultural perspective (so that entire volumes were devoted, for example, to accounts of *The Father in Primitive Society* [Malinowski 1927] or *Coming into Being Among the Australian Aborigines* [Montagu 1937]), this interest was remarkably narrowly cast. Reproduced within the better part of the modern anthropological corpus of knowledge concerning reproduction were familiar forms of androcentrism, ethnocentrism, and biological determinism that greatly limited the ways in which reproduction could be analysed or studied.[2] In particular, the nearly exclusive anthropological focus for over a century, from the mid-1800s to the late twentieth century, on *knowledge of physical paternity* indexed the limitations curtailing analysis of "reproduction." Paradoxically, then, despite its detailed interest and global reach in matters of reproduction, anthropology managed determinedly to preserve and reproduce "physical paternity" as its overriding focus and concern.

Several factors ensured the reproduction of this tunnel vision for over a century within not only anthropology, but much Anglophone and European social theory more generally. Primary among these are the relegation of "reproduction" to a domain of "natural" or biological facts that were (and often continue to be) considered prior to, and separate from, sociality. Compounding this reductivist tendency was the perception of reproduction as a private, domestic activity associated with femininity, maternity, and women, which therefore rendered it of limited importance to anthropological theory. Together, the naturalization, domestication, and feminization of reproduction ensured that it would remain undertheorized within the major paradigms of modern social theory. As Rayna Rapp has suggested, "perhaps because it was considered a 'woman's subject,' reproduction long remained on the margins of anthropological theory" (1994: 1). Supporting the reproduction of this gender bias have been taken-for-granted assumptions about the sexual division of labor, sexual difference, and the reproductive *telos* necessary to ensure human survival (i.e., Darwinism) that continue to operate as central but unexamined premises in many contemporary models of culture and society. In sum, reproduction could be described as invisibly central (along Darwinian, patriarchal, and biologically determinist lines), while remaining visibly marginalized (for example, in terms of childbirth practices) within anthropology.

Redefining Reproduction

Several developments in recent years have contributed to the contemporary reemergence of an anthropology of reproduction. With the rise of feminist anthropology in the 1970s came a wholesale reevaluation of the exclusion of women's activities from the ethnographic record and a critical interrogation of the social models responsible for this exclusion. Studies such as Annette Weiner's influential *Women of Value, Men of Renown* (1976), in which she critiqued Malinowski's neglect of women's exchange networks, to which reproductive models were central, opened up new possibilities for appreciating the embeddedness of procreative imagery in the maintenance and renewal of cultural identity and tradition. Such studies contributed to an important critique not only of the exclusion of women and "feminine" activities from the ethnographic record, but also of the enduring structuralist and structural-functionalist dichotomies of nature-culture, jural-domestic, and public-private, all of which had significant constraining effects on the theorization of gender and kinship as well as reproduction. By the early 1980s, feminist scholars had established a significant challenge to many of the reductive biologistic assumptions structuring much social scientific study. Both physical and cultural anthropology were seen to rely on a false dichotomization of social and natural facts through which, as Weiner described it, reproduction was reduced to "mere biology" while culture was defined as "everything else" (1978).

Nonetheless, assumptions about the biological basis of reproduction have proven difficult to displace. Despite more than two decades of ongoing and determined critical intervention, biologistic assumptions about reproduction that position it as a universal, timeless, essential, and ahistorical component of human existence remain ubiquitous within anthropology, as they do within the larger culture of which it is part. As Rayna Rapp has noted, "dragging reproduction to the center of social analysis is a relatively recent project for anthropologists" (1994:2). Part of this project involves widening the concept of "reproduction," as has been possible through analysis of new reproductive and genetic technologies (Helmreich 1995 and in this volume; Rabinow 1996; Strathern 1992, and Hayden in this volume). Through such studies, "reproduction" in its procreative sense is linked to informatics (artificial life), biowealth, and techniques of power-knowledge (e.g., polymerase chain reaction). Consequently, "the politics of reproduction" comprises a broad field linking human procreative activity to issues such as intellectual property, environmental activism, and genetic engineering.

"Every Technology Is a Reproductive Technology" (Sofia)

In their important review article on "The Politics of Reproduction" (1991) and their introduction to the subsequent anthology charting the global reach of this subject area (1995b), Faye Ginsburg and Rayna Rapp describe several trajectories of study through which reproduction has come to be seen as a potent site of political contestation and resistance. The control of reproduction through population policy, global planning, and international development initiatives has been the subject of numerous feminist studies. Similarly, the medicalization of reproduction and the emergence of new reproductive technologies have also attracted increasing scholarly attention. The ethnography of birth, childrearing, and the management of both fertility and infertility through indigenous systems of knowledge has developed into a significant trajectory of anthropological research, largely due to the pioneering work of Brigitte Jordan. Finally, the meanings of reproduction over the course of the life cycle, in relation to gender and kinship definitions and as resources in social movements, have also been chronicled and documented. From all these perspectives, Rapp and Ginsburg argue, reproduction can be seen both as a critical site of local/global interface and as an important site of social stratification.

This volume takes its cue both from the "local-global lens" proposed by Ginsburg and Rapp and from other recent studies arguing for a renewed appreciation of reproduction in social theory (Davis-Floyd and Sargent 1997; Davis-Floyd and Dumit 1997). Though our aim can be most broadly described as contributing to the effort to make reproduction more visibly central to contemporary anthropology, we have organized this volume to emphasize two specific strategies related to this end. The first strategy is to foreground the defamiliarizing impact of new technologies, through which many of the most deeply taken-for-granted assumptions about the "naturalness" of reproduction are displaced. By this we are referring to the many widely publicized dilemmas occasioning the rapid developments in the fields of assisted reproduction and biotechnology. Observing high-profile controversies about, for example, orphaned frozen embryos, transgenic organisms, the human genome project, or artificial life forms, it becomes more difficult to argue that reproductive acts are private, personal, domestic, and "merely biological" phenomena that have little to do with the more important business of politics, science, commerce, or the law. Quite the reverse— recent reproductive controversies span the gamut of social institutions; comprise global property debates; confound expert jurists, theologians, and ethicists; and challenge the very idea of a "natural fact."

The defamiliarizing perspective provided by technology, however, can be both superficial and dizzying. It is for this reason we have also foregrounded an ethnographic focus, which seeks to situate changing cultural definitions of reproduction in the context of their lived articulation. This traditional form of anthropological empiricism works to ground what can otherwise become overly speculative, abstract, and decontextualized accounts of the "impact" of new technology. Technology is not an agent of social change; people are. Yet the forms of instrumentalism made available through new technology are not insignificant— they shape possibilities and they comprise powerful materializations of human desire and capability. Hence, the contributions to *Reproducing Reproduction* define technology very broadly, while attempting to specify what is meant by its "cultural implications" as precisely as possible. Using technology as a defamiliarizing lens, but wary of the tendency to inflate its determinism or to become enthralled by its dazzling promises, this collection offers a series of studies that seek empirically to ground accounts of reproductive techniques *as cultural practice* within carefully specified interpretive frames.

By acknowledging the importance of culturally grounded accounts, we do not wish to contribute to an overvaluation of ethnographic representation as a uniquely privileged form of anthropological analysis. Following Marcus's elegant discussions in his account of "Ethnography in/of the World System" (1995), we seek *both* to emphasize the cultural specificity of meanings, practices, and techniques as part of lived, contested, and negotiated relations, *and* to transcend the limitations imposed by such a view—for example, its tendencies to overvalorize resistance, "experience," and the "authentic voices" of selected Others. In the context of in vitro fertilization, transnational adoption, surrogacy, and prenatal screening, it is essential to recognize not only the local, regional, or national dimensions that impinge upon a particular case study or field setting, but increasingly *also* to appreciate the international and global formations that exercise a distinctive and distinctively *cultural* influence. As Marcus notes, much as there is reason to defend the time-honored ethnographic practice of situating meanings within whole ways of life in which people resist, accommodate, and alter the messages and mechanisms they encounter, there is also a need to begin to retool ethnographic representation in such a manner that it can better attend to the character of those meanings, messages, and mechanisms *in their own right.*

Invitations such as those encouraged by Marcus, for anthropology to begin to develop approaches to forms of culture that are not necessarily bounded, locatable, or reducible to the means of their consumption or production, pose important methodological challenges to which this volume seeks to respond. Some of the tools with which to begin expanding traditional anthropological means of ethnographic representation can be drawn from cultural studies, and this interface is a lively, if contested, border within contemporary research on culture. Ginsburg and Rapp (1995b), for example, express what has become a frequently encountered criticism of cultural studies (often synonymous with textual, semiotic, postmodern, or poststructuralist) accounts of representations when they warn that:

> *Time* magazine . . . regularly publishes cover stories on everything from new infertility treatments to the search for *in utero* methods of screening for genetic diseases. . . . [T]hose using [cultural studies] methods might view *Time* magazine as an unproblematical stage for the display of scientific hegemony. From an anthropological perspective, this kind of analysis relies on outdated Durkheimian models in which the image and its interpretation are isomorphic. (1995b: 6)

This criticism is often summarized as the "culture-as-text" approach, referring to the increasing influence of textually based models within social science (see Rabinow and Sullivan 1979a, b). In addition to decontextualizing meanings, culture-as-text approaches raise concerns that representations will be read in an overly deterministic manner, described as "textual determinism." Ginsburg and Rapp, for example, refer to this slippage between textual structures and of social relations as "Durkheimian"—suggesting a rigid, anachronistic model of social action. Such a model could as well be described as "Parsonian" in its evocation of a set of norms, rules, or ideals that can be studied in their own right. David Schneider's study of American kinship as a *cultural system* (1968) invoked this type of formal analysis, whereby a set of core symbols were extracted (or abstracted) from normative statements concerning the definition of relatives within a kin universe.

As Ginsburg and Rapp go on to note, cultural studies models of reception theory (Ang 1991, Radway 1988) and media studies (Hall 1988) can also be highly attentive to the processes whereby "imagery is produced and consumed by a broad range of people who may resist, negotiate, or accommodate encoded meanings" (1995b: 6).[3] In addition, sociologists of culture who study the "culture industries," such as the media, advertising, and entertainment industries, have developed models of

consumption and *consumerism* that have much to offer anthropologists re-
searching visual, public, or mass culture (Lury 1993).

Theorists such as Donna Haraway, Marilyn Strathern, Lila Abu-
Lughod, Emily Martin, and many others have been instrumental in
developing methods of cultural research that can work across texts,
practices, and contexts, uniting several layers or sites of cultural production within coherent, empirically based analytical models. Haraway,
for example, uses the model of "materialized figurations" to describe
the agentic character of representations in and of themselves as they
work to constitute the worlds actors inhabit (1992). Representations for
Haraway have "world-building" consequences, identifiable at the level
of narrative, discursive, or figurative mechanisms. These can be traced,
specified, exemplified, and documented at every level of social practice.
In addition, and of particular importance for the anthropology of reproduction (and thus for this volume), Haraway makes the point that
representations, such as the anthropological account of the human as
a species and of species as evolutionary entities, are themselves (discursive) "technologies" and are reproductive in the sense that they are
generative of actual and possible worlds (1997).

Marilyn Strathern similarly describes culture in terms of specific types
of effects that can be documented, analyzed, and defined. The effects
of substitution, displacement, and literalization, for example, comprise
for Strathern ethnographic documentation of how culture is enacted
by individual social agents. Such accounts neither reduce the cultural
to the social vs. the individual nor inflate its agency along formal, determinist lines. Instead, as Abu-Lughod notes (1991), such innovative
accounts of culture respond to important criticisms of traditional culture models in anthropology.[4]

Emily Martin's important contributions to a refashioned ethnographic
engagement with contemporary cultural forms, or what Marcus describes as "multi-sited ethnography," emphasize the movement of cultural forms across a range of sites and locations. Hence, idioms of immu-
nity as a system travel from corporate boardrooms to clinical settings to
"lay" understandings of health and illness (Martin 1994). The means of
"tracking" such idioms, as Martin describes them, remain underspeci-
fied at present. A challenge for anthropology, therefore, is to balance
what is gained and what is lost by moving away from traditional models
of culture, ethnography, "fieldwork," and agency. Central to the question of what a more flexible ethnographic empiricism will entail is the
question of evidence—if there are to be new rules of anthropological
method, the question of what counts as a cultural fact is sure to figure
prominently among them.

Such questions emerge with particular prominence in relation to the "new" forms of culture with which anthropology has begun to seek more effective scholarly engagement, such as global, virtual, public, transnational, popular, and professional cultures. Without underestimating the degree to which there are, as ever, numerous important precedents for such forms of cultural analysis, and without overestimating the novelty or distinctiveness of these "new" cultural domains, it remains clear that, as stated earlier, a certain degree of retooling is not out of place. New forms of technology, as well as new methods for the analysis of culture as a set of representations, are central concerns for this effort to refashion anthropology's ability to engage with both the plurality of cultural forms available to it and the consequences of the culture explosion — summed up by Strathern as the fact that "culture has become all too utterable" (1992).[5]

Our interest in technology, then, is somewhat overdetermined. In the same way that new technology may be useful as a defamiliarizing lens from which to "make strange" the familiar, the often invisible assumptions through which we understand social and cultural change, so too it has the potential to effect a respatialization and retemporalization of both "culture" and "society." It is for this reason that this volume examines the cultural dimensions of reproduction not only from the traditional standpoint of participant observation as part of a community or local group, but also from the point of view of reproduction within global culture, virtual culture, popular media, and transnational capitalist exchange. In addition, therefore, to foregrounding the importance of ethnographic analysis, we seek also to challenge the traditional "sited-ness" of this enterprise by expanding what can be considered as an anthropological, or cultural, field.

Reproducing Reproduction

This book emerges out of a panel organized at the 1993 annual meeting of the American Anthropological Association. Since that time, we have added new contributors and expanded our original aims to develop this volume. In our original conference abstract, we emphasized both topical and methodological concerns related to what we perceived as the rapidly expanding corpus of ethnographic study related to changing definitions of reproduction and the "facts of life."

Reproduction, we suggested, is increasingly subject to a wide range of professional and technological forms of intervention, many of which have aroused public concern. In addition to the so-called "new" reproductive technologies, such as assisted conception and prenatal screening, there are also a number of emergent reproductive service industries, such as surrogacy, through which "traditional" reproductive activities have become both professionalized and commercialized. It is this convergence of professional, technological, and commercial "management" of conception, procreation, and pregnancy that has been the subject of widespread public debate. In turn, the intensification of reproductive intervention has contributed to the increasing visibility of a significant site of late-twentieth-century cultural contestation, namely the foundational meanings connected to reproduction. At stake are not only traditional definitions of family, disability, parenting, kin connection, and inheritance, but the conventional understandings of nature, life, humanity, morality, and the future.

Through the panel, we sought to examine the cultural dimensions of contemporary forms of reproductive intervention, professionalization, and contestation by using several different sites as contexts for one another. We thus aimed to provide an exercise in comparison, using a growing number of ethnographic and cultural studies that might be brought together for the first time. Hence, the main focus of our initial panel was the theme of how gender, kinship, disability, race, and personhood are reworked and reconstituted through "new" procreative practices that variously instrumentalize the "management" of reproduction. In turn, we sought to investigate the renegotiation of a wide range of other foundational meanings and values seen to be at stake in this process.

The means, for example, by which the transgressive potential of new techniques (e.g., professional surrogacy) is offset by their incorporation into established idioms, such as the naturalness of the desire to procreate, provided instances of the kind of cultural process we sought to make explicit. Likewise, the remobilization of traditional understandings of reproduction, or reproductive control (e.g., abortion) in the context of contemporary contestations over new transnational identities (e.g., "European" citizenship) offered a reverse example of a related process. In turn, such exemplifications raise both theoretical and methodological questions concerning the analysis of reproduction, kinship, and gender as well as race, nationality, and disability.

The contributions to this volume build on our original aims. The first two chapters introduce a recurrent theme of *Reproducing Reproduction*: the normalizing influence of new reproductive screening technologies. In both Janelle Taylor's chapter on ultrasound and that by Nancy Press, Carole H. Browner, Diem Tran, Christine Morton, and Barbara Le Master concerning a range of prenatal tests, the establishment of clinical norms to guide reproductive intervention and management is described. At the same time, these chapters also emphasize the uneven and contradictory dimensions of this process of "normalization," documenting the ways it is resisted, negotiated, ascribed to, and redefined by both practitioners and their patients. Thus new technology emerges as both determining of and determined by complex social relations.

The next three chapters address new methods of assisted concep-tion, including both in vitro fertilization (IVF) and surrogacy. In chap-ters based on fieldwork in IVF clinics in Britain and the United States, Charis Cussins and Sarah Franklin explore the experience of *achieving* conception. In this context, as Cussins notes, processes of normaliza-tion include those of naturalization and routinization. In both chapters, the naturalized narrative of the "facts of life" takes on new dimensions in the context of increasing technological assistance. In turn, assisting conception creates specific dilemmas for women seeking to exercise agency in the face of uncertain diagnostic information and the stratified relations of the clinic. Again, the ethnographic focus allows for several layers of these processes to be documented and discussed. Both Cus-sins and Franklin outline interpretive frameworks linking the analysis of reproduction to wider questions concerning the cultural dimensions of science. Continuing these themes, Ragoné addresses the complex formation of identities and motivations in the context of commercial surrogacy arrangements. In particular, her focus foregrounds the shift-ing significance of race, class, gender, and nationality in the process of establishing connections and disconnections between surrogates and commissioning couples. This chapter also provides a preliminary discus-sion of the links between different reproductive techniques, including IVF and artificial insemination (AI) in the context of surrogacy.

Reproductive disputes in the context of national and global identity formation is the theme of the next two chapters, in which both abortion and adoption are depicted as sites of intense and ongoing contestation. Recounting her fieldwork experience on the abortion controversy in the midst of Ireland's decision whether to join the European community, Laury Oaks demonstrates how deeply intertwined are issues of the con-trol of reproduction and the maintenance of cultural identity. Likewise, Judith Modell explores the conflicts between local, indigenous customs and the formal, legal apparatus of the state concerning child custody, fosterage, and adoption in Hawai'i. In both settings, reproductive con-tinuity emerges as a potent symbol of the maintenance of cultural tradi-tions and identity.

The final two chapters also address new forms of relatedness as part of both global and virtual culture. Analyzing the emergent cultural value of "biodiversity," Cori Hayden discusses both the Human Genome Di-versity project and related disputes over intellectual property rights in living organisms. Here, reproduction emerges as a key issue in the definition not only of nationality but of property, patrimony, and patenting rights. Similarly, Stefan Helmreich presents material from his ethnographic study of paternity claims by the inventors of artificial life systems. Examining models of conception, origin, and "begetting" as part of the male world of artificial life creation, he provides an unexpected perspective on some of the most traditional anthropological concerns about paternity and kinship.

Together these chapters comprise both analytical and ethnographic perspectives on reproduction in a range of settings. They demonstrate in a variety of contexts the centrality of reproduction to both social structure and social theory. Most important, these chapters document the changing meanings of "reproduction" itself, as it is transformed, reproduced, and redefined in the present as it has been in the past. A potent symbol of the future, as well as of tradition and continuity with the past, reproduction is increasingly visible as one of the most contested sites of contemporary cultural change. *Reproducing Reproduction* argues for the value of the ethnographic lens in analyzing the multiple and contradictory dimensions of these changes. In contributing to the emergence of the anthropology of reproduction, this book offers specific examples of the kinds of innovative and essential studies in which reproduction is no longer a structuring absence, but a definitive presence.

Notes

1. Recent and forthcoming anthologies addressing the anthropology of reproduction include Ginsburg and Rapp (1995a), Davis-Floyd and Sargent (1997), Davis-Floyd and Dumit (1997), Morgan and Michaels (forthcoming), Lock and Kaufert (forthcoming), and Inhorn (1996). See also Delaney (1991), Yanagisako and Delaney (1995), Inhorn (1994), Ragoné (1994), Sandelowski (1993), Edwards et al. (1993), Franklin (1997), Rapp (forthcoming), and Layne (forthcoming).

2. A more radical argument would be that many exemplary forms of androcentrism and ethnocentrism, in particular those that derive from biological determinism, *are* reproductive models—for instance, Darwinian natural selection.

3. Because the field of cultural studies comprises a diverse and disunified set of approaches to the study of contemporary culture, it includes within its broad parameters many useful critical discussions of textual determinism and culture-as-text (e.g., Stacey 1994, Chapter 2).

4. These criticisms would include the reduction of culture to place and the overemphasis of holism, boundedness, authenticity, and the "romance of resistance" (e.g., Abu-Lughod 1991, Clifford 1988, and Gupta and Ferguson 1992).

5. See also, for example, Annette Weiner's presidential address to the American Anthropological Association, "Culture and Our Discontents" (1995).

References

Abu-Lughod, Lila. 1991. "Writing Against Culture." In *Recapturing Anthropology: Working in the Present,* ed. Richard G. Fox. Santa Fe, N.M.: School of American Research. 137–62.

Ang, Ien. 1991. *Desperately Seeking the Audience.* London and New York: Routledge.

Bachofen, Johann J. 1861. *Das Mutterecht.* Trans. as *Myth, Religion, and Mother-Right.* New York: Schocken Books, 1967.

Clifford, James. 1988. *The Predicament of Culture: Twentieth-Century Ethnography, Literature, and Art.* Cambridge, Mass.: Harvard University Press.

Coward, Rosalind. 1983. *Patriarchal Precedents: Sexuality and Social Relations.* London: Routledge.

Davis-Floyd, Robbie E. and Joe Dumit, eds. 1997. *Cyborg Babies: From Techno Tots to Techno Toys.* New York: Routledge.

Davis-Floyd, Robbie E. and Carolyn Sargent, eds. 1997. *Childbirth and Authoritative Knowledge: Cross-Cultural Perspectives.* Berkeley: University of California Press.

Edwards, Jeanette, Sarah Franklin, Eric Hirsch, Frances Price, and Marilyn Strathern. 1993. *Technologies of Procreation: Kinship in the Age of Assisted Conception.* Manchester and New York: Manchester University Press.

Engels, Friedrich. 1884. *On the Origins of the Family, Private Property, and the State.* Reprint New York: International Publishers, 1972.

Franklin, Sarah. 1997. *Embodied Progress: A Cultural Account of Assisted Conception.* London: Routledge.

Frazer, James G. 1910. *Totemism and Exogamy: A Treatise on Certain Early Forms of Superstition and Society.* 4 vols. London: Macmillan. Reprint London: Dawson, 1968.

Ginsburg, Faye and Rayna Rapp. 1991. "The Politics of Reproduction." *Annual Review of Anthropology* 20: 311–43.

———, eds. 1995a. *Conceiving the New World Order: The Global Politics of Reproduction.* Berkeley: University of California Press.

———, eds. 1995b. "Introduction." In *Conceiving the New World Order: The Global Politics of Reproduction,* ed. Ginsburg and Rapp. Berkeley: University of California Press.

Gupta, Akhil and James Ferguson. 1992. "Beyond 'Culture': Space, Identity, and the Politics of Difference." *Cultural Anthropology* 7, 1: 6–23.

Hall, Stuart. 1988. *The Hard Road to Renewal: Thatcherism and the Crisis of the Left.* London: Verso.

Haraway, Donna J. 1992. "The Promises of Monsters: A Regenerative Politics for Inappropriate/d Others." In *Cultural Studies,* ed. Lawrence Grossberg, Cary Nelson, and Paula A. Treichler. New York: Routledge, pp. 295–337.

———. 1997. *Modest Witness@Second Millennium—FemaleMan© Inc. Meets OncomouseTM: Feminism and Technoscience.* New York: Routledge.

Helmreich, S. 1995. *Anthropology Inside and Outside: The Looking-Glass Worlds of Artificial Life.* Ph.D. dissertation, Department of Anthropology, Stanford University.

Inhorn, Marcia Claire. 1994. *Quest for Conception: Gender, Infertility, and Egyptian Medical Traditions.* Philadelphia: University of Pennsylvania Press.

Layne, Linda. Forthcoming

Leach, Edmund R. 1967. "Virgin Birth." *Proceedings of the Royal Anthropological*

Institute: 39–49. Reprinted in Leach, *The Structural Study of Myth*. London: Jonathan Cape, 1969.

Lury, Celia. 1993. *Cultural Rights: Technology, Legality, and Personality*. London and New York: Routledge.

Maine, H. J. S. 1861. *Ancient Law: Its Connection with the Early History of Society, and Its Relation to Modern Ideas*. Reprint Tucson: University of Arizona Press, 1986.

Malinowski, Bronislaw. 1913. *The Family Among Australian Aborigines*. London: University of London Press.

———. 1927. *The Father in Primitive Society*. New York: Norton.

———. 1937. Foreword. In Ashley Montagu, *Coming into Being Among the Australian Aborigines: A Study of the Procreative Beliefs of the Native Tribes of Australia*. London: Routledge, pp. xix–xxxv.

Marcus, George E. 1995. "Ethnography in/of the World System: The Emergence of Multi-Sited Ethnography." *Annual Reviews of Anthropology* 24: 95–117.

McLennan, John Ferguson. 1865. *Primitive Marriage: An Inquiry into the Origin of the Form of Capture in Marriage Ceremonies*. Ed. Peter Riviere. Chicago: University of Chicago Press, 1970.

Montagu, Ashley. 1937. *Coming into Being Among the Australian Aborigines: A Study of the Procreative Beliefs of the Native Tribes of Australia*. London: Routledge. 2d ed. rev. London: Routledge, 1974.

Morgan, Lewis Henry. 1871. *Systems of Consanguinity and Affinity in the Human Family*. Smithsonian Contributions to Knowledge. Washington, D.C.: Smithsonian Institution. Reprint Oosterhout, Netherlands: Anthropological Publications, 1970.

Morgan, Lynne and Meredith Michaels, eds. Forthcoming. *Fetal Positions*. Philadelphia: University of Pennsylvania Press.

Rabinow, Paul. 1996. *Making PCR: A Story of Biotechnology*. Chicago: University of Chicago Press.

Rabinow, Paul and William Sullivan, eds. 1979a. *Interpretive Social Science: A Reader*. Berkeley: University of California Press.

———. 1979b. "The Interpretive Turn Emergence of an Approach." In *Interpretive Social Science: A Reader*, ed. Rabinow and Sullivan. Berkeley: University of California Press.

Radway, Janice. 1988. "Reception Study: Ethnography and the Problems of Dispersed Audiences and Nomadic Subjects." *Cultural Studies* 2, 3: 359–76.

Ragoné, Helena. 1994. *Surrogate Motherhood: Conception in the Heart*. Boulder, Colo.: Westview Press.

Rapp, Rayna. 1994. "Commentary." *Newsletter of the Council on Anthropology and Reproduction* 2, 1: 1–3.

———. Forthcoming.

Rivers, W. H. R. 1910. "The Geneological Method of Anthropological Inquiry." *Sociological Review* 3.

Sandelowski, Margarete. 1993. *With Child in Mind: Studies of the Personal Encounter with Infertility*. Philadelphia: University of Pennsylvania Press.

Schneider, David Murray. 1968. *American Kinship: A Cultural Account*. Englewood Cliffs, N.J.: Prentice-Hall.

Spiro, Melford E. "Virgin Birth, Perthenogenesis, and Physiological Paternity: An Essay in Cultural Interpretation." *Man* 3: 242–61.

Stacey, Jackie. 1994. *Star Gazing: Hollywood Cinema and Female Spectatorship*. London and New York: Routledge.

Strathern, Marilyn. 1992. *Reproducing the Future: Anthropology, Kinship, and the New Reproductive Technology.* Manchester: Manchester University Press.

Van Gennep, Arnold. 1906. *The Rites of Passage.* Trans. Monika Vizedom and Gabrielle L. Caffee. London: Routledge.

Weiner, Annette B. 1976. *Women of Value, Men of Renown: New Perspectives on Trobriand Exchange.* Austin: University of Texas Press.

———. 1978. "The Reproductive Model in Trobriand Society." *Mankind on Trade and Exchange in Oceania and Australia,* special issue, ed. Jim Specht and P. White.

———. 1995. "Culture and Our Discontents." *American Anthropologist* 97, 1: 14–20.

Westermarck, Edward A. 1891. *The History of Human Marriage.* 5th ed. London: Macmillan, 1921.

Yanagisako, Sylvia J. and Carol Delaney, eds. 1995. *Naturalizing Power: Feminist Cultural Analysis.* New York: Routledge.

Chapter 1
Image of Contradiction: Obstetrical Ultrasound in American Culture

Janelle S. Taylor

> The more we explore the world of ultrasound, the more we learn of the world within. We gain fresh perspective on familiar territory. We rediscover ourselves.
> —Siemens Quantum ultrasound equipment marketing brochure

In early December of 1994, Paul Hill was sentenced to life in prison on federal charges stemming from his July 1994 murder of Dr. John Britton and Mr. John Barrett outside a Pensacola, Florida abortion clinic. In response to his sentencing, Hill declared that in order to understand his motivations the judge need only watch an ultrasound of an abortion being performed (West 1994). Few incidents could illustrate more starkly the paradoxical relationship between the medical uses of obstetrical ultrasound and the meanings it has acquired in the broader culture than this invocation of ultrasound technology to "justify" the murder of precisely those medical professionals who use it. How are we to understand the relationship between Paul Hill's use of ultrasound and the ways Dr. Britton might have used it in his work? How do the polarized politics of reproduction relate to the everyday practices of reproduction more generally in contemporary American culture?

This essay draws on ethnographic research to show how the uses of obstetrical ultrasound within medicine are linked to its uses outside the medical context. The research setting was a hospital-based obstetrics and gynecology (ob/gyn) ultrasound clinic in Chicago, where I spent one or two days each week over a period of nearly a year, interviewing women patients and observing medical practice.[1] This sort of clinic is one among a variety of sites at which obstetrical ultrasound may be performed in the United States at this time. Obstetricians and other doctors in private practice may also own their own equipment,[2] and may either perform scans themselves or hire sonographers to do so.[3] Alternatively, obstetrical exams may be performed by sonographers working in hospital-based radiology clinics, in freestanding medical-imaging clinics (which may also offer computerized tomography [CT], magnetic resonance imaging [MRI], X-ray, and so forth), or in mobile ultrasound services that contract to come regularly and perform ultrasound scans in clinics or private practices. The hospital-based clinic is thus not necessarily typical of the kind of site to which most women would go for ultrasound exams during pregnancy, and one would naturally expect that medical practice might differ somewhat in different types of settings. There are, however, certain distinctive features of the obstetrical ultrasound exam that I believe remain relatively constant, and it is with these that we shall concern ourselves.

Beginning with the puzzle of why medical practice so far outstrips official policy with regard to ultrasound use during pregnancy, we shall then move to consider in detail the theory of "psychological benefits" of obstetrical ultrasound, which I argue may in some part account for this gap. "Psychological benefits" encompass both "reassurance" and "bonding," which, as we shall see, embody two quite contradictory views of pregnancy, the fetus, and the function of ultrasound imagery. Indeed, I argue that the tension between these two forms of "psychological benefits" points to a deeper contradiction, which I have termed "the prenatal paradox"—namely, that the fetus is constructed more and more as a consumer commodity, and pregnancy as a "tentative" condition,[4] *at the same time and through the same means* that pregnancy is also constructed more and more as an absolute and unconditional relationship, and the fetus as a person from the earliest stages of development. We shall consider in some detail the manner in which this contradiction shapes the practice of the obstetrical ultrasound examination.

Next, we shall examine some of the ways in which ultrasound is taken up and used outside the medical context, by patients and their families, by advertisers, and by antiabortion advocates. We shall see that the promise of "reassurance," and ultrasound's function as prenatal diagnostic technique, drop entirely out of view, in favor of a greatly expanded notion of "bonding," as sonographic imagery is taken up and used outside the medical context. By thus tracing a path from medical applications of ultrasound to those uses apparently farthest removed from (and antagonistic to) medicine, it is hoped that such an ethnographic approach may shed some light upon the relationship between the practices and the politics of reproduction.

Medical Applications: Policy Versus Practice

The advent of ultrasound technology has had an enormous impact on medical knowledge and treatment of pregnancy. Indeed, although as recently as the early 1970s ultrasound remained a quite rare and experimental technique in obstetrics, today

> practitioners under the age of 40 or 45 have difficulty imagining that pregnancy can be managed or gynecological disease dealt with unless high frequency sound waves have been caused to traverse a woman's body.[5]

From an obstetrician's perspective, it might seem that ultrasound has come to be so widely used because . . . well, because it is so *useful*. The safety of diagnostic ultrasound use during pregnancy continues to be debated in the medical literature, but it is widely believed to be very safe at levels used in diagnostic procedures. (Ironically, because ultrasound was widely introduced into practice before large-scale controlled studies were conducted, the primary evidence for its safety is the apparent absence—thus far—of ill effects in the millions of women and their children who have already been exposed.) Practitioners generally downplay possible health risks of obstetrical ultrasound as insignificant in comparison with the wealth of information ultrasound provides, much of which could otherwise be obtained only through invasive procedures, or would simply not be available at all.

Today, an ultrasound exam performed by a competent individual can tell how many embryos or fetuses there are, how the fetus is positioned in the womb, whether its heart is beating, where the placenta is located, and how much amniotic fluid there is. Measurements of the fetus are also taken via ultrasound, measurements of features such as the diameter of the head and the circumference of the abdomen, which are then compared to standard charts that researchers have developed over the years. These measurements are then used to estimate the "gestational age" of the fetus—in order to establish a "due date," to identify possible growth problems, or in preparation for elective abortion. By visually examining the anatomical structures of the fetus, many gross anatomical abnormalities may be detected, such as anencephaly (in which the skull and brain fail to develop), spina bifida (in which the spinal column is open), diaphragmatic hernia (when a deficiency in the diaphram allows the contents of the abdomen to ride up into the chest), cleft lip and palate, and dwarfism. Sophisticated new equipment that indicates the direction and speed of flow allows for the detection of a variety of circulatory problems (notably of the heart and the kidneys) as well.

Ultrasound is also used in conjunction with invasive procedures, a common example of which is amniocentesis; the image on the screen shows exactly where the needle is, allowing the obstetrician to guide it to the right location, in order to extract a sample of amniotic fluid for genetic testing without harming the fetus. Ultrasound examination of the ovaries, as a means of monitoring ovulation, is also important in the treatment of infertility. The strictly medical value of ultrasound is thus twofold. On the one hand, it is itself used as a technique for prenatal diagnosis, and is also used in conjunction with other tests (although no treatment is available for many of the problems that can be detected). On the other hand, obstetricians use ultrasound to make decisions about the medical management of abortion, pregnancy, and birth (for example, whether to induce labor, if the "gestational age" of the fetus as determined by ultrasound measurements is judged to be beyond accepted limits).

To say that ultrasound is used because it is useful, however, evades the question of how and why a whole generation of practitioners—and patients—have become convinced that they need, even for apparently unproblematic pregnancies, the kinds of information that ultrasound can offer. Clearly, practice has far outstripped policy in this regard. In the absence of any national health care system, the closest thing to a national policy that exists in the United States are the guidelines issued periodically by national organizations of medical professionals, such as the American Medical Association (AMA), the American College of Obstetricians and Gynecologists (ACOG), and the American Institute of Ultrasound in Medicine (AIUM). Though routine screening has long been instituted as national policy in various European countries, these U.S. guidelines have consistently recommended *against* the routine screening of all pregnancies by ultrasound, instead insisting that ultrasound should be ordered only on the basis of certain specified medical indications. A list of twenty-eight approved indications was issued in 1984 in a statement developed by a consensus conference convened by the National Institutes of Health (NIH).[6]

Nonetheless, ultrasound quickly moved from a technology reserved for use in pregnancies with known or suspected complications to one routinely prescribed even in apparently normal pregnancies. The most recent national survey available (already long out of date) indicates that between 1980 and 1987, the percentage of all pregnancies that were scanned by ultrasound in the United States increased from 35.5 percent to 78.8 percent (Moore et al., 1990). Eight more years have passed since then, and all evidence indicates that this percentage has since increased dramatically. Indeed, it's probably safe to say that in the United States today, nearly every pregnant woman who has access to any form of health care will have at least one ultrasound scan during pregnancy, and most of those who do not will have consciously resisted it.

Many factors have played into the routinization of obstetrical ultrasound, including the growth of new industries and new professions associated with this new technology, the increasing cost and importance of insurance, and the gradual expansion of the category of "medical indications." Perhaps most interesting for our purposes is the way that medical practice has been shaped by the theory that ultrasound has "psychological benefits." As we shall see, an examination of the relationship between "medical indications" and "psychological benefits" of ultrasound within medical practice provides an interesting angle on the relationship between reproductive medicine generally and the broader culture and politics of reproduction.

"Psychological Benefits": Behavior, Bonding, and Reassurance

Compared to its many clinical applications, the meanings that ultrasound may carry as an image for pregnant women and their partners is of strictly secondary significance from a medical point of view. However, obstetricians and sonographers alike make frequent reference to ultrasound's "psychological benefits," both in informal conversation and in the medical literature. This concept of "psychological benefits" is worth considering in some detail, not only because it has shaped both medical practice and patient expectations of obstetrical ultrasound, but because the logic of "psychological benefits" echoes that of Paul Hill's very different invocation of ultrasound noted above. In both cases, the sight of the ultrasound image is expected to work upon the viewer an emotional transformation, which will in turn inspire the desired behavior.

Seeing Is Behaving

One reason that "psychological benefits" are considered important is because it is thought that if ultrasound increases a woman's awareness of the fetus, and if this awareness leads a woman to modify her behavior, then ultrasound's "psychological benefits" could potentially improve the physical health of the fetus.[7] For example, one often-cited study of "the short-term psychological effects of early real-time scans" concludes that, if viewing the fetus via ultrasound "enhances awareness of the fetus and influences compliance with health-care recommendations such as stopping smoking and alcohol intake, then, as scanning accomplishes this at an earlier stage of pregnancy, there will be greater potential benefit to the fetus" (Campbell et al. 1982).

Used in this sense, the term "psychological benefits" would probably be more accurately glossed as "behavioral benefits." Since the mind of a woman thus appears to provide one therapeutic route to the body of a fetus, and since images are apparently thought to make more of an impression upon women's minds than words (of explanation, advice, or persuasion), it has become possible to understand "psychological benefits" as a *medical side effect* of obstetrical ultrasound (Fleishman 1995), or indeed as medically sound grounds for ordering a scan, even though this is still not approved under official policy.[8]

The "awareness of the fetus" that ultrasound is thought to facilitate encompasses two different ideas of how the sight of the fetus on the ultrasound screen affects a pregnant woman's state of mind—on the one hand, the notion that it promotes maternal *bonding*, and on the other hand the notion that it provides *reassurance*. For example, a consumers' guide to prenatal testing (one of the two authors of which is an obstetrician who specializes in ultrasound) begins its response to the question, "Why is a scan so important?" by citing the importance of "reassurance" and "bonding":

> Obstetricians are increasingly recommending that an ultrasound examination to check the structure of the baby be carried out during pregnancy. The advantages of doing so are as follows:
> (i) It provides enormous reassurance to parents. Most parents worry a great deal about the normality of their baby during pregnancy. The reassurance of seeing normal structures, plus the added bonding that a normal ultrasound examination provides, is reason enough for the examination for many people. (de Crespigny and Dredge 1991: 64)

Often, as in the passage above, "reassurance" and "bonding" are used together as more or less synonymous terms. The difference between them, however, is crucial.

"Reassurance"

The word "reassurance" in this context evokes thoughts of health, happiness, and security; ultrasound, it would seem, dispels fear and doubt from the mind of the happily pregnant woman by assuring her that her fetus is healthy and normal. But the "reassurance" that ultrasound offers is always limited—not all problems can be detected by ultrasound, and problems can also arise later in pregnancy. An apparently normal exam offers no guarantee of a live birth or a healthy baby. The "reassurance" that ultrasound may provide thus exists only in relation to its repressed opposite, which is dread—of the loss of a pregnancy, of fetal abnormality or death, of agonizing dilemmas, of abortion.

When "reassurance" is invoked as one of the "psychological benefits" of ultrasound, it is on the presumption that ultrasound will in most cases *not* reveal fetal death or abnormalities. However, the only medical justification for ordering the examination in any individual case is the reasonable suspicion that it *will* reveal problems, and one of the primary justifications for offering ultrasound screening to all women on a routine basis is the expectation that fetuses exhibiting anomalies will be aborted. Medical articles on ultrasound explicitly make this link between "reassurance" and selective abortion, especially in connection with cost-benefit assessments—for example, a recent article on "Routine Versus Indicated Scans" concludes that:

The short-term gains resulting from routine ultrasound would be reassurance that patients receive from the knowledge that the ultrasound study is normal. . . . Long-term gains would include identification of a major anomaly and termination of pregnancy, thus avoiding the birth of a child with an anomaly who is likely to survive but with a poor quality of life. . . . (Gabbe 1994: 72)

Thus, if ultrasound offers women "reassurance" that their individual pregnancies are normal, it does so by granting tentative exemptions on a case-by-case basis from the broader conviction that pregnancy in general is inherently prone to go badly awry. And if a pregnant woman has reason to feel "reassured" when problems are *not* detected, the obstetrician who provides care for her has some reason to feel reassured when they *are*. Given the realities of practicing medicine in the American context, another "long-term gain" from routine ultrasound is the protection that prenatal diagnosis can afford against possible "wrongful birth" or "wrongful life" lawsuits.

In short, ultrasound as a prenatal diagnostic technique, in combination with selective abortion, is enlisted to attempt to minimize the possibility of a less than perfect child, while ultrasound for "reassurance" offers to dispel the dread that may attend the "tentative" pregnancy under these conditions.

"Bonding"

If the notion of "reassurance" contains repressed fears that the health of the embryo or fetus will not conform to expectations, the notion of "bonding" contains similar fears regarding the emotional disposition of the pregnant woman.

The notion of maternal "bonding" has come to be so completely taken for granted that it is startling to learn that the term is in fact only twenty-three years old. It was only in 1972 that two pediatricians,

John Kennell and Marshall Klaus, published a study in the *New England Journal of Medicine* arguing that mothers who were allowed sixteen extra hours of contact with their infants right after birth showed better mothering skills, and their infants did better on developmental tests, than mothers and infants who did not have this extra contact (Klaus et al. 1972). Klaus and Kennell attributed these dramatic effects to the "bonding" that takes place between mother and infant during a sensitive period following birth, when women are hormonally primed to accept or reject their offspring. The authors were inspired by research with animals, especially rats and goats, which showed that hormones exerted an especially powerful effect upon maternal behavior in the period during and after birth. Though it has since come under considerable criticism, the theory of maternal-infant bonding was widely embraced throughout the 1970s, and was instrumental in the progressive reform of hospital birthing practices during that period, providing a scientific rationale for allowing new mothers to see and hold their newborn babies immediately after birth.[10]

In a letter to the *New England Journal of Medicine* in 1983, Drs. Fletcher and Evans suggested that ultrasound performed in the first trimester might facilitate earlier maternal "bonding" with the fetus, and that women who had "bonded" in this way might be less likely to choose to abort (Fletcher and Evans 1983). Subsequent studies published in the medical literature paint a more nuanced picture, locating the ultrasound exam within cognitive and psychological models that distinguish between the various stages of "attachment" thought to take place during pregnancy, and the "bonding" that supposedly takes place immediately after birth.[11] However, it is a cruder concept of maternal "bonding" via ultrasound—elevated from speculative suggestion to stated fact—that has entered the common parlance of people both inside and outside the medical community. We would therefore do well to consider what is entailed in adopting this term to describe the pleasure women are thought to (and often do) feel upon seeing the ultrasound image of the fetus.

First of all, the "bonding" theories of Kennell and Klaus and their followers had focused on the period immediately *after* birth, whereas obstetrical ultrasound by definition takes place *before birth*—that is, during pregnancy. Earlier maternal-infant bonding theories attempted to account for why some women were apparently better than others at "mothering"—they presumed that women are instinctively disposed to love and care for their offspring, but that an alienating birth experience might upset the natural development of the mother-infant relationship. By the time Fletcher and Evans transferred this notion of "bonding" to ultrasound during pregnancy in 1983, a decade of increasingly heated public controversy over the legalization of abortion had shifted the terrain of public debate (and the locus of anxieties) about women and reproduction from issues of child rearing to issues of procreation, and the question of why so many women have abortions. It is thus not surprising that the ultrasound "bonding" theory was first put forth in the context of suggesting how women who feel ambivalent about their pregnancies might be persuaded not to abort.

A second way in which Fletcher and Evans's proposal differs from older maternal-infant "bonding" theories is that it emphasizes not *when* mothers would form an emotional "bond" with their babies, but *how*. Discussions of maternal-infant "bonding" in the 1970s had tended to focus on the problem of establishing the time frame for the "sensitive period" during which women were primed to form emotional attachments to their newborns: was it the first few minutes, the first days, the first months, or the first year? The proposal that ultrasound might facilitate "bonding" shifted this time frame from the period after birth to the period of pregnancy, as we have seen. In the process, it also made a more radical suggestion, that emotional and social ties between a mother and child might form in an altogether new manner—not through physical and social interaction, but through *spectatorship*. Klaus and Kennell's theory of maternal-infant "bonding" had been welcomed by advocates of natural childbirth, because it argued that medical professionals must step aside after birth and allow women themselves to establish direct relations with their newborns. Ironically, this newer version of the "bonding" theory implicitly suggests that women *need* both medical technology and the assistance of the medical professionals in order to form the proper emotional attitude toward their fetuses.

As we have seen, the theory of "bonding" has undergone several transformations as it has migrated from the hospital labor and delivery room to the ultrasound examination room, with important implications. The notion of ultrasound "bonding" equates pregnancy with the relationship between a woman and her newborn child. In this regard, it presumes a view of pregnancy as absolute, a relationship of unconditional maternal love for the developing fetus. At the same time, however, the ultrasound "bonding" theory suggests that this relationship forms through technologically and professionally mediated spectatorship, and even implies that it is the technology itself that in some sense "gives birth," to the fetus, construed as a child. On some level, this amounts to an unstated recognition that without such technological and professional interventions, women are in fact *not* naturally inclined to feel and act with the same maternal concern toward the embryo or early fetus that they might have for a fetus in the later stages of pregnancy, or for a newborn child.

Prenatal Paradox: Commodity, Person, Fetus

The contradiction between "reassurance" and "bonding" should be obvious. The notion of "reassurance" emerges from ultrasound's function as a prenatal diagnostic technique, which as we have seen enacts a view of pregnancy as a highly conditional matter, contingent upon the embryo or fetus successfully passing certain tests and measuring up to the scrutiny of a critical scientific gaze that evaluates its condition and its development in light of an ever more elaborate body of knowledge about what is normal. As Barbara Katz Rothman, among others, has pointed out, the fetus appears in this context as a sort of consumer commodity:

The commodification process has transformed pregnancy, as society encourages the development of prenatal testing. This process—genetic counseling, screening and testing of fetuses—serves the function of "quality control" on the assembly line of the products of conception, separating out those products we wish to develop from those we wish to discontinue. Once we see the products of conception as just that, as products, we begin to treat them as we do any other product, subject to similar scrutiny and standards. (Rothman 1989: 21)

The notion of "bonding," by contrast, presumes that pregnancy should be a relationship of unconditional maternal love, the natural development of which ultrasound technology may speed up and enhance—here the fetus, as object of a loving maternal regard, is construed as a person. The contradiction, which we might for brevity's sake term "the prenatal paradox," is that, ironically, pregnancy is constructed more and more as a "tentative" relationship, and the fetus as a "commodity," *at the same time and through the same means* that pregnancy is also constructed more and more as an absolute and unconditional relationship, and the fetus as a "person" from its earliest stages.

It often does happen that ultrasound in fact reveals no fetal abnormalities, and that a pregnant woman in fact does derive some pleasure from viewing her fetus on the screen. In such cases, this contradiction might not ever fully surface to consciousness. Many women do indeed experience the ultrasound exam as a moment of both "reassurance" and "bonding." Yet the dominant narrative of ultrasound's "psychological effects," which tells of an intentionally pregnant woman happily reassured and bonded with her provisionally certified-normal fetus, always contains within itself repressed counternarratives of guilt and dread in the possibility of a different ending. The ever-present possibility of a "positive" diagnosis threatens to force this contradiction to the surface by putting the pregnant woman in the anguishing position of deciding whether to selectively abort, or to knowingly carry a fetus that is in some way anomalous, demanding, in the terms set by the abortion debate, that she declare it either a "commodity" or a "person." It is this dreaded possibility that lends such drama to the routine ultrasound examination—the agonizing suspense of waiting and wondering, the climactic moment of diagnosis, the joy (or despair) that follows.[12]

We have seen how a contradiction between opposing views of pregnancy and of the fetus may be discerned in the gap between policy and practice regarding ultrasound use during pregnancy, and in fissures within the concept of "psychological benefits." Let us now turn to look at social practice, and we shall see how the same contradiction emerges in the form of tensions about the boundaries of the medical domain, in the context of the obstetrical ultrasound examination.

The Ultrasound Examination: A Hybrid Practice

In the United States, the medical task of obtaining certain views and measurements of the fetus and placenta is combined with a number of other practices. A pregnant woman is usually allowed to bring a companion (often her husband or boyfriend) into the examining room, and the sonographer usually shows them the screen, points out certain features of the fetus, offers the pregnant woman the option of finding out the fetal sex if this can be visualized, and gives her an image to take home. While practice naturally varies, and not all examinations include all of these elements, sonographers tend, at the very minimum, to at some point show the pregnant woman the screen—it is widely agreed that women generally want to see the image of the fetus, that they are entitled to, and that to do so is beneficial (for reasons we have explored above). The ultrasound examination is thus a hybrid practice, in that assumptions about the nonmedical meanings and functions of ultrasound are incorporated into medical practice.

These conventions are not only enshrined in widely shared expectations, but indeed built into the very architecture of equipment and clinic. Many U.S. ultrasound companies, for example, now build into their equipment a swivel monitor, which facilitates turning the screen and "showing the baby," as well as a special printer for producing "souvenir photos" to give to patients. The dual aspects of obstetrical ultrasound, as high-tech medical device and as a form of consumer product, also enter into equipment design in more subtle ways, in the overall design of the visible exterior of the machine, as a design engineer at a major U.S. ultrasound company explains:

What feelings should this system convey, when you walk in the door? Is it a very ominous black box that magically produces an image, so are you in awe of this machine? Or are you a buddy with this machine? A lot of the forms that we play with in creating an overall aesthetic, how we use those forms and colors can really send a different signal. Like a very soft, curvaceous form may be something that's more consumerish, as opposed to sharp angles and hard edges, rectilinear shapes. But you have to strike a balance. . . . You may look at it and say, "Wow, that's fun. Let's have an ultrasound today." Or, "Wow, that's a serious product there, it looks lethal." . . . We will try to strive for *one* image with this product, a combination of "high-tech," because that still means a lot to people in a positive way, but at the same time "friendly."

Similarly, examination rooms in OB/GYN ultrasound clinics are often furnished with an extra chair for the woman's companion—typically the father of the expected child, but often a female friend or relative.[13]

Professional practices, equipment features, and public expectations congealed around this particular ritualized form sometime around the mid-1980s, according to sonographers who have worked in obstetrics for many years. By now, ten years later, it has become difficult to do things otherwise. As a hybrid practice, the ultrasound exam highlights the fact that medicine is *not* a completely distinct domain of knowledge and practice. As we shall see, much of the cultural "work" that goes on around the practice of ultrasound involves struggles to *establish* clear boundaries between medicine and the broader consumer culture within which it is located—between medical indications and "psychological benefits," between medical professionals and patients-as-consumers, between medical procedures and visual entertainment.

Between Medical Indications and "Psychological Benefits"

Officially, ultrasound examinations may be ordered only on the basis of certain specified "medical indications," as we noted earlier. Some exams clearly are ordered because the practitioner has reason to suspect a problem, and there is reason to believe that others are actually ordered solely for "psychological benefits," but most cases are in fact not clear-cut. At the clinic where I did research, sonographers usually began each scan by asking the patient why she was having an ultrasound. With remarkable regularity, women answered, "The doctor ordered a scan just to check and make sure everything's okay."

What does this mean? Does it mean that the doctor has reason to think something is *not* okay, or does it mean that the scan was ordered to reassure the patient by "checking and making sure" that everything *is* okay? Both may be the case—this ambiguity is inherent in the hybrid character of the ultrasound examination. According to sonographers, the majority of problems discovered via ultrasound are totally unsuspected, so that an exam ordered, in good faith, for "psychological benefit" may nonetheless unexpectedly reveal major or minor abnormalities or fetal death.

Perhaps because they deal with the tension between medical applications and "psychological benefits" on a daily basis, sonographers I observed at work sometimes attempted to draw the line between them, by exhorting women to demand from their doctors a *medical* reason for ordering an ultrasound. One exam started out this way:

S: Now tell me why she ordered the ultrasound.
P: I don't know.
S: You have to ask why. If somebody sticks a needle in your arm, don't you ask why? It's the same thing.

At the same time, however, sonographers could hardly help but conflate the two, since the convention of "showing the baby" for the "psychological benefit" of the patient is firmly entrenched in medical practice.

For a woman who is *already* focusing on medical indications, this may sometimes only heighten the intrusiveness of ultrasound as a medical procedure. Savita,[14] a thirty-three-year-old administrator in a nonprofit organization, pregnant with her first child, described her experience:

We spoke to the genetic counsellor, because there are some problems in my family and some in his family, and so we had an ultrasound just to look for any problems with the organs. And I must say I didn't enjoy that at all. First of all it took a very long time, they were looking at the heart, the four chambers of the heart, and the valves and the ventricles and the this and the that, and they looked at the kidneys, looked at them very closely. Just somehow . . . I felt like the baby you know, until now, had been just fine and I could tell how it was doing by its kicking movements inside, and then. . . . Somehow I just felt that I didn't want to know all this. It just felt like, too much. I got actually quite emotional, kind of crying a little bit. I didn't really want to look at the screen at all. . . . They were very willing to explain things, but I kind of didn't want to know.

Between Professional and Patient

Still, the incorporation of such practices may, in subtle ways, shape women's experience of the medical procedure itself, especially for those less well positioned to make demands as consumers in a medical setting. The convention of "showing the baby," for example, provides an opening for women to interrogate sonographers about the medical procedure, in a way that might be unusual in the context of other diagnostic tests, or in interactions with doctors. Consider this exchange between Linda (the sonographer) and Charlotte, a thirty-nine-year-old African-American woman expecting her first child, previously employed as a nurse's aide, who was referred for an ultrasound scan from a prenatal care clinic operated by the Board of Health:

Charlotte: You still lookin' at the head?
Linda: Yeah . . . are you sure of your dates?
Charlotte: Why, you think it's coming sooner?
Linda: I'll have to do all the measurements. Here's baby's nose, and mouth.
Charlotte: How can you tell? I mean, I expected to see like a human form. . . . So there's really a baby in there? This is the head and stuff up here, right? . . . Now what are we looking at?
Linda: Baby's like all stretched out . . . there's the heartbeat, see it moving?
Charlotte: Yeah. . . . Well, it's alive. What are those two holes there?
Linda: Vessels.
Charlotte: (to screen) Well why don't you turn over so we can see what you are. . . . (Then, to the sonographer:) Is he turned over?
Linda: This is baby's belly. . . .
Charlotte: Where at, right here? (she touches the screen).
Linda: This is baby's bladder, this is baby's thigh. . . .
Charlotte: Gettin' close, huh?
Linda: Sometimes when they're breach, butt down, we can't see. . . . This is where the cord goes into the body. . . .
Charlotte: (looking at the machine) Every time it hits a point it beeps, huh? What was that?

In practice, then, "showing the baby" often also means "showing the anatomy," "showing the procedure," and "showing the equipment." As we left the room after this particular exam, Linda whispered to me, "She's driving me nuts!!"[15] In my observation, Linda generally talked to women with respect and answered questions patiently and clearly, but she and other sonographers did sometimes express frustration when patients asked too many questions. (I most often heard such complaints about women who, like Charlotte, were "clinic" patients—those without private health insurance who must rely on Medicare and Medicaid for coverage.)

More than merely complicating the sonographer's task, the convention of "showing the baby" poses a subtle challenge to the hierarchy that separates the sonographer as medical professional from the patient. On the one hand, the sonographer's professional responsibilities require that she perform scans accurately and relatively quickly,[16] obtaining a series of specific anatomical views in a fixed sequence, looking for abnormalities and problems—and if she sees any, according to protocol she is *not* to communicate that information to the patient, but is instead to notify the attending physician, who will then arrange for the patient to be informed in a counselling session.[17] It is thus assumed that the sonographer commands specialized medical knowledge and skills to which patients cannot have immediate access. On the other hand, however, the sonographer is also expected to show the patient the screen and give a play-by-play account what she is seeing, both to "reassure" the patient and to facilitate "bonding"—it is thus also expected that the sonographer can and will make ultrasound understandable to people with no medical training at all.[18]

This tension surrounding the sonographer's professional status emerged particularly clearly on one occasion during my ethnographic research, when the friend of a young "clinic" patient, who had accompanied her into the examination room, pointed to the screen and gleefully declared, "It's a boy! I can tell, it *looks* like a boy!" Turning to me (as I sat in the back of the room taking notes), the sonographer said, with some irritation, "You know, it's amazing to me, we go through a very rigorous training to do this, and then patients come in and after one minute they think they know!" Those whose professional identity is bound up with their expertise in ultrasound may perceive that their own status as medical professionals is eroded when people appear to assume that this medical technology is comparable to television, photography, or other forms of imagery that require no special skills to interpret. As one obstetrician complained, "To us this is a deadly serious medical procedure, but to them it's just a form of entertainment!"

Between Medicine and Entertainment

Because women patients and others outside the medical profession do not necessarily distinguish between the pleasures of "bonding" or "reassurance" and the pleasures of "entertainment," the notion of ultrasound's "psychological benefits" can in fact open the way for a serious challenge to both the integrity and the authority of the medical practice of ultrasound. Some sonographers get around this issue by separating the "medical" portion of the exam from the "entertainment" portion, as distinct moments in time, with statements such as the following:

What I'm going to do is run through these pictures first, then I'll show you the baby in its entirety. So if I'm not talking much, that's because I'm trying to concentrate, okay?

In this way, the sonographer in effect divides the exam into two distinct parts. This allows her to first step into the role of medical professional, wordlessly performing a diagnostic procedure, and then step into the role of educator, providing a demonstration of fetal anatomy that often focuses on those features thought to be of interest to parents, such as the face, the hands, and the heart.

Dividing the ultrasound exam in this manner reestablishes the autonomy of the medical diagnostic procedure, within the examination. At the same time, however, instituting a scan for "psychological benefit" alongside the medical procedure may tend to validate the performance of obstetrical ultrasound for nonmedical reasons, and this in turn poses a challenge to medical control. When the nonmedical exam is separated *entirely* in space and time from the medical procedure, then medical authority may step in to put a stop to it. Thus, the Food and Drug Administration recently shut down a widely publicized enterprise in Texas that offered ultrasound videos purely for entertainment purposes because, in the words of the FDA spokesperson:

It is an approved device, but an unapproved use. . . . The FDA only allows ultrasound to be used for specific conditions, and entertainment, or just the pleasure of knowing what's going on in the uterus, is not approved. (News Wave 1994)

Such blatantly entrepreneurial operations aside, however, scanning for "entertainment, or just the pleasure of knowing what's going on in the uterus" is commonly incorporated into the practice of medically indicated scans, as we have seen. Even within the medical context, the "entertainment" portion of the exam may spin off to become quite separate from the medical procedure, as in this case described to me by a sonographer who has been working in an obstetrical clinic for many years:

At the clinic where I work, the doctors are very responsible, very conservative, but I guess they think that if it's safe at this level of exposure, it's just always safe no matter what. So, they will send a patient for an ultrasound exam, and if we can't see the sex that first time, then the patient herself can call back and schedule a second exam. At first it was just a matter of, you know, if we've done the exam and they want to know the sex, I could spend ten minutes just looking for the sex, but why not come back another time and do that ten minutes another time, when you'd have a better chance of seeing it? So it started out as a "sex check" for people who couldn't get the sex the first time, but it evolved into a situation where they'll schedule a "sex check" for a videotape, or so that grandma can come along, 'cause grandma didn't get to see it. . . . They bill the patient directly for this, they charge $35, just for our time really, it doesn't go through the third-party system at all. So basically it's home entertainment video, but it's done in a doctor's office.

Cast in this light, allowing patients to schedule ultrasound scans on their own, purely for viewing pleasure, sounds like a case of questionable medical ethics—yet it is not, perhaps, so very different from ordering an exam for "psychological benefits," which appears to be a relatively widely accepted practice.

One consequence of the hybrid character of the practice of obstetrical ultrasound is that practitioners have to some extent apparently ceded to women as consumers the authority to decide whether and when to order an ultrasound scan. Even some nurse-midwives I have spoken with now routinely offer ultrasound, for just such reasons—even though their clients are women already defined as "low-risk" (and thus presumably less likely to "need" an ultrasound exam for medical indications) and, by choosing to work with midwives, have already opted for a more "natural" pregnancy and childbirth.[19] Two nurse-midwives working in a hospital-based practice explained:

About a year and a half ago we began offering structural ultrasound to patients at twenty weeks, because so many of our patients were asking for ultrasound. You know, they see all their friends having two or three or even four ultrasounds during pregnancy; they get worried that something might be missed, medically. Also, they look forward to it. It's real reassuring, especially for women who've had a miscarriage in the past. . . . And they read about ultrasound in all the women's magazines; they expect it. . . . As midwives, we believe in less intervention, but we're also committed to the idea that women should be active participants in their own care. . . . And there is a big difference in the kinds of people that choose to work with midwives now, compared to when we started out in the seventies—maybe it's because we're more accepted now? But it's much more technological. Women request ultrasound, they request induction. . . . So we offer them a structural scan, and about 80 percent choose to have one.

Some women, to be sure, resist having ultrasound during pregnancy, and many more simply agree to a scan because their prenatal care provider recommends it. Yet women themselves, as avid consumers of prenatal care, are also clearly agents in the routinization of ultrasound. In an environment where pregnancy is often experienced as a quest for scientific knowledge, and where medical wisdom and practices are constantly changing, women pass along to each other information about ultrasound along with other advice about pregnancy, birth, and childcare[20]:

At our Lamaze class, you know, everyone was kind of comparing notes, and one woman said she hadn't had a sonogram yet and didn't think she was going to have one, and this other woman said to her, very sternly, "You go right back there and you tell that doctor you want a sonogram! You can get one!" (Debbie, a 36-year-old white lawyer)

I requested [an ultrasound]. I explained my fears, about me being over 35 years old, and [the doctor] said it's rare now a woman goes through a full pregnancy without one. . . . A woman in the waiting room showed me her ultrasound picture. And I got disappointed because I didn't have one. . . . People kept asking me, "What is it? What is it?" Everybody kept asking me, "Did you have your ultrasound yet?" I felt cheated. I wanted to see that it was normal, and also, I didn't want to miss out on that experience. (Charlotte, who appeared earlier in this essay)

Between the two halves of that sentence—"I wanted to see that it was normal" and "I didn't want to miss out on that experience"—you can see all of the contradiction that we have been tracing. On the one hand, Charlotte wanted to be "reassured" that the fetus she carried was normal—she wanted it to pass the test of prenatal diagnosis, to be assessed a valuable commodity. On the other hand, she also didn't want to miss out on the experience of having an ultrasound examination, as a valued part of the overall experience of pregnancy. She wanted the pleasure of seeing and "bonding" with her eagerly awaited baby. The paradox is there in women's experience of pregnancy, and we've seen how it is built into medical practice itself.

What we'll find as we move to look at the ways ultrasound is used outside the medical context, however, is that the pattern of emphasis is reversed. What's primary in the medical context (ultrasound as prenatal diagnostic technique) drops out of view, and what's secondary in the medical context (ultrasound as a tool for promoting bonding) becomes primary as ultrasound moves into popular kinship rituals, into advertising and consumption, and into abortion politics. The critical, measuring, professionally trained gaze of the sonographer likewise gives way to the yearning, ardent gaze of the viewer seeking an emotional connection.

Stretching the "Bond"

As we have seen, the application of the notion of maternal-infant "bonding" to obstetrical ultrasound implies, among other things, that kinship bonds may form in an entirely new way, through *spectatorship* of technologically mediated imagery, as well as through physical or social contact. In this regard, the concept of ultrasound-facilitated "bonding," and the practices that (as we have seen) have sprung up around it, ironically work to undermine the distinctiveness of the relationship between mother and fetus, at the same time that they supposedly strengthen it, because *as a spectator*, the pregnant woman does not enjoy any special access to the fetus. Given the convention of allowing the patient to bring a companion (usually the husband or boyfriend) along to the examination, ultrasound offers to expectant fathers and mothers alike an equivalent experience of the fetus. Both equally become spectators, viewing the expected child on the ultrasound screen, and both may (or may be expected to) feel an emotional "bonding" to the child as a result.[21]

Those who take home with them from the ultrasound examination a "snapshot" image or a videotape further extend this notion that spectatorship may effect "bonding," when they show (or give) the image to others. For the majority of women with whom I spoke, the people to whom they had shown or planned to show their take-home sonograms were family members—their older children, their own parents, their siblings, aunts, cousins, and so forth. Even for those who acknowledged that they themselves could not really make visual sense of the image, or who expected that others would not understand what they were looking at, the sharing of the sonogram image thus appears as a means of establishing or strengthening kinship links with the fetus, well beyond the mother-child relationship. Indeed, the sonogram itself might be understood to work in part as a sort of "shared substance" of kinship, which moves along the social networks of kin whose relationships are conceived as emerging out of their sharing of "blood" (Schneider 1968). That it can be faxed to relatives residing in another part of the country (a phenomenon encountered more than once in my research) only enhances the appeal of the sonogram as a device for "bonding" kin together in contemporary American society.

Bonding and Selling: Ultrasound Imagery in Product Advertisements

In the last few years, advertisers have picked up on this idea that ultrasound promotes "bonding" among family members, and used it to sell products. This makes sense, of course, insofar as advertisements, like ultrasound when used for "psychological benefits," employ imagery to attempt to manage the viewer's fears and desires. Once the idea has taken root that technology helps create or enhance the bonds of kinship, then it becomes possible to try to channel the desire for strong relationships with one's children (as well as the fear that such relationships may weaken or unravel or simply fail to form properly in the first place) into the purchase of better technology—needed, it would seem, to forge stronger family ties.

Ultrasound Equipment

In the Siemens advertisement reproduced here (Figure 1.1). ultrasound imagery is used in this manner to advertise ultrasound technology itself, in a kind of perfect feedback loop. The main theme in this ad, which carries through both in the imagery and the captions, is the idea that ultrasound allows an expectant parent, or a doctor, to "see" the baby before it is born. We have already noted that in the case of ultrasound, "seeing" is invested with very different meanings and resonances, depending on which aspect of this hybrid practice is highlighted: its ability

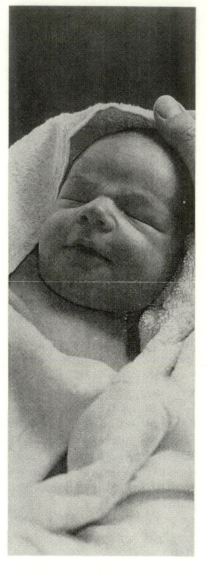

SIEMENS

Hey, I've seen you before!

As we see it, monitoring health begins in the prenatal phase. That's why we've engineered ultrasound scanners to see a developing child's condition clearly, quickly and safely, providing internal images of exceptional high quality. At Siemens, we're committed to improving the quality of health care for everybody – by helping doctors make faster, more complete health examinations. In fact, it's an appproach that stands behind all our non-invasive scanners. Because a better diagnosis means better treatment. Of course it's our hope that you never have to see a doctor for other than a routine check-up. But when you do, it's good to know that today, medical professionals can see you better than ever before.

Siemens medical imaging meets human needs.

Ultrasound scanner image of an embryo

Figure 1.1. Siemens ultrasound advertisement.

to allow medical professionals to "see" potential problems and abnormalities, or its ability to allow expectant parents to "see" and form emotional attachments to the baby.

In this advertisement, the ultrasound image of the fetus, juxtaposed with the image of the newborn baby, and the large caption, "Hey, I've seen you before!" all reinforce the point that ultrasound establishes a relationship with the fetus before birth. The kind of "seeing" implied here is a loving parental gaze, a recognition of an individual person's visage. That which is the primary purpose of ultrasound technology from the medical point of view—prenatal diagnosis—is by contrast very much played down, referred to only in small print, at the end of the paragraph, and couched in the vaguest possible terms at that:

Of course it's our hope that you never have to see a doctor for other than a routine check-up. But when you do, it's good to know that today, medical professionals can see you better than ever before.

This reversal of emphasis is perhaps consistent with a remark made to me by the director of marketing of a different ultrasound company (not Siemens). When asked how marketing obstetrical ultrasound is different from marketing ultrasound for other segments of the medical profession, such as cardiology or radiology, he replied: "Well, the difference is, that in obstetrical ultrasound we're really marketing just as much to the patient as to the physician."[22] As a marketing strategy, this of course presumes that patients as consumers of prenatal care have a role in creating demand for ultrasound.

After all, if ultrasound technology can be used to promote mother-love, it stands to reason that mother-love can also be used to sell ultrasound technology.

Telephone Service

The notion that ultrasound helps strengthen kinship bonds can also, by analogy, be used to suggest that other technologies have similar effects. This approach has been exploited most visibly in advertisements for telephone service (not coincidentally, perhaps, the very networks along which the faxed sonogram travels). The most notable example of this is an AT&T television spot that aired frequently on national networks for a number of months in 1994.

This advertisement centers around the narrative of a pregnant woman who has come for an obstetrical ultrasound examination, but whose husband couldn't be with her. Slightly eerie, space-age-sounding music accompanies our first glimpse of a pretty blonde woman in her thirties, lying on the examination table with her pregnant belly exposed for the examination.

"Excited about your sonogram?" asks the sonographer, standing by her side (strangely enough, on the side *opposite* the ultrasound machine).
"Yeah."

"Not even a little nervous?"

"Well . . . ," she confesses, "Sam was supposed to call. I guess he's going to miss it." (Is he not in any case "missing it" by not being there?). The sonographer applies the transducer to the belly, and the fetus appears on the screen. Then the phone rings, and the sonographer hands it over to the woman patient. As she talks to her husband, we see alternating shots of her in the examination room—touching the image of the fetus on the ultrasound screen, twisting the phone cord around her finger, putting her finger in her mouth—and Sam, briefcase in hand, speaking to her from a phone booth on a busy city street. Sam asks, "How's our kicker?"

"He's almost as gorgeous as you! Same long legs . . . big head. . . . Hey," we see her mouth ask, "wanna say hi?" She puts the receiver to her stomach in place of the transducer.

Sam speaks to the fetus, "Hey big boy, wanna come out and play?"

A rapid series of close-up shots show the woman's mouth opening, her eye blinking, the image on the screen jumping. "Oh Sam, he kicked!"

We see Sam's smiling mouth at the receiver, "Really?"

"Yeah!" she responds, laughing happily, her hair spread out around her face on the pillow.

A male narrator speaks. "With AT&T True Voice Long Distance, the clearest, truest sound ever will soon be coming your way. So everyone you call will hear everything you feel."

Sam asks, "Do you think he heard me?"

"Yes," the woman laughs, "he did!"

Sam closes his eyes and smiles, leaning his head against the phone booth, weak with happiness. A female voice sings, "The real you / Coming through / Your True Voice," as the screen fades to black and an AT&T logo appears, over a phone number: 1-800-BE-CLOSE.

This advertisement clearly plays on the idea that ultrasound technology facilitates bonding between members of the family, but attempts to transfer the emotional significance from ultrasound technology to telephone technology. A number of details in the advertisement are rather unrealistic as a portrayal of an actual ultrasound exam. For one thing, the sonographer is pretty much absent from the picture, standing on the opposite side of the woman from the ultrasound equipment—it is as if the woman is there alone, watching the ultrasound as she might watch TV. The image of the fetus, furthermore, remains on the screen even when the transducer is removed and the telephone receiver is put there in its place—implying, of course, that the telephone itself acts as a sort of transducer. The advertisement implies, moreover, that the telephone is even *more* powerful than ultrasound as a technology for promoting "bonding," because the "bonding" that takes place via ultrasound is all one-way—the mother sees the fetus and feels love, while the fetus just sits there passively. The telephone, on the other hand, seems to make the fetus "bond" actively with its father, kicking in response to the sound of his voice, perhaps an early form of Oedipal response to the distant father's inevitable intrusion into the mother-child relationship.[23]

Even the camera style in this AT&T advertisement is deliberately odd, in an attempt, it would seem, to mimic the visual style of ultrasound imagery. Thus, when we are looking at the woman, we see her in the same way that one sees the fetus on the ultrasound screen, focusing on a series of distinct anatomical features in turn—the eyes, the fingers tangling in the cord, the fingers in the mouth, etc. The implication here, of course, is that through the television we "bond" with the pregnant woman, while through the ultrasound screen she "bonds" with the fetus, and the fetus in turn "bonds" with the father through the telephone.[24] Not only the product being advertised here, but even the medium of television itself can, it would seem, like obstetrical ultrasound forge "bonds" between viewer and viewed.

"Bonding" the Public: Ultrasound in Abortion Politics

A similarly expanded notion of "bonding" may also be discerned in the use of obstetrical ultrasound in antiabortion propaganda materials.

By the time Fletcher and Evans proposed a possible connection between ultrasound and maternal "bonding," in 1983, abortion had of course been legalized already for over ten years, and controversy over abortion had steadily gained prominence in national politics, most notably with the election of Ronald Reagan. One characteristic feature of antiabortion rhetoric, which had already emerged clearly at that time —and which has remained more or less constant throughout the various shifts that have taken place in the political strategies and religious and gender composition of the antiabortion movement—is an emphasis on visual imagery of the fetus. Faye Ginsburg, who carried out her groundbreaking ethnographic study of the abortion debate during the 1980s, writes that:

The idea that knowledge of fetal life, and especially confrontation with the visual image of the fetus, will "convert" a woman to the pro-life position has been a central theme in both local and national right-to-life activism. A popular quip summarizes this position: "If there were a window on a pregnant woman's stomach, there would be no more abortions."[25]

Given this emphasis on visual persuasion, it did not take long for the antiabortion advocates to seize upon the idea that ultrasound could promote "bonding" with the fetus. In 1984, the videotape *The Silent Scream* was released, and it was viewed by hundreds of thousands of people across the country over the ensuing decade (it is still available today).

This videotape, billed as a view of abortion "from the point of view of the unborn child," is narrated by Dr. Bernard Nathanson (a prominent activist for legalization of abortion in the early 1970s who had later converted to the antiabortion position), and features what is supposedly a real-time ultrasound image of a first-trimester abortion taking place. The title of the videotape refers to a moment at which the fetus appears to be opening its mouth, in what the narrator tells us is a "silent scream."[26] In this case, it would seem that the ultrasound image is supposed to have a "bonding" effect not merely upon the pregnant woman, but upon the entire viewing public. As we saw in the case of the AT&T advertisement, here too we see the concept of "bonding" extended from ultrasound to other technologies (in this case videotape and television), such that they too appear to possess the power to forge unbreakable bonds of love between viewer and viewed.

The DeMoss Foundation has used ultrasound in the same manner in a more recent television spot, part of its "Life: What a Beautiful Choice" campaign, which was aired off and on during 1993 and 1994. In this commercial, a split screen shows an extremely cute newborn baby in a diaper on one side, and on the other side a real-time ultrasound image of a fetus moving around in the womb. A male narrator's voice points out certain highly symbolic physical capabilities that they share: "The baby on the left can feel pain; so can the baby on the right. . . . The baby on the left can suck its thumb; so can the baby on the right . . . ," and so forth. The narrator then concludes: "The difference is, that the baby on the left has just been born, and the baby on the right would very much like to be." The screen then shows, in white script against a black background, the slogan "Life: What a Beautiful Choice." Again, I would argue that this advertisement works to expand the limits of the supposed "bonding" effect of ultrasound, from the pregnant woman to the entire American public.

This expansion of the "bonding" concept entails certain serious implications. First of all, it implies that the crucial factor in "bonding" is not the mother-infant relationship (as assumed by Fletcher and Evans, and by Kennell and Klaus before them), but rather simply the fact of viewing the ultrasound image. Not only is the pregnant woman visually excluded from the picture in ultrasound depictions of the fetus (a point made by a number of feminist commentators),[27] but, more important, the conditions have been established for arguing that the public may form a relationship with the fetus that is equally emotionally profound as that of the pregnant woman—or indeed *more* profound, if the viewers have "succeeded" in bonding with the fetus and the pregnant woman has, for whatever reason, "failed." In other words, the notion of ultrasound "bonding" lays the groundwork for arguing that a relationship with an abstract image or idea of "the fetus" can be just as deep and valid as, or indeed more profound than, an actual concrete specific relationship of a particular woman and her particular pregnancy.

It is here that we see most clearly the manner in which the notion of ultrasound as a tool for promoting maternal "bonding" may ironically work to *undermine* the integrity of the relationship between the pregnant woman and the fetus. We see too how the tensions inherent within the hybrid practice of obstetrical ultrasound may finally explode, as the theory of ultrasound "bonding" sets the stage for antiabortion advocates to use the authority and power and tools of medical science *against* a medical procedure, and the medical professionals who perform it.

Conclusions

Paul Hill's statement, to the effect that obstetrical ultrasound can explain and justify the ideologically motivated murder of a physician who performs abortions, does not come from nowhere—it is the logical (or rather, the very illogical) conclusion of the curious role that obstetrical ultrasound plays in the construction of what I have termed the "prenatal paradox." Pregnancy is constructed as a highly tentative and conditional affair, subject to prenatal testing and quality control, and at the same time, the very technology that is used to perform the diagnostic test is also used to construct pregnancy as an experience of unconditional bonding. More generally, the fetus is increasingly constructed as a consumer product, at the same time that it is constructed more and more as a "person" from the earliest stages of development. Obstetrical ultrasound is intricately involved in many aspects of these contradictory processes, and the resulting tensions, which as we have seen are implicit within medical practice itself, become glaring as ultrasound is taken up outside the medical context, in the broader culture. An ethnographic focus on obstetrical ultrasound thus allows us to see, in part, how the black-and-white polarities of abortion politics emerge out of a level of practice that is, like ultrasound imagery itself, an ever-changing composition in many shades of gray, as ambiguous as it is emotionally charged.

The research on which this essay is based was supported in part by a Jacob K. Javits graduate fellowship from the U.S. Department of Education, for which I am very grateful. For practical assistance with the research and/or helpful comments on earlier drafts of this essay, I wish to thank Madeleine Akrich, Joan P. Baker, Daphne Berdahl, Jean Comaroff, Sarah Franklin, Shao Jing, Linda Layne, Dr. Gary Loy, Mary Mahowald, Lynn Morgan, Anne McCleary, Helena Ragoné, Michael Rosenthal, Dr. Z. Sheikh, Mary Scoggin, Jean Lea Spitz, and Dave Wight.

Notes

1. As they waited in the clinic waiting room, I explained the nature of my research to women who had come for obstetrical scans, and those who were interested agreed to allow me to accompany them into the examination room during the scan and conduct a semistructured interview afterward. Participants were thus self-selected, and no attempt was made to limit the study only to women who were pregnant for the first time, or who had never had an ultrasound examination before, or who had planned their pregnancies jointly with a partner in the context of a stable monogamous relationship (see note 8). Just over one hundred women eventually took part. This research in the clinic was supplemented by interviews with approximately thirty women residing in the vicinity of the clinic, whom I contacted through personal connections and through the informal circulation of a letter explaining my research. Again, participants were self-selected; some had had obstetrical ultrasound exams many years ago, some very recently, and some on a number of occasions over a period of months or years. I also formally interviewed fifteen sonographers (some practicing clinically, some working in the ultrasound industry, some working in educational institutions), a few other medical professionals (midwives, radiologists, and obstetricians), and several engineers employed by a company that manufactures ultrasound equipment. This research will be discussed at greater length in the dissertation I am currently completing in the department of anthropology at the University of Chicago.

2. Although the most sophisticated ultrasound equipment may cost as much as $150,000, low-end devices may be purchased new for as little as $10,000, and there is also a thriving market in second-hand equipment. The cost of acquiring ultrasound equipment thus is not prohibitive for doctors in private practice, unlike other medical imaging technologies. A member of the marketing department of one leading U.S. producer of ultrasound equipment estimated that some 60 percent of equipment sales are to private practices.

3. In European countries, ultrasound examinations are often performed by physicians, radiologists, or midwives. In the United States, by contrast, a separate profession of "diagnostic medical sonography" has been established, and people specially trained and certified in ultrasound, called "sonographers," perform the majority of ultrasound examinations. Formal training programs established since the early 1970s, which range in length from one to four years, prepare sonographers to specialize in one or more of several major areas, such as vascular, cardiac, and abdominal or ob/gyn. At the end of this training, sonographers who pass a registry examination are certified competent to accurately obtain ultrasound views of anatomical features as ordered by a physician. These ultrasound images must then be reviewed, approved, and interpreted by a physician or radiologist.

4. On the manner in which prenatal diagnosis has redefined pregnancy as a "tentative" condition, see Rothman (1986).

5. Pitkin, cited in Gabbe 1994: 67.

6. U.S. Department of Health and Human Services (1984). The list of approved indications (edited slightly in the interest of brevity) is as follows:

- Estimation of gestational age for patients with uncertain clinical dates, or verification of dates for patients who are to undergo scheduled elective repeat caesarian delivery, indicated induction of labor, or other elective termination of pregnancy.
- Evaluation of fetal growth (e.g., when the patient has an identified etiology for utero-placental insufficiency, such as severe pre-eclampsia, chronic hypertension, chronic renal disease, severe diabetes mellitus, or for other

medical complications of pregnancy where fetal malnutrition, i.e., IUGR or macrosomia, is suspected).

- Vaginal bleeding of undetermined etiology in pregnancy.
- Determination of fetal presentation when the presenting part cannot be adequately determined in labor or the fetal presentation is variable in late pregnancy.
- Suspected multiple gestation based upon detection of more than one fetal heartbeat pattern, or fundal height larger than expected for dates, and/or prior use of fertility drugs.
- Adjunct to amniocentesis.
- Significant uterine size/clinical dates discrepancy.
- Pelvic mass detected clinically.
- Suspected hydatidiform mole on the basis of clinical signs of hypertension, proteinuria, and/or the presence of ovarian cysts felt on pelvic examination or failure to detect fetal heart tones with a Doppler ultrasound device after 12 weeks.
- Adjunct to cervical cerclage placement.
- Suspected ectopic pregnancy or when pregnancy occurs after tuboplasty or prior ectopic gestation.
- Adjunct to special procedures, such as fetoscopy, intrauterine transfusion, shunt placement, in vitro fertilization, embryo transfer, or chorionic villi sampling.
- Suspected fetal death.
- Suspected uterine abnormality (e.g., clinically significant leiomyomata, or congenital structural abnormalities, such as bicornate uterus or uterus didelphys, etc.).
- Intrauterine contraceptive device localization.
- Ovarian follicle development surveillance.
- Biophysical evaluation for fetal well-being after 28 weeks of gestation.
- Observation of intrapartum events (e.g., version/extraction of second twin, manual removal of placenta, etc.).
- Suspected polyhydramnios or oligohydramnios.
- Suspected abruptio placentae.
- Adjunct to external version from breech to vertex presentation.
- Estimation of fetal weight and/or presentation in premature rupture of membranes and/or premature labor.
- Abnormal serum alpha-fetoprotein value for clinical gestational age when drawn.
- Followup observation of identified fetal anomaly.
- Followup evaluation of placenta location for identified placenta previa.
- History of previous congenital anomaly.
- Serial evaluation of fetal growth in multiple gestation.
- Evaluation of fetal condition in late registrants for prenatal care.

7. Such modifications in a woman's behavior might be expected to improve her own physical health as well, of course, but I have not seen this point made in the context of discussions of ultrasound's "psychological benefits" in the medical literature.

8. One might expect that practitioners would seek such "behavioral benefits" from ultrasound in women who are considered likely to engage in harmful behaviors such as drinking, smoking, and drug use. It is very difficult to gauge accurately when an expectation

of "behavioral benefits" comes into play in the decision to prescribe an ultrasound exam, since the ordering physician is required in each case to list one of the officially approved indications, and neither the patient nor the sonographers would likely be aware of this intention. Anecdotal evidence suggests, however, that the practice of ordering ultrasound for "behavioral benefits" is not so uncommon, and my own impression is that this primarily involves low-income or "clinic" patients (women without private health insurance who rely on Medicare or Medicaid for coverage and receive care in a publicly funded clinic).

Published studies suggesting that ultrasound can have "behavioral benefits," however, are *not* based on research among women who are known to engage in harmful behaviors during pregnancy, nor indeed among socially and economically disadvantaged women who, as a group, are perhaps considered more likely to do so. The study cited above, for example (Campbell et al. 1982), included as subjects only women "of Caucasian origin, aged between 18 and 32, married or within a stable relationship . . . having planned the pregnancy jointly with their partner . . . and all having attended [prenatal care] early in pregnancy," who furthermore had no history of infertility, no previous miscarriages, and no known risk of congenital malformations. Indeed, it is most unlikely that the women included in the study would ever be thought to *need* ultrasound in order to behave properly during pregnancy, because the very criteria that qualified them for the study (planned pregnancy in the context of a stable relationship, early prenatal care attendance, etc.) already exhibit the desired forms of behavior.

9. See Rothman (1986) on the "tentative pregnancy." For discussions of the impact of amniocentesis, see Rapp (1993, 1995).

10. This account draws on Eyer (1992). Eyer criticizes both the "bonding" research and the earlier "maternal attachment" research upon which it drew as being more myth than science, and argues that it has served to cloak prevalent attitudes toward motherhood in a mantle of scientific authority.

11. See, for example, Milne and Rich (1981), Eichmann (1992).

12. For a discussion of the ways in which ultrasound imagery is used by parents mourning pregnancy loss, see Layne (1992).

13. Aside from the clinic in which I conducted research, I have visited two other clinics, both of which also organized examination rooms in this way. Conversations with sonographers (many of whom have worked in a number of different settings) and with women who had had ultrasound examinations at different sites suggest that this arrangement is typical.

14. All names are pseudonyms.

15. Charlotte, perhaps emboldened by her experience working as a nurse's aide, took a rare degree of initiative. Not only did she ask a great many questions *during* the exam, but when left alone for a few minutes to dress herself afterward, she seized the transducer and attempted to see for herself whatever it was she felt Linda had not shown her. "After she left I did it myself. I put the gel on and I moved it around myself, and I could see things."

16. I was told that in this clinic over the course of several years, the number of scans (especially more extensive "Level II" scans) scheduled each day had increased significantly.

17. Sandelowski (1994) discusses the way in which this arrangement turns the sonographer herself into a sort of spectacle, as patients and those accompanying them attempt to read from the sonographer's facial expressions the information that she is not authorized to deliver to them.

As well as challenging the hierarchy that separates the sonographer as medical professional from the patient, this convention thus also highlights the hierarchy that separates the sonographer as a "technician" from the supervising physician, who alone has the authority to make diagnoses. In fact it sometimes happens that the supervising physician, whose signature is required on each examination and who receives a fee for reviewing the images, is less competent in ultrasound than the sonographer working under him or her. In practice, the distinction between "production" and "interpretation" of ultrasound imagery is not as clear as protocols would suggest, and one might argue that a certain amount of "interpretation" or even "diagnosis" is inevitably involved in the sonographer's work.

18. I use the feminine pronoun because all but one of the sonographers I encountered in this clinic were women, and nationwide 87 percent of registered sonographers are women. The proportion of men is even lower in the specialized field of ob/gyn ultrasound, though there are more male sonographers in fields such as cardiac ultrasound and vascular ultrasound.

19. However, the notion of what may count as "natural" is very flexible (see Wertz and Wertz, 1989).

20. On pregnancy experienced as a quest for scientific knowledge, see Davis-Floyd (1992).

21. Perhaps for this reason, I found in my research that couples who were committed to a vision of shared parenting especially valued the father's presence at the ultrasound examination. Alternatively, women sometimes expressed the hope that seeing the ultrasound might facilitate "bonding" between a father and his child, when paternal sentiment seemed lacking; see also Rapp (1995: 80). On the manner in which ultrasound makes expectant fatherhood and expectant motherhood "less unequal," see Sandelowski (1994).

22. Members of the marketing department of Siemens Ultrasound whom I interviewed disagreed with the notion that ultrasound equipment marketing does or should directly target patients. Instead, they insist, their marketing efforts must be aimed at sonographers and doctors, since these are the parties likely to have a say in equipment purchasing decisions. Still, given the manner in which this particular advertisement is addressed (toward a viewer who is clearly construed as patient rather than doctor), I believe this interpretation is fair in this case.

23. Other AT&T advertisements elaborate upon this subtle suggestion that telephone technology helps "bond" family members together in the proper hierarchical order. For example, a recent magazine advertisement (appearing in the July 17, 1995 issue of *The New Yorker*), states:

Now when mothers speak, daughters can have an easier time listening. And when fathers make pronouncements, their sons may actually find themselves nodding in agreement. As many AT&T customers are discovering, the barriers between loved ones are giving way to bridges of understanding. For example, family members are finding it easy to comprehend even the subtlest inflections of a familiar voice. . . .

24. Ameritech (another telephone service company) has also recently released an advertisement featuring an obstetrical ultrasound image, drawing attention to the role of telephone technology in the new and rapidly developing field of teleradiology.

For an in-depth discussion of one of the earliest product advertisements—for Volvo cars—to feature obstetrical ultrasound, please see Taylor (1992). This advertisement is also discussed in Stabile (1993) and Kaplan (1994).

25. Ginsburg (1988: 102).

26. For a discussion of *The Silent Scream* and its use of ultrasound imagery, see Petchesky (1987). See also Taylor (1992).

27. See, for example, Petchesky (1987), Stabile (1993), and Duden (1993).

References

Campbell, S., A. E. Reading, D. N. Cox, C. M. Sledmere, R. Mooney, P. Chudleigh, J. Beedle, and H. Ruddick. 1982. "Ultrasound Scanning in Pregnancy: The Short-Term Psychological Effects of Early Real-time Scans." *Journal of Psychosomatic Obstetrics and Gynecology* 1, 2: 57–60.

Davis-Floyd, Robbie E. 1992. *Birth as an American Rite of Passage.* Berkeley: University of California Press.

de Crespigy, Lachlan and Rhonda Dredge. 1991. *Which Tests for My Unborn Baby? A Guide to Prenatal Diagnosis.* Melbourne: Oxford University Press Australia.

Duden, Barbara. 1993. *Disembodying Women: Perspectives on Pregnancy and the Unborn.* Cambridge, Mass.: Harvard University Press.

Eichmann, M. A. 1992. *Impacts of Ultrasound on Maternal-Fetal Attachment (Bonding).* Ph.D. dissertation, Northwestern University.

Eyer, Diane E. 1992. *Mother-Infant Bonding: A Scientific Fiction.* New Haven, Conn.: Yale University Press.

Fleishman, S. 1995. "Too Young to Be Movie Stars? FDA Warns Firms Making 'Keepsake' Sonogram Videos." *Washington Post,* February 13, section D.

Fletcher, J. C. and M. I. Evans, 1983. "Maternal Bonding in Early Fetal Ultrasound Examinations." *New England Journal of Medicine* 308, 7: 392–93.

Gabbe, S. G. 1994. "Routine Versus Indicated Scans." In *Diagnostic Ultrasound Applied to Obstetrics and Gynecology,* ed. Rudy E. Sabbagha. Philadelphia: Lippincott.

Ginsburg, Faye D. 1988. *Contested Lives: The Abortion Debate in an American Community.* Berkeley: University of California Press.

Kaplan, E. A. 1994. "Look Who's Talking, Indeed: Fetal Images in Recent North American Visual Culture." In *Mothering: Ideology, Experience, and Agency,* ed. Evelyn Nabato Glenn, Grace Chang, and Linda Rennie Forcey. New York: Routledge.

Klaus, M., P. Jerauld, N. Kreger, W. McAlpine, M. Steffa, and J. Kennell. 1972. "Maternal Attachment: Importance of the First Postpartum Days." *New England Journal of Medicine* 286, 9: 460–63.

Layne, Linda. 1992. "Of Fetuses and Angels: Fragmentation and Integration in Narratives of Pregnancy Loss." *Knowledge and Society* 9: 29–58.

Milne, L. S. and O. J. Rich. 1981. "Cognitive and Affective Aspects of the Responses of Pregnant Women to Sonography." *Maternal Child Nursing Journal* 10, 1: 15–39.

Moore, R. M., Jr., L. L. Jeng, R. G. Kaczmarek, and P. J. Placek. 1990. "Use of Diagnostic Imaging Procedures and Fetal Monitoring Devices in the Care of Pregnant Women." *Public Health Reports* 105, 5: 471–75.

News Wave. 1994. "FDA Investigates Fetal Sonogram Video Businesses." *News Wave* 15, 4.

Petchesky, R. P. 1987. "Fetal Images: The Power of Visual Culture in the Politics of Reproduction." *Feminist Studies* 13, 2: 263–92.

Pitkin, R. M. 1991. "Screening and Detection of Congenital Malformations." *American Journal of Obstetrics and Gynecology* 164: 1045.

Rapp, Rayna. 1993. "Accounting for Amniocentesis." In *Knowledge, Power, and Practice: The Anthropology of Medicine and Everyday Life,* ed. Shirley Lindenbaum and Margaret Lock. Berkeley: University of California Press.

———. 1995. "Heredity, or: Revising the Facts of Life." In *Naturalizing Power:*

Essays in Feminist Cultural Analysis, ed. Sylvia J. Yanagisako. New York: Routledge.

Rothman, Barbara Katz. 1989. *Recreating Motherhood: Ideology and Technology in a Patriarchal Society.* New York: Norton.

———. 1986. *The Tentative Pregnancy: Prenatal Diagnosis and the Future of Motherhood.* New York: Viking.

Sandelowski, Margarete. 1994. "Separate, But Less Unequal: Fetal Ultrasonography and the Transformation of Expectant Mother/Fatherhood." *Gender & Society* 8, 2 (June): 230–45.

Schneider, David Murray. 1968. *American Kinship: A Cultural Account.* Englewood Cliffs, N.J.: Prentice-Hall.

Stabile, Carol A. 1993. "Shooting the Mother: Fetal Photography and the Politics of Disappearance." *Camera Obscura* 28: 178–205.

Taylor, Janelle S. 1992. "The Public Fetus and the Family Car: From Abortion Politics to a Volvo Advertisement." *Public Culture* 4, 2 (Spring): 67–80.

U.S. Department of Health and Human Services, National Institutes of Health, Office of Medical Applications of Research. 1984. "Diagnostic Ultrasound Imaging in Pregnancy." *National Institutes of Health Consensus Development Conference Consensus Statement* 5, 1.

Wertz, Richard W. and Dorothy C. Wertz. 1989. *Lying-In: A History of Childbirth in America.* New York: Free Press.

West, Cindy. 1994. "Hill Sentenced to Life in Prison on Federal Charge." Reuters News Service, December 2.

Chapter 2
Provisional Normalcy and "Perfect Babies": Pregnant Women's Attitudes Toward Disability in the Context of Prenatal Testing

Nancy Press, Carole H. Browner, Diem Tran, Christine Morton, and Barbara Le Master

The past decades have witnessed the transformation of reproduction by advances in technology for the prenatal detection of birth defects and other developmental disabilities. Independently, yet concurrently, America has been engaged in a struggle to redefine the meaning of disability and the place of the disabled in society. The question of how advances in prenatal diagnosis and changes in our ways of viewing disability may affect each other is of great concern to all those interested in issues of disability and of reproduction.

The disabilities rights movement has fueled much important change. Today many persons with disabilities are forcefully asserting their right to be accepted as full participants in society. In contrast with times past, they are choosing not to mask their handicaps and are challenging other Americans to deal with any discomfort this may cause. They are demanding changes in insurance and employment law and in the structure of public space so they may participate more fully in work and in social life. At the same time, many feminists, bioethicists, and disability rights activists fear that the growing acceptance of prenatal diagnosis and the practice of selectively aborting defective pregnancies will generalize to more intolerance of the disabled and heightened stigma of families with disabled children (Kaplan 1993; Retsinas 1991; see also Wertz and Fletcher 1993 for one response to this concern). So far there has been little empirical research on pregnant women's attitudes toward disability. Yet the attitudes and actions of pregnant women are at the nexus of the social forces created by advances in prenatal diagnosis and the disabilities rights movement.

Research on attitudes toward disability has focused primarily on the populations most directly affected, such as families of children with disabilities or teachers and other professionals who work with individuals who are disabled (Horne 1985; Yuker 1988). Most prior research has been informed by the field of psychology. This work has assumed that attitudes toward disability are static, measurable entities that explicitly correlate with personality or sociodemographic indicators and directly predict behavior. The research has also presupposed that attitudes can be extracted from the locally occasioned character of their production. Consequently, insufficient attention has been given to the contingent and contextual nature of social interaction in forming attitudes of any sort.

Recently, however, some disability researchers have displayed concern with how individuals construct the meaning of particular disabilities in general or in specific contexts, how they come to determine what it means to be "human" or "normal," and the importance of these qualities for social relationships or social interaction (Asch and Fine 1988; Bogdan and Taylor 1992; Deshen and Deshen 1989; Ferguson et al. 1992).

In keeping with this recent contextual approach to studying attitudes toward disability, this paper will examine the images of, and attitudes toward, disability held by a group of pregnant women, as well as their hypothetical willingness to terminate a pregnancy for a variety of disabling conditions. The women, who all had low-risk pregnancies, represent the general population in that they lacked special prior knowledge or experience with disability. While their views, images, and attitudes are likely to be representative of those of the general public, the context of pregnancy and the prenatal diagnostic testing they were offered are likely to have made the issue of disability particularly salient for them.

The Context of MSAFP Screening

Until recently, women under 35 with no personal or family history of birth defects were generally not offered prenatal testing. The available procedures were invasive, carried some risk to the fetus, required considerable procedural skill, and were expensive to perform. However, the development of the maternal serum alpha fetoprotein (MSAFP) screening test changed this situation. MSAFP screening uses a venous blood draw from the arm of the pregnant woman and can indicate the possible presence of several serious birth defects in the fetus. It is thus procedurally simple, noninvasive, and inexpensive. Following its widespread availability in the 1980s, MSAFP screening was rapidly incorporated as part of standard prenatal care in many parts of the United States and Europe (Macri et al. 1979; Crandall 1980; Wald 1980; Cunningham and Kizer 1990). As of 1989, over half of all pregnancies in the United States were screened by MSAFP (Meaney et al. 1993). However, while the mechanics of the test are trivial and benign compared to invasive pre-natal procedures, such as amniocentesis and chorionic villus sampling, the ethical and moral implications are identical. In almost all cases, a woman's only options following a confirmed positive diagnosis are termi-nating the pregnancy or continuing it knowing her child will be affected. Thus the routine offer of MSAFP testing has been seen to constitute a transformation of the experience of pregnancy in that it encourages *all* pregnant women to think about prenatal diagnosis and disability as something with particular relevance to their own lives. We will present data below that speak to both the meanings and the hypothetical actions of pregnant women in regard to disability in the context of pregnancy.

Description of the Research

The Study Population

Our data come from a larger study of the role of noninvasive prenatal screening in the transformation of pregnancy and prenatal care in the United States. The data presented here come from 140 of our infor-mants, all of whom were pregnant at the time of entry into the study. Of these 140, 63 percent (n = 86) were European-American (born in the United States to parents of European-American backgrounds), 37 percent (n = 54) were Mexican-American (born in the United States to parents of Mexican ancestry or immigrated to the United States by the age of ten). Of the European-Americans, 52 percent (n = 45) had been raised Roman Catholic, and 48 percent (n = 41) had been raised non-Catholic Christian; all but one of the Mexican-Americans had been raised Catholic.[1] The mean age of the group was 26.6 years. They had had between 0 and 6 children (mean = 1.3, standard deviation [SD] = 1.04) and from 0 to 9 previous pregnancies (mean = 2.2, SD = 1.69). Slightly over one third had had at least one induced abortion. Their me-dian household income was $30,000 to $35,000, with 24 percent having incomes below $15,000 and 26 percent over $50,000. Nineteen percent had not completed high school, 67 percent had earned high school degrees, and 14 percent had more than a high school education. We re-cruited only women between the ages of 18 and 35 because we wanted to exclude pregnancies that health care providers and/or women them-selves would routinely deem "high risk."[2]

Abundant research has documented the role of ethnicity and social class in shaping attitudes toward health and illness and health-related behavior (Brown 1989; Mechanic 1986; Waitzkin 1983). In addition, religion is often assumed to be an important factor in women's decisions about prenatal testing. This is because many religions prohibit or place restrictions on the use of abortion, which is generally the only way to avert the birth of a child found to have a birth defect. We therefore stratified our sample according to these variables in an effort to capture these differences. However, few significant differences related to ethnicity, religion, or social class were found with regard to the issues we discuss below. We believe this was the case partly because of the relative homogeneity of our study population. The sample showed little variation in educational level, often found to be an important predictor of health and illness behavior (Mechanic 1986), and there was a high level of acculturation among the Mexican-Americans, according to their scores on standardized instrument (Marín et al. 1987). In addition, as other research has shown, ethnic differences are often overwhelmed by the homogenizing effect of interaction with the biomedical system (Lazarus 1994); we found such an homogenizing process in the interactions of our informants with the health maintenance organization (HMO) where they were prenatal care patients (Press and Browner 1993). For these reasons, we will not differentiate, for the most part, by ethnicity, religion, or socioeconomic status (SES) in discussing our results.

Methods

We conducted lengthy face-to-face interviews with pregnant women who were patients at five branches of a southern California HMO. All interviews took place after the twenty-fourth week of pregnancy, by which time pregnant women had received MSAFP test results as well as results from any suggested follow-up testing. The interview included semistructured and open-ended questions covering a broad range of topics, including women's understandings and attitudes about, and experiences with, pregnancy, prenatal diagnosis, and disability. The data we will discuss below come from two series of interview questions relating to disability and a ranking device developed by the investigators to assess attitudes toward specific disabilities.

The first series asks about the informant's general experience with disability: *Have you ever known anyone with a handicap, disability, or serious medical condition, or whose child had a handicap, disability, or serious medical condition? What seemed to you to be the most difficult thing about that person's condition? Was there something you particularly admired in the way that person dealt with his/her condition?* The second series of questions, taken from a later portion of the interview, ask about disability specifically in the context of the woman's pregnancy: *If a child of yours were born with a handicap or severe medical problem, how do you think you would react? What do you think the greatest challenges of the situation would be for you? for the rest of your family? If all the [prenatal diagnostic] tests had shown that your baby had a problem, what do you think you would have done? Under what conditions, if any, do you think you would have terminated the pregnancy?*

At the end of the interview we administered the investigator-designed Developmental Disabilities Attitudes Measure (DDAM). A four-point Likert scale, the DDAM comprises two sequentially administered sorting tasks. The symptoms of seventeen conditions that are genetically transmitted are listed, one to a card. The informant was first asked to sort the cards according to the degree of concern she would feel if told that her fetus would be born with the condition characterized by the symptom on each card. Cards could be placed under one of four headings: *Extreme Concern, Considerable Concern, Mild Concern,* or *Slight or No Concern.* She was then handed another card deck, with the same symptom descriptions, and asked to sort them according to her hypothetical willingness to terminate her pregnancy if she were told that the fetus would be born with the condition characterized on each card. Cards again could be placed under one of four headings: *Would Definitely Terminate, Would Probably Terminate, Would Probably Not Terminate,* and *Would Definitely Not Terminate.*

Pregnant Women's Views on the Meaning of Disability

The prenatal detection of conditions that cannot be cured logically entails the belief that these conditions are so devastating that pregnant women should be given the opportunity to avoid the birth of babies so affected. Some disabilities rights activists hold that this logic implies a wider belief that many disabled people would be better off dead, or at least not having been born (Asch and Fine 1988). This view runs directly counter to an emerging disabilities rights discourse, which argues that the primary obstacles facing people with disabilities are located in the body politic rather than in the physical body. Thus, as the number of women offered prenatal testing is increasing, the choices they must make to accept or decline testing are also increasingly subjected to influences from two quite divergent views of the meaning and nature of disability. An examination of the words of the pregnant women we interviewed suggests that both views are being heard and that the tension between them has yielded views of disability that are compartmentalized, self-contradictory, and very much in flux.

Our informants' responses to our questions about disability reveal partial and undigested acceptance of positive, often romanticized images of disability alongside negative views of disability as stigmatizing and deeply feared. Perhaps the most striking discontinuities were seen between the upbeat and strongly positive attitudes women frequently expressed toward people with disabilities, both as a general category and those whom they had actually known, versus their extremely fearful and negative attitudes regarding the possibility that their own child might be disabled. For instance, Beth Thompson,[3] pregnant with her first child, said "Handicapped kids are probably the most beautiful beings in the world; they have a bigger heart than anybody and they know what love is all about more than anybody." Victoria Young also spoke of the handicapped as special. She stated, "Actually, you can learn a lot from a handicapped person. . . . They become better than the average person." Similarly, in discussing children with disabilities as a general category, Eileen Calvert declared that "mentally retarded children are some of the most loving kids I've ever met." She went even further, claiming as her best friend an adult woman who is mentally retarded and whom she terms "an equal." Shawna Franklin had more experience with disability than the others, having grown up with a disabled foster brother. She was eloquent in discussing the needless discrimination he suffered due to his speech and motor impairments, yet, in keeping with the generally positive, and almost casual, voice many of the women used in discussing disability, she denied that her brother's conditions created any sort of problem for her parents and stated that, while he "had it rough for a while, [he has] gotten over it fine."

Yet, when each of these women was asked about the implications of a possible disability in a child of her own, not only their opinions, but their entire tone changed from casual and upbeat to emotionally charged, frightened, and negative. Thus, for example, when Beth Thompson talked about her possible response if she were to be told her child had been born with a handicap, she answers that she would cry. Victoria Young said that if prenatal tests had shown a problem with her fetus she would have done whatever the doctor directed, including abortion. Although the interviewer only mentioned a prenatally detected "problem," the image of disability spontaneously conjured up by Victoria was a baby "who is going to be a vegetable and have to live off life support." Eileen Calvert, who claimed as a "best friend" a woman who was mentally retarded, stated later in the interview that, if she found out early enough in her pregnancy, she would terminate a pregnancy if the baby would be born mentally retarded, because "it would be selfish on my part to have this child that could never amount to anything. . . ." But perhaps most surprising was Shawna Franklin, whose foster brother was disabled. Shawna also said she might terminate a pregnancy because of a fetal abnormality. She feared that the child might ask, "Why did you even have me?" and added, "I wouldn't want to bring a child into the world to suffer."

Although this inconsistent stance may be due in part to women's greater sense of protectiveness about their own children, this view is belied by the fact that similar tensions within women's views of and reactions to disability were apparent in responses to many other question areas, as seen below.

Provisional Normalcy and the Image of the "Supercrip"

In order to tap a full range of our informants' images of disability, we asked them to talk about someone they had personally known with a disability. Among other things, we asked, "Was there something you particularly admired in the way that person dealt with his or her problem?" The wording of our question, with its emphasis on "admirable" qualities, activated many positive images, many of which appeared to have been influenced by the media and the new public discourse on disabilities.

Writers on disability issues have suggested that the media focus on the achievements of persons with disabilities has created an image of the "supercrip": someone who has "overcome" her or his disability to the extent of leading not simply an acceptable life but an exemplary one. They claim the "supercrip" image reinforces core American values of self-reliance, independence, and the determination to overcome adversity, but that by doing so it perpetuates false standards for all members of society. Many in the disabilities community prefer to emphasize the natural, common, and even inevitable aspect of disability in the life course.

Our data provide support for the concerns of writers on disability. Thus, for example, what many of our informants found most admirable about the way a person lived with a disability was that she or he overcame it. An individual who was admired was frequently described as someone who "keeps on keeping on," "never gives up," or "doesn't let it get them down." For example, Caroline Booth admired a coworker, who used crutches, for her determination "not to use a wheelchair, not to go on disability" and because "she wants to keep working." Paula Black's uncle was paralyzed from the waist down. When asked if there was something she particularly admired in the way he dealt with his situation, she responded, "I've never seen him not be able to do anything or go anyplace. . . . He hasn't let it stop him from doing anything." And Claudia Sanchez stated specifically, "I've known a few people [with disabilities], but it's like I've never thought of it as a disability because . . . they've always been able to overcome it."

Another trait admired by our informants was a lack of negative affect in the person with the disability. Thus the disabled nephew of one informant was lauded for his "positive attitude" and the way he made a joke of his disability. Another informant admired a cousin who was "in a wheelchair," because "it really never seemed to bother him." Another person with a serious paralysis was admired because "he didn't sit at home and pout about it."

When disabled people exhibited these attitudes and behaviors, they were frequently awarded a sort of provisional normalcy, often expressed with a simile whereby disabled individuals were said to act *as if* they were normal. In fact, the word "normal" appeared over and over again in responses to this question. Patricia Jones said that what she remembered most about an aunt with a handicap was that, "to me, she was just a normal person that does everyday normal things." She admired the way her aunt kept "trying to lead a normal life." Maggie Haynes similarly lauded a disabled uncle who "tried to act like he was just as normal as anybody else."

Parents and other relatives were similarly admired for treating their disabled children "just as if they were normal" or "just like any other child." Debbie Broder criticized her parents for being overprotective of her brother, who had a developmental disability. She and her husband, on the other hand, liked "to take him places and treat him regular."

Interestingly, whereas adults were lauded for being essentially no worse off and acting no differently because of their handicap, children with disabilities were valued for the ways in which they were better than other children. They were often described as very "lovable" or "particularly loving." Roseanne Vaughan had volunteered to work with "handicapped kids." She enjoyed it, she said, because "they're so easy to love . . . [and] they just wanted to be loved." Linda Macklin believed that the handicapped daughter of a friend was "one of the happiest children I'd ever known." And Marina Salcedo said children with Down's syndrome, in particular, have "feelings [that] are more soft than ours. . . . they're very special . . . very loving and funny." For a few informants, such children were even superior to normal children. Thus, for Lynne Koenig, "a handicapped child is even a little better off [than others] because . . . they are already perfected spirits and don't have to prove themselves down here."

Conflicting Discourses: The Example of Down's Syndrome

One of the most striking examples of the tension that may be created by a burgeoning disabilities rights discourse in the context of prenatal testing was seen in our informants' beliefs about Down's syndrome. The

MSAFP test was developed to screen for neural tube defects and is only secondarily used to detect Down's syndrome. For this reason almost no emphasis was put on Down's syndrome when our informants were told about MSAFP screening at the HMO. Yet the detection of Down's syndrome is the primary reason for performing amniocentesis, and Down's syndrome is currently one of the most commonly known birth defects. Thus it is not surprising that we found that virtually all the women had heard of, and had opinions about, Down's syndrome. These opinions, however, appeared to have been strongly influenced by recent popular media images of Down's syndrome, including television programs with Down's syndrome actors, made-for-TV movies about parents helping Down's syndrome children achieve in school, and Down's syndrome children pictured on the same cereal boxes as major athletes. The result was statements that show a dynamic and somewhat confused mix of old images of mental retardation and incapacity juxtaposed with new images of different but "special" children.

Thus, in responding to the question, "Can you tell me what Down's syndrome is?" Rosie Schutz said she couldn't exactly, "just that it's not retardedness, not exactly. . . . It looks like they have mental retardation because of their movements, but their minds are fine." Angela Garcia believed that Down's syndrome children could often be pretty much normal, and that it is primarily when their parents don't have high expectations and "treat them as if they're handicapped" that they wind up appearing mentally deficient. Finally, when asked to define Down's syndrome, Brandy Morris said the only thing she knew was that "their eyes bulge out a little; they're actually smart, but their mentality just isn't like ours."

Carla Baker was one of many informants who directly referenced the television series *Life Goes On*, which includes a child with Down's syndrome as one of the actors. She said, "I always thought [Down's syndrome] was mental retardation, [but] my husband corrected me the other night when we were watching *Life Goes On*." Similarly, Susan Bradshaw said that "people with Down's syndrome can grow up to have a normal life." When asked by the interviewer what was the basis of this belief, she answered, "TV—that program on television [about the child with Down's syndrome]. Talk shows, things like that."

The struggle of these women to define the relationship between Down's syndrome and mental retardation is particularly crucial since, elsewhere in the interviews, these same women reacted to a mention of the term "mental retardation" with great fear and indicated that it was one of the disabilities for which they would be most likely to consider abortion. The positive images they held of Down's syndrome and "special children" had apparently not so much transformed their fears of mental retardation as led to the creation of a new subcategory for Down's syndrome, one that lacked some of the negative attributes they attached to mental retardation in general.

The view among many of our informants that Down's syndrome is not really mental retardation, and is therefore not terribly handicapping, is significant, since it contrasts with what most in the medical establishment believe—that Down's syndrome is one of the more serious forms of mental retardation. The question that arises, then, is which image of Down's syndrome would prevail if a pregnant woman were counseled by a physician or genetic counselor following prenatal testing? Our data suggest that if a medical provider depicted Down's syndrome as mental retardation, the more positive new media image loosely held by many pregnant women would rapidly dissolve. This supposition is borne out by statistics that show that the vast majority of women whose fetuses are diagnosed with Down's syndrome do in fact seek abortion (Deukmejian et al. 1990).

Negative Images and Societal Disapproval

It should also be noted that not all our informants held positive images of persons with disabilities. For a small minority, negative and fearful attitudes were all that existed, unmitigated by any positive views about disability or the disabled, either children or adults. Karen Root, for example, felt that a disability meant the complete absence of a worthwhile quality of life. She equated disability with the decrepitude of age and with the dying. Like extreme old age, it was a defensible reason for euthanasia. Kathy Corbin talked about how she and her husband had purposely distanced themselves from acquaintances who had a disabled child. She said her husband felt "he picked right in the woman who is having his children, because I've given him these healthy, strong children. We do separate ourselves [from those with disabilities]." When asked by the interviewer precisely what she meant by "separate ourselves," Kathy said it was as if "it's going to rub off . . . if I'm being honest. . . . I hate to say this, but they're almost unclean, like they're not whole human beings." Although few informants were this negative, sometimes what began as a generally positive statement about individuals with disabilities moved on to an uncomfortable admission of mixed feelings. Thus, for example, Caroline Booth, cited earlier for her admiration of a coworker who was trying to stay out of a wheelchair, admitted, "I am not comfortable with [her disability]. . . . I had to force myself to stay around and say hello to her."

For some of the women, a powerful negative aspect of having a disabled child was the attendant social embarrassment. This fear of disapproval sometimes appeared to reflect what they, themselves had felt when looking at mothers with disabled children. Thus Maria Torres said that what she would find hardest about having a child with a handicap or severe medical problem was "how other people would look at you." Kathy Griffith spoke of a woman in her church who wheeled her mentally retarded son into services each week. She admired this woman, but said that in the same situation she would "be afraid of what people would think. 'Oh, she had a retarded baby.' They'd make fun of me and . . . I don't know if I could handle that." And Joelle Wyatt said that having a disabled child would be difficult for her because "I always care about what other people think." She went on to talk about how disturbing she found it to have to watch odd-looking children clinging to their mothers when she went to the mall. She did not want to be on the receiving end of the sort of censure she felt.

Other women focused on a fear of being judged negatively by specific family members who would devalue the baby and, perhaps by extension, the mother. Cindy-Dawn Apted thought the greatest challenge of having a child with a disability would be "hearing people making fun of my child." This included her family, whom she felt "would be embarrassed." Doreen McMillan thought her family would "eventually accept the [disabled] child. . . , [but] I have a feeling that some of them would put this one off to the side. Especially if it was a physical handicap . . . something that would be more readily noticeable to a person walking down the street. . . . And as a parent I would feel more . . . burdened." Kyla Boone first described the social rejection she would fear for a disabled child. According to Kyla, "Life is difficult enough, so when you come out and have a disability marked against you, people discriminate so badly and they're so prejudiced and judgmental." However, when asked to imagine her own reaction to the birth of a child with a disability, her tone changed from the general and political to the very personal. She answered, "I would just want to crawl away and die . . . [and] my mom wouldn't have anything to do with [the child]." She ended by stating, "I just want to produce perfect children."

"Perfect Babies" and Accepting What's Not "Normal"

This last response is particularly interesting. Social critics who are concerned about the transformation of pregnancy by routine prenatal diagnosis have frequently expressed a fear that women will seek to have only "perfect babies." We believe that our data shed a somewhat different light on this issue. Careful analysis of our informants' statements indicates that the great majority are not seeking "perfect" children but, rather, "perfectly normal" children. Anna Grant eloquently presented this position when she said that "everyone wants to be handed this little person who is perfectly normal." It is considered normal, in the sense of usual and proper, for babies to begin life perfectly healthy. "Everyone prays for a healthy and normal child," said Beth Thomson. Linda Carson responded to the question, "what would be the greatest challenge of having a child with a disability?" with the following: "That feeling that it wasn't supposed to turn out this way."

"Normal" was a word the informants used very frequently. If individuals with disabilities were accorded a provisional normalcy, expressed with the simile of acting *as if* they were normal, the birth of a child with a disability seemed to be always, and by definition, "not normal." Responses to questions such as, "Have you ever worried that your child might be born with a disability?" drew affirmative responses that typically included the assertion, "Everyone wants a normal child." Such responses were just as likely to come from women who felt they could fairly easily accept having a child with a disability as from women who admitted being highly fearful of this possibility. Thus Angel Kerokian, who felt that she could easily accept a child with a disability, expressed this by saying, "I think I would feel the same [as] if it was a normal child." Katie Hammel, on the other hand, said the situation of a disabled child "would be very hard. With a normal child it is hard enough." But Martha Pratt was perhaps clearest in her view of the distance between children with and without disabilities. She worried about raising a child with a disability because "they require a lot of attention; a lot more than a normal baby would. I think that you have to be a special person, because it's different than what's naturally bred into a woman, [which is] to take care of a normal child."

Most informants felt that the birth of a child with a disability would be a major life challenge and that the first hurdle to get over would be the struggle to "accept" this not-normal pregnancy outcome. Although most informants had little doubt that they would love the child and would be able to accept it, some feared that their families might contain people who could or would react by definitively rejecting a child with a handicap. The husband of Benita Hernandez, for example, had a brother who was mentally retarded and institutionalized. She wondered whether, if her child were born handicapped, her husband would reach back to his personal experience and "just push it away [and] keep it hidden." And, for an even smaller number of women, adoption or institutionalization were mentioned openly as something they felt they would choose due to their own incapacity to cross the hurdle of acceptance. Marsha Letts said she didn't know what she would do, "if I would give it up for adoption or if I would keep it." Celia Drury said, "I wouldn't know. I don't think I would want [the child]. . . . Maybe adoption."

Thus a disabled child is the "other," neither normal, perfect, healthy, nor the customary occurrence. One implication of these data on disabilities springs logically from this continuing belief in the "otherness" of a disabled baby. If a disabled child is an unexpected, odd, and accidental event, then this lapse from the norm appears to open up a choice about the acceptance or rejection of that child. Thus, in answer to our question, "If a child of yours were born with a handicap or severe medical problem, how do you think you would react?" we were struck by the repeated use of phrases such as "I would accept it," "I would keep the child," "there wouldn't be any reason to institutionalize it," or "I wouldn't lock it in a closet." The fact that our informants were consciously considering and then rejecting these options was underscored by responses in which hypothetical "other people" who decided to institutionalize or adopt out a handicapped child were mentioned.

Attitudes Toward Disability in the Context of Abortion Decision-Making

Prenatal diagnosis today presents another alternative to women—that of preventing the birth of a child with a disability. Since our informants viewed the birth of a child with a disability as an out-of-the-ordinary occurrence that raised for them the issue of acceptance or rejection of the baby, it is noteworthy that few appear to have undergone MSAFP testing determined to end the pregnancy if a birth defect were diagnosed. In fact, as we have discussed elsewhere (Press and Browner 1997), women's decisions to accept prenatal screening seem to speak more to a generalized willingness to do everything possible to ensure a healthy pregnancy than to a specific intention to avoid the birth of a baby with a disability. Thus, although over 76 percent of our informants had agreed to undergo MSAFP testing, when asked whether they would have terminated their pregnancies if all test results had been positive, only about 13 percent said that they would have. In contrast, almost 40 percent said they were certain they would have continued the pregnancy.

Of course these data reflect only hypothetical actions, not actual ones. In fact, the majority of women in California do act to end their pregnancies following confirmation of a positive prenatal diagnostic test result.[4] Thus it is possible that what women say they would do is simply an expression of their discomfort in admitting their interest in terminating a pregnancy for a birth defect and cannot be taken as a true expression of their actual thoughts and feelings about disability and abortion. However, to assume this as the only plausible explanation for the discrepancy between women's statements and their subsequent actions masks an assumption. The assumption is that the period between when a woman gives her assent to prenatal screening and when she decides to terminate her pregnancy is a transparent stretch of time marked only by the single event of receiving a positive test result. In fact, the time following an initial positive MSAFP result is filled with a variety of new and intense experiences. At the HMO where we conducted our research, these include telephone notification of a potential problem with the pregnancy and immediate referral for genetic counseling; the genetic counseling includes discussion of potentially serious disabilities of which women often have little or no prior knowledge (Browner et al. 1996; Faden et al. 1985). The woman who eventually terminates her pregnancy will first undergo ultrasound and, often immediately following, amniocentesis. All of this will occur within a very rushed time frame in the few weeks remaining before the twenty-fourth week of pregnancy, and all of it takes place in a highly technological and medicalized setting. We believe that all this, in concert, has the potential to reframe what may have seemed like a personal and ethical decision as a medical emergency in which there is little room for parental choice. Therefore, although the hypothetical data we have may not accurately reflect what these women would actually have done if faced with a confirmed positive result, it may be equally inaccurate to assume that one can simply read women's attitudes toward disability and abortion from their ultimate, binary decision. The data we collected from our interviews and the DDAM present a far more nuanced and complex view of how women feel about disabilities and about their ideal decisions should they be faced with the prospect of giving birth to a child with a disability.

The DDAM data in particular allowed us to analyze several dimensions of women's attitudes toward disability. Table 2.1 presents the mean scores for the seventeen conditions that comprise the DDAM, ranked first in terms of informants' level of concern (from most concerned = 4.0 to least concerned = 1.0) and then in terms of willingness to terminate a pregnancy (from most willing to terminate = 4.0 to least willing to terminate = 1.0).[5]

As can be seen, there is little variation between the rankings of conditions in terms of degree of concern and willingness to terminate — the things that women most fear for their children are those things for which they would be most likely to end their pregnancy. However, women's general reluctance to terminate a pregnancy, even in the face of a disabling condition they fear, is shown by the significant difference between the mean Level of concern (3.36 out of 4.00) and the mean Level of willingness to terminate (1.55 out of 4.00). That is, despite positive statements about the lives and experiences of adults and children

TABLE 2.1. Mean Scores on the Developmental Disabilities Attitudes Measure (DDAM).

Degree of concern (from most to least concerned)	Mean rank (4.0 = most concerned) (N = 140)	Willingness to terminate (from most to least willing)	Mean rank (4.0 = most willing) (N = 140)
(1) Death before age 5	3.88	(1) Death within days of birth	2.44
(2) Death within days of birth	3.85	(2) Severe mental retardation	2.15
(3) Quadriplegia	3.78	(3/4) Quadriplegia	2.11
(4) Severe mental retardation	3.77	(3/4) Death before age 5	2.11
(5) Death in 20s	3.61	(5) Physical deformity	1.90
(6) Paraplegia	3.57	(6) Severe illness throughout life	1.84
(7) Severe illness throughout life	3.52	(7) Paraplegia	1.78
(8) Physical deformity	3.44	(8) Death in 20s	1.71
(9) Blindness from birth	3.42	(9) Mild retardation, unusual appearance	1.68
(10) Mild retardation, unusual appearance	3.36	(10) Heart disease or cancer as adult	1.55
(11) Adult-onset heart disease or cancer	3.29	(11) Blindness from birth	1.54
(12) Blindness as adult	3.17	(12) Mild retardation, normal appearance	1.47
(13) Total deafness	3.14	(13) Blindness as adult	1.40
(14) Mild retardation, normal appearance	3.10	(14) Total deafness	1.30
(15) Aggressive behavior problems as child	3.04	(15) Aggressive behavior problems as child	1.29
(16) Some hearing loss	2.60	(16) Sterility	1.15
(17) Sterility	2.55	(17) Some hearing loss	1.12
Mean degree of concern	3.36	Mean willingness to terminate	1.55

with disabilities, our informants were very concerned about the possibility of virtually all the disabilities presented to them. At the same time, they expressed little willingness to terminate a pregnancy, even for many of those conditions they considered very disabling.

How Specific Disabilities Are Perceived

Thus our data suggest that the assumption that is at the base of much discussion of prenatal screening—that women's acceptance of prenatal screening implies an equal interest in ending a pregnancy subsequent to a positive test result—is overly simplistic (cf. Press and Browner 1997). This is in part because this assumption is itself predicated on an implicit belief that concern about disability and willingness to terminate a pregnancy are comparable cognitive arenas that share an underlying logical structure. Our data from the DDAM challenge this assumption. A factor analysis performed on the DDAM data demonstrates not only that women's levels of concern were significantly higher than their willingness to terminate, but that the ways they thought about these two issues were fundamentally different. Thus, when the data for willingness to terminate were subjected to a factor analysis, it appeared that the binary decision of whether or not to have an abortion produced a similar binary division of conditions into those that appeared more severe and those that appeared less severe. However, when a factor analysis was performed on the data for degree of concern, quite a different configuration emerged, in which more nuanced aspects of life with each disability, rather than simple degree of severity, appeared as underlying organizing principles.

Table 2.2 shows the results of the factor analysis performed for the 17 disabling conditions of the DDAM according to "willingness to terminate."

Table 2.3 shows a similar factor analysis of data on women's Level of concern about the 17 disabling conditions. As can be seen, the responses here loaded onto four factors rather than two.

The conditions in Factor 1, Table 2.3, appear to share the quality of being "globally disabling." One of the most interesting aspects of this factor is the inclusion of severe mental retardation along with more obviously physical impairments. Supported by informants' gloss, in other parts of the interview, of severe mental retardation using the term "vegetable," it implies that, in contrast to the milder forms of cognitive deficit, severe mental retardation may be seen as globally *physically* as well as mentally handicapping. It is possible that this factor also comprises conditions which are seen to present an extreme parental burden because, in a phrase used by several informants, these are children who "couldn't

TABLE 2.2. Conditions Considered More or Less Severe Among the 17
Disabling Conditions of the DDAM in Terms of Willingness to
Terminate a Pregnancy.

Factor 1: more severe	Factor 2: less severe
Death before age 5	Blindness from birth
Death within days of birth	Blindness as adult
Death in 20s	Total deafness
Severe mental retardation	Some hearing loss
Severe illness throughout life	Mild mental retardation, normal appearance
Quadriplegia	Sterility
Paraplegia	Aggressive behavior problems as a child
Physical deformity	
Mild mental retardation, unusual appearance	

TABLE 2.3. Factor Analysis of Scores for the 17 Disabling Conditions of
the DDAM in Terms of Level of Concern.

Factor 1: globally disabling	Factor 2: sense handicap	Factor 3: involving death of child	Factor 4: part of normal human experience
Physical deformity	Some hearing loss	Death before age 5	Heart disease or cancer as adult
Severe mental retardation	Mild mental retardation, unusual appearance	Death within days of birth	Severe illness throughout life
Quadriplegia	Mild mental retardation, normal appearance	Death in 20s	Aggressive behavior problems as child
Paraplegia	Total deafness		
	Sterility		
	Blindness from birth		
	Blindness as adult		

do anything for themselves." Factor 2 conditions appear linked as "sense
handicaps." It is interesting that mild mental retardation sorted with
the rest of this group, indicating the possibility that less severe cognitive deficits are considered another type of sensory loss. The clustering
of conditions under Factor 3 indicates that "death" is seen as a thread
of similarity overriding the age at which death occurs. Factor 4 appears

to comprise conditions that are seen as a "normal part of the human experience."

But perhaps the most interesting aspect of this analysis is that conditions whose numerical rankings in Table 2.1 indicated that they were viewed with very similar degrees of concern often loaded onto different factors, as, for example, "severe mental retardation" (Factor 1: globally disabling conditions) and "death before age 5" (Factor 3: conditions involving death as a child). Thus, at the most general level, the factor analysis revealed that our informants had complex cognitive schema in regards to these disabilities and handicaps that could not simply be mapped onto a binary abortion choice.

Conclusion

Anthropological and historical data indicate that pregnant women in most societies try to avoid being exposed to people with disabilities, or even thinking about the subject, for fear their own fetus will somehow be affected (Huet 1993). However, today the routine offer of prenatal diagnostic screening implies that women *should* consider the possibility of disability for the fetus they are carrying. It also clearly implies support for the selective abortion of fetuses diagnosed with many types of disabilities. Ironically, this implicit acceptance of pregnancy termination in the case of disability is happening at a time when hiding a disabled child or subjecting it to passive euthanasia is no longer a societally acceptable option. It is also happening while disabilities rights activists are making inroads toward making disability not only acceptable, but normalized as part of the human life course.

Thus prenatal testing not only represents a profound change in women's relationship to pregnancy, it also makes pregnancy the place where the streams of two deeply contested themes in contemporary U.S. public life—abortion and disability—converge. Pregnant women, in fact, have become the actors whose individual choices will decide the shape of the accommodation between these two debates. For this reason, it is crucial and pressing to understand how women themselves see these issues. This chapter is hoped to have provided some initial insight into the complexity of women's views of disabilities in general, in terms of their meaning for their own lives and those of their families and, especially, in the context of prenatal testing and the prospect of selective abortion.

The research was supported in part by NICHD grant HD11944 and grants from the UCLA Chicano Studies Research Center and Academic

Senate. The authors would like to thank Dr. Donald Guthrie for his invaluable assistance with analysis of the data from the Development Disabilities Attitude Measure.

Notes

1. We chose to oversample Catholic women. We speculated that, because of their church's objection to abortion, these women might be more likely to hold strong opinions on the subject of prenatal diagnostic testing.

2. Health care providers generally consider teen-age pregnancies and pregnancies of women over 35 as high risk and due for special monitoring. Women over 35 are routinely offered amniocentesis to detect Down's syndrome, the incidence of which increases rapidly after 35, at which point it also begins to exceed the miscarriage risk from amniocentesis itself.

3. All proper names are pseudonyms.

4. According to figures from the California State Genetic Disease Branch, over 90 percent of women who were diagnosed, through MSAFP and follow-up testing, to be carrying a fetus with a neural tube defect or Down's syndrome in 1988–89 elected to terminate their pregnancies (Deukmejian et al. 1990).

5. As an analysis by socioeconomic status and ethnicity did not reveal significant differences between groups, we have collapsed the data from all informants into a single table.

References

Asch, Adrienne and Michelle Fine. 1988. "Shared Dreams: A Left Perspective on Disability Rights and Reproductive Rights." In *Women with Disabilities: Essays in Psychology, Culture and Politics*, ed. Fine and Asch. Philadelphia: Temple University Press.

Bogdan, Robert and S. J. Taylor. 1992. "The Social Construction of Humanness: Relationships with Severely Disabled People." In *Interpreting Disability: A Qualitative Reader*, ed. P. M. Ferguson, D. L. Ferguson, and S. J. Taylor. New York: Teachers College Press.

Brown, Phil, ed. 1989. *Perspectives in Medical Sociology*. Prospect Heights, Ill.: Waveland.

Browner, C. H., H. M. Preloran, and N. A. Press. 1996. "The Effects of Ethnicity, Education and an Informational Video on Pregnant Women's Knowledge and Decisions About a Prenatal Diagnostic Screening Test." *Patient Education and Counseling* 27: 135–46.

Crandall, B. F. 1980. "Workgroup Paper: Counseling and Education." In *Maternal Serum Alpha-Fetoprotein: Issues in the Prenatal Screening and Diagnosis of Neural Tube Defects. Proceedings of a Conference Held by the National Center for Health Care Technology and the Food and Drug Administration, July 28–30, 1980*, ed. Barbara Gastel, James E. Haddow, John C. Fletcher, and A. Neale. Washington, DC: U.S. Government Printing Office.

Cunningham, G. C. and K. W. Kizer. 1990. "Maternal Serum Alpha-Fetoprotein Screening Activities of State Health Agencies: A Survey." *American Journal of Human Genetics* 47: 899–903.

Deshen, Shlomo and H. Deshen. 1989. "Managing at Home: Relationships Between Blind Parents and Sighted Children." *Human Organization* 48, 3: 262–67.

Deukmejian, G., C. L. Allenby, and K. W. Kizer. 1990. "A Report to the Legislature: Review of Current Genetic Programs." Berkeley: State of California, Health and Welfare Agency, Department of Health Services, Genetic Disease Branch.

Faden, R. R., A. J. Chwalow, E. Orel-Crosby, N. A. Holtzman, G. A. Chase, and C. O. Leonard. 1985. "What Participants Understand About a Maternal Serum Alpha-Fetoprotein Screening Program." *American Journal of Public Health* 75: 1381–84.

Ferguson, P. M., D. L. Ferguson and S. J. Taylor, eds. 1992. *Interpreting Disability: A Qualitative Reader.* New York: Teachers College Press.

Horne, Marcia D. 1985. *Attitudes Toward Handicapped Students: Professional, Peer, and Parent Reactions.* Hillsdale, N.J.: Lawrence Erlbaum.

Huet, Marie-Hélène. 1993. *Monstrous Imagination.* Cambridge, Mass.: Harvard University Press.

Kaplan, D. 1993. "Prenatal Screening and Its Impact on Persons with Disabilities." *Fetal Diagnosis and Therapy* 8 (suppl 1): 64–69.

Lazarus, E. 1994. "What Do Women Want? Issues of Choice, Control, and Class in Pregnancy and Childbirth." *Medical Anthropology Quarterly* 8, 1: 25–46.

Macri, J., James E. Haddow, and R. R. Weiss. 1979. "Screening for Neural Tube Defects in the United States: A Summary of the Scarborough Conference." *American Journal of Obstetrics and Gynecology* 133, 2: 119–25.

Marín, Gerardo, F. Sabogal, Barbara VanOss Marín, and R. Sabogal-Otero. 1987. "Development of a Short Acculturation Scale for Hispanics." *Hispanic Journal of Behavioral Sciences* 9, 2: 183–205.

Meaney, F. J., S. M. Riggle, and G. C. Cunningham. 1993. "Providers and Consumers of Prenatal Genetic Testing Services: What Do the National Data Tell Us?" *Fetal Diagnosis and Therapy* 8 (suppl 1): 18–27.

Mechanic, David. 1986. *From Advocacy to Allocation: The Evolving American Health Care System.* New York: Free Press, 1986.

Press, Nancy and C. H. Browner. 1993. "'Collective Fictions': Similarities in Reasons for Accepting Maternal Serum Alpha Fetoprotein Screening Among Women of Diverse Ethnic and Social Class Backgrounds." *Fetal Diagnosis and Therapy* 8 (suppl 1): 97–106.

———. 1997. "Why Women Say Yes to Prenatal Diagnosis." *Social Science and Medicine* 45, 7: 979–89.

Retsinas, J. 1991. "The Impact of Prenatal Technology upon Attitudes Toward Disabled Infants." *Research in the Sociology of Health Care* 9: 75–102.

Waitzkin, Howard. 1983. *The Second Sickness: Contradictions of Capitalist Health Care.* New York: Free Press.

Wald, N. J. 1980. "The Interpretation of AFP Values and the Effect of AFP Assay Performance on Screening Efficacy." In *Maternal Serum Alpha-Fetoprotein: Issues in the Prenatal Screening and Diagnosis of Neural Tube Defects: Proceedings of a Conference Held by the National Center for Health Care Technology and the Food and Drug Administration, July 28–30, 1980,* ed. Barbara Gastel, James E. Haddow, John C. Fletcher, and A. Neale. Washington, DC: U.S. Government Printing Office.

Wertz, Dorothy C. and John C. Fletcher. 1993. "Feminist Criticism of Prenatal Diagnosis: A Response." *Clinical Obstetrics and Gynecology* 36, 3: 541–67.

Yuker, Harold E., ed. 1988. *Attitudes Toward Persons with Disabilities.* New York: Springer.

Chapter 3
Producing Reproduction: Techniques of Normalization and Naturalization in Infertility Clinics

Charis Cussins

Producing the Socionatural World of an Infertility Clinic

The Argument

In this chapter I argue that the stated aims of infertility medicine — diagnosis and treatment for the "involuntarily childless" — are not achieved simply as results of the application of medical knowledge about the human reproductive system. Rather, the diagnostic and treatment options and knowledge about human reproduction are mutually dependent. The frames of reference and modes of practice that at once enable infertility to be understood, and diagnosis and treatment to be performed, are various. There are many strategies of demarcating the objects of study and treatment, and several codes of conduct toward them. Many of these strategies can be understood as processes of either normalization, naturalization, or routinization.

This chapter has two aims served by the argument that infertility medicine in practice is not a straightforward matter of the application of medical knowledge about human reproduction. First, it aims to illuminate the socionatural world of the (re)production of reproduction in infertility medicine as a part of contemporary culture.[1] It highlights the coordination of moral and technical and scientific discourses and techniques required to give the site meaning and effect. Second, the paper uses the related notions of normalization, naturalization, and routinization to illustrate the interconnections between social lives, material reality, and expertise that must be wrought to settle the existence and character of the infertility clinics. It aims to show the constitutive links between normalization, naturalization, and routinization.

The definitions of normalization, naturalization, and routinization being employed will be exemplified in the course of the narrative, but I will start with some preliminary comments on the explanatory work the notions will do in this paper. Normalization is taken to include the means by which "new data" (new patients, new scientific knowledge, new staff members, new instruments, new administrative constraints, and so on) are incorporated into preexisting procedures and already recognized objects of the clinic. But just as important, it is taken to include the ways in which the grid of what is already there, and what counts as preexisting, is produced, recognized, reproduced, and changed over time. This use of the concept of normalization incorporates both "normal" and "normative." This use is beholden to Foucault,[2] particularly in its extension in the science studies and feminist literature.[3]

By naturalization I refer both to the rendering of states of affairs and facts in a scientific or biological idiom, and to the means by which certain uncertainties, questionings, and contingencies are rendered unproblematic, "natural," or self-evident.[4] This second meaning of naturalization can be thought of as the means by which what sometimes gets referred to as "bedrock"[5] is established and maintained. Its examination invites an analysis of the role of specific configurations of bedrock in establishing the moral, epistemic, and technical taken-for-granteds essential to the practice of infertility medicine.

The concept of routinization is being used here to refer to the repertoires of skilled local knowledge exercised by practitioners and patients in conjunction with the medical technologies. The acquisition of skills and expertise, and the differentials between kinds of skills and expertise that the notion tags, are the aspects of routinization that are most salient in this paper.

The quasitechnical use to which I am putting these notions may be somewhat impoverished, but it has the virtue of allowing me to show the links between these conceptually separable notions. What is "normal" is very often stabilized by what is "natural" in this site (for example, a mother-and-father family is normative for the clinics because it is assumed to be the natural state of affairs, so clinics do not need to invoke the "social" convention of marriage in selecting their patient couples; it is sufficient that patients present as stable heterosexual couples). What is normal or normative also helps fix what is naturalized (for example, compliance with treatment protocols is normative, and failure to suppress even those "psychological side effects" that are seen as integral to the Western experience of infertility, such as stress, is frequently naturalized as a side-effect of taking hormones). Likewise, a routinized skill such as reading a scan screen to determine numbers of follicles is often used to determine both what is natural and what is normal and enables the diagnostic separation of the normal from the abnormal. What skills and expertise are routinized depends in turn on what is normal and natural; values for diagnostic tests, possible explanations for responses to drugs, and so on, are routinely recognized and recorded from the range of possible (normal and natural) values.

Infertility clinics are intriguing and dynamic cultural sites where human reproduction is the production goal. They draw on culturally specific meanings of reproduction and change those meanings in their version of the reproduction of reproduction. They are superb places to examine the ways in which processes of normalization, naturalization, and routinization conspire to produce a real world replete with moral, social, technical, and intellectual texture.

Some Methodological Constraints

Like many who have studied technical practice, I have remained more or less within my own culture to do so. This presents a Scylla and Charybdis of ethnographer's temptations. The first is that, although one is less likely to be tempted to find internal symbolic or functionalist coherence than one might be if faced with the exotic otherness of a far-off culture, one is frequently tempted to go epistemically native; to confer truth values in line with actors' categories.[6] The opposing temptation is to assume that one is somehow able to improve upon actors' accounts of what is going on, even to *expose* what is really going on. My sense after doing ethnographic work in clinics over a number of years is that the practitioners are themselves variously self-conscious participants in the generation of accounts of what is "really going on" in the clinic.

Among the practices of normalization that struck me as particularly salient were the filtering mechanisms operating from within the infertility unit that restrict who can be an infertility patient. It is known, thanks in particular to a number of feminist writings on reproductive technologies, that the politics of sex, race, able-bodiedness, and class, and the intricately related politics of being an experimental subject, are all important aspects of the development and use of these technologies.[7]

The ethnographic approach I have taken is politically deflationary in a significant sense. I looked for mechanisms of exclusion in such things as the making of appointments and the persistence of some treatment protocols rather than others. I didn't look at personal agendas or macro political factors except insofar as these were translated within the clinic into actions or representations that served to narrow the range of possible patients.[8] Let me say two things about this deflationism. First, infertility clinics all over the United States, despite some demographic variation, *do* treat predominantly rich and predominantly white couples ("boutique medicine"), and their pharmacies often buy their drugs from Serono's Mexican factory, where the predominantly female work force is poorly paid and part of the target audience for public population control campaigns. There are times when a louder story about whose reproduction is valued and whose is not is the story that needs to be told. For this purpose the approach taken here is insufficient.

Second, and on the other hand, many of the mechanics of exclusion and objectification are wholly mundane, and are built into the fabric of the functioning clinic. The ethnographer can aim to show how external political effects get created out of, and sustained in, everyday local practices. This paper discusses ways that are internal to the functioning of the clinic that restrict access to treatment, and ways in which women's body parts come to stand in for the couple in treatment, and ways in which the statistical epistemic culture exerts pressure on women to try open-ended numbers of treatment cycles. I thus take my project, despite its deflationism, to be part of the feminist dialogue about access, objectification, and technological imperatives in reproductive medicine and in modern society.

Becoming an Appropriate Observer

This section briefly charts aspects of my socionaturalization into the office and then into surgery at the first clinic where I worked. Almost identical events occurred at the next clinic at which I worked. The implicit and informal "training" I underwent to fit into this setting was revealing about the filtering processes of normalization, naturalization, and routinization.

The Human Investigation Committee felt that my research interests were innocuous enough to be given a waiver on formal passage,[9] and a preliminary meeting with the director of the clinic took place. On the first day of my fieldwork the director, Dr. T., hastily greeted me, and, with no further ado, dispatched his nurse to find a white coat that would fit me.[10] Once enrobed, I was informed that my title was to be "Dr. Cussins, a visiting scientist," and from then on that is how I was introduced to patients. The white coat and descriptive title normalized my presence (fitted an unclassified outsider in by assimilating me to one kind of thing that is normal in clinics—doctors and scientists in white coats) and naturalized my work and my role (for example, my presence during the physical examinations and consultations was the presence of the neutral researcher[11] for whom the public/private dimension was not salient because I was not there "in person," so it did not constitute a breach of privacy). Being white-coated[12] socionaturalized me *up*—it conferred on me not just fittingness, but some of the high mobility associated with the status and expertise of the physicians and research scientists.

Observing surgery presented new hurdles. The white coat and being in the company of a physician allowed me entry into the operating room area, but I was then directed, alone, to the women's changing room to change into scrubs. This is quite a challenge first time through, because little or no explicit instruction is given on how to look like everyone else in the operating room (OR). Operating rooms are governed by strict rules of entry, of sterility, and of appropriate behavior. As a measure of the greater depth of the rituals of belonging in the operating room relative to the rest of the clinic, my first attempt at appropriate comportment was marred by several blunders. I'll recount one such episode.

On my first day observing surgery, having finally negotiated the stacks of clean linen, hats, and shoe covers, and the difference between the clean and dirty entrances to the changing room, and having taken that first bedizened walk out of the changing room, I arrived outside the laparoscopy operating room. I was introduced to the head scrub nurse, who took pity on me and tied my mask on for me and found me the perspex glasses to protect my eyes from the laser surgery. On the second day, however, I was unaided. Without realizing it I covered only my mouth with the mask, leaving my nose free, and entered the room before surgery began. I was sternly reprimanded—and, as residents and visitors to the OR will attest, being scolded by the head nurse is serious. A brief discussion ensued, during which she decided whether or not to consider this a contamination and instigate formal procedures of decontamination. What saved me was the in vitro fertilization (IVF) nurse's reminder to the head nurse that Dr. T. never covered his nose in the operating room, and that it was possible I had just copied him (Figure 3.1). They concluded that if his nose was sufficiently clean, mine probably was too. I was let off, but cautioned that only physicians could take liberties with sterility procedures.[13]

Who Can Be an Infertility Patient?

In this section I explore some of the mechanisms by which normalizing concepts are imported from the wider society into the clinic. The routine and mundane ways in which the norms of heterosexuality, the ability to pay, appropriate comportment, and compliance are invoked and enforced are discussed. This translation of societal norms into the everyday practice of the clinic in turn reinforces and changes (through applying them in these new contexts) the various expressions of these

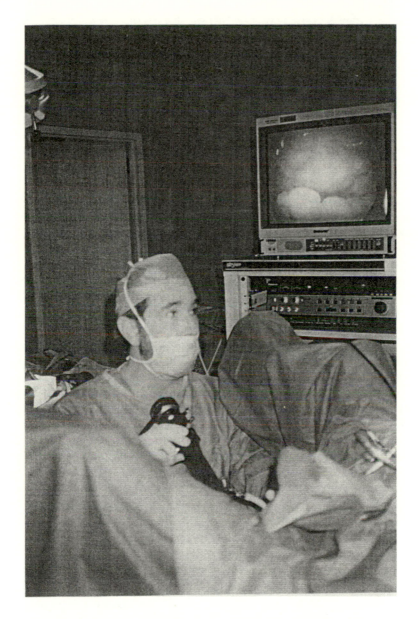

Figure 3.1. Infertility clinic, physician with nose uncovered.

norms in wider society. These norms are discussed in terms of the restrictions on, and fashioning of, the patient.

De Jure and De Facto Restrictions on Access — Heterosexual Couples with the Ability to Pay and Civil Comportment

Almost every patient is one half of a heterosexual couple at the clinics where I have worked. Clinics have variously codified guidelines as to who may be treated, and will discuss patients among themselves and at group meetings if there is any doubt about the appropriateness of a patient.[14] The frame of discussion is based on the perceived needs of a future possible child. It is thought to be preferable to evince a *stable family* environment, and that is almost always interpreted to mean that anyone seeking treatment should be heterosexually partnered, although not necessarily married.

The requirement of stable heterosexuality is invoked in implicit ways as well. While I was working, a number of calls to the office were reported to me in which a woman identified herself as single or lesbian and requested information about the sperm donation program. These callers were referred to a commercial sperm bank. The frozen donor sperm in most clinics is positioned within a matrix of diagnosis and treatment that implicitly restricts it to the couple. The frozen sperm is viewed as a stand-in for the component in successfully achieving pregnancy that is assigned to the husband's or male partner's sperm. If the husband's sperm is diagnosed as the reason why the couple cannot get pregnant and the problem is considered too serious for treatment, the use of donor sperm is suggested. Mainstream heterosexual infertility clinics bank sperm, but are not licensed or set up for the sperm to be mobilized outside of patient couple context.

Most patients have done some contact work with the unit before the first appointment, during which the ability to pay is assessed. Prices for "typical" treatment trajectories are quoted over the phone, in conversation with one of the secretaries. In several clinics, nonanglophone callers are routed through hospital translation services, adding an additional step to successful access. If you can afford the treatment, or have adequate insurance coverage, an appointment will be made on the telephone for an initial consultation with one of the doctors.[15] Scheduling an appointment initiates a material trail whereby the nurses expect you, a file is retrieved or prepared for you, and so on. If you are not covered for the treatment and are not prepared verbally to attest that you can personally cover the costs, no scheduling will occur. If you have already been seen but have reneged on a payment, no subsequent appointments will be made either.

The norm of "the ability to pay" references those whose reproduction in the wider society is taken to be valuable enough to warrant the pursuit of infertility treatments and the concentration of resources. Some physicians describe an element of their job satisfaction in terms of the kind of patients they are able to work with, and one "reassured" me that most people who cannot afford to pay already have several children.[16] Among other things, this again invokes the stereotype that the population divides into those who have too many children and those who don't have enough—those for whom there is contraception, if they would only use it, and those for whom there are infertility treatments. Nonphysician team members are typically more sceptical of the exclusivity of infertility treatment. As one embryologist expressed it:

(Availability) should be assessed by need only. . . . I think it's very unfair that only the wealthy can have this sort of procedure. . . . Its an ongoing concern of mine. . . . I don't feel the knowledge we have should be given out as to who can pay for it. I think it should be "if we have the knowledge it should be given to everyone universally." [17]

For many infertility physicians, having an elite "clientele" is an active and valued element of their working culture, whereas for others it is a moral issue and contravenes a responsibility of the possessors of knowledge to surrender that knowledge without prejudice. Pressure is being put on this dimension of the physicians' culture, however.

As more and more clinics open up,[18] the supply of infertility procedures has outstripped demand. For example, in the United States, a highly organized political lobby on behalf of the American Society for Reproductive Medicine is pushing for insurance coverage for infertility procedures, and for a reclassification of the now mundane procedures such as IVF from "elective" to nonelective (involuntary childlessness is being made into a medical problem, so that its treatment is therapeutic, rather than voluntary/cosmetic). These measures are intended to ensure the growth of the field by opening up access to the services it offers. Relative to a few years ago, the emphasis placed on attracting patients has grown and the emphasis on being a practitioner of an elite subspecialty has correspondingly declined.[19] It will be interesting to see whether this affects normative judgments embodied in current practice about whose reproduction is valued.

Apart from the ethos of an elite clientele, in the infertility clinics where I have observed, patient comportment is an important dynamic. At all points, a couple undergoing treatment must behave appropriately or they risk forfeiting their status as patients. When the patient couple does not stay in control, remain civil, and, above all, manifest their stability as a couple, their public persona as an appropriate patient couple breaks down. Examples of lapses of civility include the couple openly disagreeing with each other or otherwise being hostile toward each other in front of the physician or reacting sceptically or cynically to treatment suggestions from the physician. In these circumstances, which occur infrequently—it is stunning how well most couples do conform to the cooperative, civil participant mode—the physician is loathe to recommend treatment, and frequently ends the meeting suggesting that the couple think about some option and get back to the secretary about whether or not they want to proceed. Occasionally, a couple can reconstitute the patient/physician relation and rescue a consultation that is going badly by emphasizing their underlying goodwill toward each other and their enthusiasm for treatment. During one consultation, the couple redeemed themselves by explicitly explaining their imperfect public facade as a reflection of anxiety about the treatment options and the draining effect of being unsuccessful thus far.

The norm of civility seemed to be doing two kinds of work. The first was expressed by one staff member as follows: "There's no point everyone going through all this, not to mention the cost, if there's not going to be a functional home for the baby at the end of it. If they're doing it to save the marriage, that's not the reason to get into this."[20] Civility here is standing in proxy for the baby-centered, heterosexual nuclear family mentioned above that is normative for the society in which the clinics are positioned.

The second reason for the emphasis on civility has to do with the management of patient stress and "psychological factors" and the implicit gendering of these notions. Infertility clinics expect infertility treatments to be stressful, and almost all clinics have in-house psychologists to counsel patients (at an additional cost).[21] Infertility is classed by practitioners as a major life crisis,[22] especially for women, and the treatments are acknowledged to be inherently stressful because of the time and financial commitment required and because of the poor success rates. The hormones that regulate the female cycle and that are administered in large additional exogenous doses during many forms of infertility treatment are psychophysical surrogates for stress in contemporary Western culture. The liaison between naturalized stress, or stress naturally provoked by high female hormone levels, and the inherently stressful nature of infertility treatments, means that stress is doubly coded, gendered, and generally in need of containment and management if it is not to get in the way of practice-as-usual. There are places where the expression of stress is appropriate and even seemly (as in consultations with the psychologist or nurse coordinator or at home), and places (such as all meetings with the physician) where evincing high levels of stress indicates unsuitability for, and a lack of appreciation of, treatment. Appropriate comportment simultaneously guarantees a patient's fitness to receive treatment and maintains the physician's moral justificatory framework in which she or he is offering salvation.

Compliance—Normalizing the Patient Couple for Rational Treatment

This section discusses a number of ways in which the patient couple is normalized to fit diagnostic and treatment protocols and available practices. An infertile couple has to be directed to specific physical sites at which practitioners can intervene with medical equipment and procedures. Patient compliance consists in behaving in accordance with the reduction to (mostly female) body parts that this requires, as well as in accepting the epistemic logic on which these procedures are based. This means that treatment has a number of paradoxical effects: "couple" becomes, almost exclusively, the female partner; treatment is exclusive, but it is open-ended and stopping is almost impossible; and "natural cycles" give way to disciplined cycles, regardless of the diagnosis for the infertility.

Epidemiological statistics suggest that the male partner is implicated in at least 50 percent of infertility cases worldwide. Yet it is women who take most of the drugs and undergo most of the ultrasounds, hysterosalpingograms, surgery, and other invasive procedures.[23] The success of clinics is wholly dependent on the establishment of in utero pregnancies, and the reinstatement of a "normal" pregnancy trajectory. This makes the female reproductive organs the necessary focus of the treatment. A treatment works if and only if a woman becomes pregnant—success is operationalized not in terms of the child that the couple desires, or in terms of the particular problem to which the infertility is attributed, whether in the man or woman, but in terms of the normal functioning of the woman as pregnant.[24]

The rigors of repeated invasive techniques and hormonal hyperstimulation on women, and the associated culture of perseverance, have been much criticized in infertility medicine. Patients feel that if the treatments exist they have to try everything. Why is it so hard to give up? The lack of alternative operationalizations and an epistemic culture based on statistics were both elements contributing to the culture of perseverance in clinics.

One day one of the physicians came dashing in and told me that if I ran I could catch up with a patient and possibly interview her. It would interest me greatly, he thought, because she had just decided to stop treatment even though she was not pregnant. "Is that so rare?" I asked. "Put it this way—you may not see another case while you are with us."

I did run, I did catch her up, and she did agree to be interviewed. And she *was* the only person I saw during my time at that clinic who gave up treatment without a recommendation from the physician, without severe financial pressure, and without being pregnant. On being interviewed, the unusual commodity this woman appeared to possess was a network for interpreting her infertility outside of the medical one—she credited her Mormon religion—that was at this point in her treatment as powerful as the medical operationalization.

Clinic psychologists give couples advice on pursuing alternatives such as life without one's own children and on how to adopt. Nonetheless, the structuring of treatment is open-ended in the sense that there is always another combination of hormones, another cycle of artificial insemination, another go at IVF that can be embarked upon, age and finances permitting. The physicians have guidelines as to a sensible number of times to try things that are systematically relayed to patients, as are the success rates (packaged, see below) associated with each procedure. They do not, however, refuse to treat patients who want to supersede those guidelines, and in practice a rationale for not counting one or another cycle can always be found.

As all success projections are based on statistics, the argument of cumulative probabilities plays a large part in superseding guidelines. Despite the fact that independent probabilities on a given cycle may be low (which, of course, remain true for each given cycle) the fact that one in three or one in five cycles are successful translates for physicians and patients alike into a rule of thumb justifying trying three or five times.

Projections based on statistics license doing the same thing again in the face of failure. This is a distinctive epistemic element of treatment cultures based on statistics. In practice, it is an extremely difficult epistemic standard to live with because it disregards mechanism. If the very same thing only works one in five times, then there is no positive answer to the question of the cause and effect of the infertility. This epistemic difficulty is managed on a daily basis so that it doesn't interfere with practice.

When a new cycle is begun, the parameters are fine-tuned, sometimes in response to specific things like poor oocyte maturation or past hormonal responses to the drugs, and sometimes just to be "doing something different,"[25] so as to reinstate mechanism and the idea that there was some reason why the last cycle didn't work that can be taken care of this time around. Nonetheless, for the cumulative probabilities argument to work (after all, that was why another cycle was started), the two cycles must still be relevantly *the same.* The combination of cumulative probabilities and fine tuning means that the treatment plan is infinite. Cycles can always be ruled crucially not the same and so not counted;

statistics will always say that this might just be the time that the same procedure will work. Accepting the epistemic rationale on which infertility medicine is predicated involves accepting this open-endedness.

The problem of the limited agency of patients, and the problem of excessive medical monitoring and intervention (medical "disciplining" of the patient body), are frequently discussed by academics, patients' rights groups, hospital administrators, women's groups, and individual patients, amongst others. An initiative to increase patient autonomy and reduce costs in infertility medicine by decreasing the extent of the disciplining of the woman's body in IVF—"natural cycle" IVF—has failed to become integrated into most practices, giving way instead to the predominant disciplined superovulatory cycles.

A "natural cycle" involves underoing IVF, except that the woman doesn't take the hormonal drugs designed to make several eggs mature at once. Instead, her hormone levels and "natural" single dominant follicle development (the typical monthly ovulation) are monitored with blood tests and vaginal ultrasound. The advantages to the patient are that costs are lower per cycle and that the ovaries are not hyperstimulated but continue functioning as usual. When the follicle reaches the optimal size, as measured by its appearance on the ultrasound screen and blood hormone levels, human chorionic gonadotropin is given to bring on final maturation and to have the patient ready for egg retrieval approximately thirty-five hours later, just as in "stimulated" cycles. The patient is taken to surgery, and ultrasound aspiration is performed to collect the egg. This is done under local anesthetic, or sometimes just with pain killers. It can even be performed in the office, reducing costs still further. Thereafter, the egg is cultured with the partner's sperm in the lab, and, if fertilization occurs, the embryo is loaded into a catheter and transferred back into the woman's uterus two days later.

At a conference in 1990, one of the British pioneers of natural cycles[26] told me that he was confident that natural-cycle IVF would become the protocol of choice for some diagnoses. Not only did it give women more biological and personal autonomy, he thought, but it also had better success rates and fewer side effects. The director of the program I was studying concurred with all of this, and said that he also had assumed that natural cycles would sweep the country. Likewise, patients initially greeted the news with approval.

The British doctor explained that the rationale for superovulating women, apart from the fact that that's just what they do in the rest of animal embryology (i.e., with mice) was that it seemed that the success rates rose arithmetically with the number of embryos that were replaced in the woman's uterus. Thus, the argument went, if one embryo was replaced, you had a certain chance of success, and if two were replaced, a greater chance, and so on, up to around four embryos, where the success rates flattened out. He maintained, however, that this was an artifact of the way the data were collected: the data were assembled on the basis of women who had been superovulated. This specialist's claim was that a superovulated woman who only produced one egg that fertilized was obviously adversely affected by the hormones in the drugs, and so would not be able to sustain a pregnancy, and so this was the reason that she did not get pregnant. In fact, he said, the low rate of implantation when only one embryo was transferred related not to the advantages of transferring several embryos, but to the disadvantages of superovulatory drugs on implantation in women who responded poorly to these drugs. He said that his data collected on women who had had natural cycles showed a success rate comparable to the best results achieved for IVF with superovulation.

Just a few years later, superovulation is still the protocol of choice, and the nice arithmetic graph is still drawn to explain the chances of pregnancy to patients about to undergo IVF, and the plateau at four embryos is still used to limit numbers of embryos transferred and to determine how many embryos to freeze. Why do so few patients undergo "natural cycles"? The short answer is that the physicians rarely push it, treating superovulation as the default protocol and continuing to show the graph.[27] A longer answer includes the experience of the staff and patients undergoing natural cycles.

In the natural cycles I observed, or read the records for, a significant number of cycles were canceled because the patient spontaneously ovulated, or the single egg was lost at retrieval, or was not properly mature, or didn't fertilize. The strain of having all one's eggs in one basket (almost literally) negated the feeling patients had of increased agency. With superovulation there was some slack; embryos could be frozen for a later cycle, and if some eggs were not mature or did not fertilize, there would still be some that were fine. Relying on one's own body also increased the feeling of failure if something went wrong. For the staff, monitoring and retrieval are more nerve-wracking than usual in natural cycles because they might lose or damage the single egg. As an embryologist told me, "No one likes going through natural cycles. They're too stressful; they're too hit or miss."[28] It is of course possible that the sense of being hit or miss only arises by comparison with the superovulatory protocols where things go wrong but not usually at the point where eggs are retrieved and fertilized. Certainly, this comparative failure was always pointed out, and seemed to alarm patients and thus possibly unnecessarily (i.e., not as a direct result of comparing overall success rates) to discourage them from undergoing natural cycles.

For "natural cycles" to have been successfully incorporated into practice, it would have been necessary to generate a livable dynamic at the level of practice for both patients and practitioners. This would have required thorough integration into the evaluative structure of the clinic, not a simple grafting onto existing protocols.

The Diagnostic Form, the Physician's Hands, the Laparoscope, and Other Beautiful Philosophical Objects[29]

In this section the variously instrumentalized and embodied procedures I shall talk about are all philosophical, or epistemically normative. They all preserve information about spatial distribution or quantity and so allow the objects of study to be transported and mobilized as results, diagnoses, or treatment indicators, with only the most elementary of mathematical or quasimathematical transformations. The procedures are normative because of the epistemic work they do—faced with semen, ovaries, uterus, and hormones, there is nothing useful to be concluded about infertility. Blood, urine or semen in the office would simply be a mess, not a source of knowledge. The skills and collecting and analyzing devices enable quasimathematical properties to be rendered that are not the same as the objects of study, but which are faithful to the object of study and preserve this fidelity through the necessary transformations. The procedures do epistemic work because they can be transported to and within the office and are subject to transformations. Hence they can yield knowledge.

Topographies of Normality[30]

The aim of infertility clinics is to find out why each couple is not getting pregnant, and then to do something about it, within the range of procedures offered. Finding out why a couple is not getting pregnant—diagnosis—most importantly involves assimilating the female patient's body to a familiar topography and then locating the relevant physical or functional deviations from "normal." This assimilation is achieved through a number of procedures. The ultrasound, the hysterosalpingogram, and postcoital tests all involve producing an isolated image that can be fitted into representational parameters of normality. Semen analysis and blood hormone tests involve counting aspects of what is rendered visible by the production of a mathematized image. The image-producing residues are thrown away, not turned into traces. In the pelvic exam and during diagnostic surgery, the female body is turned into an object of study in situ, with the parameters of normality embodied in the physician's skilled looking and manipulation of instruments.[31]

Treatment is not always a discrete set of operations from diagnosis—for example, laparoscopies are typically diagnostic and simultaneously occasions for treatment—but the logic of the treatment step is to bypass, override, subvert, or simulate to compensate for the digression from normality.

New patients are asked how long they have been trying to get pregnant; whether they have seen an infertility specialist before; their age, height, and weight; how often they have sexual intercourse; and their occupations. The woman is asked if her periods are regular, and the man is asked if he has any potency problems or visible abnormalities of his genitalia. Their answers are entered on a diagnostic form that becomes the central inscription around which the treating physician structures a plan of action, arrives at a diagnosis, and initiates treatment.

In the examination room the program on the diagnostic form is implemented. Each examination starts with a pelvic exam. This involves the undressed and draped patient lying back with her legs over padded leg rests, as for a gynecological exam. The physician sits on a mobile stool, at the foot of the table, with his or her gaze delineating the physical zone of treatment and study. The physician uses one hand to examine the vagina and cervix. The other hand palpates the pelvic region from on top of the stomach. She or he may separately feel the breasts and check the body for "unusual"[32] amounts of secondary hair.

In this procedure the physician is interested in establishing the gross anatomical normality of the woman's body. Nothing is (usually) extracted from the body, no images are derived from traces of the pelvic area, no grid for counting, aligning or extrapolating is imposed on any organs to decide whether or not something is awry. Yet nonetheless, judgments of normality and abnormality are routinely made, fibroids are distinguished from uterine walls, nonovulatory cysts from ovulating ovaries. Diagnostically unimportant differences, such as the angling of the uterus or the length of the vagina, are ignored for diagnostic purposes, even if they are noted for subsequent procedures such as embryo transfer. The physician is aided by asking questions such as "Does this hurt?" In deciding whether or not a pelvic exam is normal, the physician has to decide which of the palpable physical parameters constitute sameness with some norm and which constitute difference.

It is perhaps feasible that the physician holds something like an idealized topographic representation in his or her head that is derived from anatomy class texts on woman's pelvic area.[33] This would then be a standard against which to make judgements about relevant sameness versus individual difference. I suspect, however, that it is much more likely that such topographic knowledge is embodied in the physician's skilled "recognizing things as thus and so" rather than as an ideal mental type.

There are two main arguments for this. First, it is not clear how the graphic properties of a picture on a page and those of a pelvic area could coincide. What topographic transformation could possibly yield an accurate prescription for all and only those pelvic areas that conformed to the image? And how would such a transformation from representation to gestural recognition be implemented? Second, an account that posited a mental representation against which judgments about sameness were made would make very poor use of the physician's resources. A physician has an enormous body of practical knowledge built up around doing the same thing time and again. She or he has a gestural repertoire of recognition. The graphic parameters of the textbook diagram provide a recognitional grid, a set of answers to the question "What am I looking for?" in the form of graphic relations and linguistic labels. But these do not function as separate from the ways to look for and find those structures. The physician's talk during the exam consists of phrases like "Here's the right ovary; the cyst seems to have gone," suggesting an itinerary-like movement through the area. Much as one sees someone in the street as *that person* first, rather than a prototypical person with *that person* properties, so the physician seems to recognize the pelvic organs as specific.

In making the woman's body into an object of study and treatment, not all procedures involve explicitly producing or working from representations with graphic properties. In some procedures the physician embodies, through his or her skilled gestures and manipulation of instruments, the normalizing work required to render that which is seen or felt as something that is, in the very seeing or feeling of it, normal or abnormal. The quasimathematical properties of sameness and difference-in-this-respect are merged with the patient's body through the process of skilled looking and feeling.[34]

Women patients usually undergo several ultrasounds in any given treatment cycle. This can be to see whether the patient is ovulating, to monitor superovulation, or to confirm the presence of a cyst, tubal pregnancy, or intrauterine pregnancy. Vaginal ultrasound probes are used almost exclusively in infertility clinics. The ultrasonographer sheaths the ultrasound probe in a sterile condom, coats it with cold jelly, and inserts the probe in the woman's vagina. By rotating the probe in different directions, the ultrasonographer brings first one ovary into view on the screen and then the other.[35]

Follicles can be measured and compared. If, for example, the woman is undergoing a cycle of IVF, the ultrasonographer (sometimes the physician and sometimes not) will be looking for several simultaneously developing follicles of roughly equal size. She or he measures each visibly developing follicle, and Polaroid® photos are produced that record all the images and the associated follicle measurements. When the physician doesn't watch or perform the ultrasound, she or he bases the decision to continue treatment or not on the ultrasonographer's hand-collated list of numbers of ripening follicles and their sizes, plus the photos. She or he also decides whether to continue medication, whether to alter doses, and what and when the next phase of treatment should be on the basis of this information.

Ultrasound images are rudimentary but diagnostically powerful. The image on the computer screen preserves many spatial characteristics of the phenomena it is transmiting, so that it reconstitutes a seeing event. For its use in monitoring superovulation, the absence of nonovulatory cysts and the relative size and number of follicles is a full complement of the information required to proceed in treatment.

In hysterosalpingograms, radioactive dye is squirted into the uterus to see if it spills freely out of the fallopian tubes. They indicate whether or not the tubes are open, permitting an egg to enter and normal fertilization to occur. This procedure involves the production of an image that provides diagnostic evidence. Unlike ultrasound, there is a time delay while the photographic image is developed. Its particular interest as a diagnostic image is that it captures the results of a dynamic experiment: the dye is what shows up on the plate, so all the cavities that the dye reaches are illuminated. If the dye is constrained in a shape looking more or less like a textbook diagram of a uterus and tubes, then the tubes are probably occluded. If, however, the dye flares out into the pelvic cavity, apparently flowing free-form, then it is concluded that the tubes are open and that dye passed easily through them.[36] What happened over time is captured in the image and tells one about the functioning of the tubes.

In the operating room,[37] the laparoscope enables the surgeon to visualize the peritoneum of women patients. The laparoscope is inserted through a half-inch cut at the navel, whereupon the surgeon looks through the eyepiece of the laparoscope. After a thorough look around, she or he connects a camera to the eyepiece and takes a number of photos of the woman's uterus and tubes, then hooks up the video system to the laparoscope, so that an image of everything in the line of sight of the laparoscope appears on two monitors placed one on either side of the patient's body. The surgeon talks everyone in the room through the pictures on the screen, pointing out her or his diagnosis, or her or his opinion that all is normal. If all is deemed normal, the surgeon removes the laparoscope and sews the patient back up again, once the public witnessing of her pelvic region is complete. If something is found that is considered relevantly abnormal, and to need treatment, two or more tiny incisions are made, through which ports are inserted so that instruments for cutting, cauterizing, or grabbing can be introduced as needed. The monitors on which the pelvic region appears during laparoscopic surgery, called "slave monitors" (sic), give a high-resolution real-time image for the surgeon's eyes from which they guide their gestures. The laparoscope allows "as-if-unmediated" looking without the hazards associated with major surgery.

Routinization: The Variety, Gendering, and Culture of Skill

Possessing the routinized skills by which the epistemic norms of seeing/feeling and knowing (things like being able to read ultrasound scans or hysterosalpingograms or carry out surgery or pelvic exams) are enacted is a large part of what it means to be a practitioner in this site. Infertility medicine is very like other arenas of expert technical culture in that marking and differentiating skills and expertise (and the social/hierarchical roles that go with those notions) are an intrinsic part of the culture. I shall discuss just one example of this pervasive phenomenon.

A consideration of who can do the looking, embody the treatment skills, and assume responsibility during laparoscopic surgery illustrates well the divisions of labor that normalize the practice and accountability of infertility medicine. At one hospital I watched laparoscopies in a dedicated endoscopy operating room over a period of several weeks. For almost all the procedures I watched, the same nurse was one of the people working the laparoscopic instruments. Toward the end of my internship at that clinic I interviewed her between two operations. In this interview I was interested in how the nurse would describe what she did relative to what the surgeon was doing, and how she would describe her own skills and knowledge. I asked whether or not she felt she could do all the things the surgeon could do. She replied:

I feel the roles are very distinct. Sometimes I feel I could do some of the stuff, do the assisting and that kind of thing; I wouldn't be able to do the surgery per se. I mean it looks like I could, but I wouldn't want to take that responsibility because I don't have the training, and they know exactly what they're looking at. Even though I can say, "Oh yes, that's an ovary, and that's this and that's that," I'm not real, real sure.[38]

She limits her ability here first in terms of professional roles of the surgeon versus the nurse, which she says are very distinct. In this hospital, gender was an almost perfect predictor of role: the nurses were women and the surgeons were men. Feminists have pointed out that where gender predicts the differentiation of professional roles, the sexual division of labor usually works by underrewarding/remunerating what women do, while simultaneously justifying the pay differentials in terms of the properties required to undertake the job, which are properties that get at least part of their relative value from the strength to which they are naturalized to "women's roles" such as caring.[39] After marking the primary distinction between nurses and surgeons, the nurse modifies this role-based account of skill slightly, saying she could maybe do the "assisting" done by a second surgeon in more complicated cases. It is not just being a surgeon, but taking the primary surgeon's responsibility and having his or her training that she isolates as critical. She makes a distinction between what it might seem to me as an observer that she could do and what the real parameters of skill are. She holds instruments and operates the camera, and occasionally makes cuts, uses the coagulator, cauterizes, and lazes just like the surgeon, but only at the surgeon's direction. The skill is not confined to the gestures, then, but knowing and deciding which ones to do when, and bearing the responsibility that implies.

At the end of this quote, the nurse distinguishes being able to *name* things such as an ovary from *knowing*, or at least being "real, real sure," what they are. This is a familiar theory of knowledge in which perception and recognitional capacities are eminently correctable and not guaranteed as certain knowledge. The surgeons know "exactly what they're looking at." We are not told what she thinks you need in addition to her recognitional capacities to have certain knowledge; perhaps a combination of experience with like cases, a knowledge of and responsibility for this patient's history, a particular interactive role with the recognized organs during surgery, and so on. But it is interesting that role is taken to *coincide* with this crucial epistemic distinction. If role is gendered, then so is access in this setting to certain knowledge.

Despite the restrictions the nurse places on her expertise, at other points in the interview she describes episodes in which she made active decisions during surgery. This is what has been described as the difference between nominal and real divisions of labour.[40] Her "job description" institutionally, and as she apparently understands it, does not include surgical decision-making. Nonetheless, there are times when there is some role overlap between herself and the surgeon. This lends flexibility to the whole system, providing a built-in guard against the breakdown of one part of the system. It also illustrates a paradoxical aspect of technical practice: the flexibility of the staff is required to keep intact the strong partitions between roles that structure infertility medicine. It was clear in this interview and in other occasions of talking to staff that these role overlaps and skill and responsibility "mobility" were occasions in which they took great pride. But it is also possible that role overlap is itself a mechanism that ultimately reinforces the categories by which role differentiation is maintained.[41]

Playing the Statistics Game and Dealing with Bad Numbers

Statistics as Normative Epistemology

Statistics are a major product of infertility clinics, and they regulate and calibrate the kinds of treatment procedures described in the preceding section. The whole "epistemic culture"[42] of the unit is based on the production of statistics. By this I mean that what it is for a procedure to work and be an indicated therapy is expressed statistically, rather than, say, as a matter of experiment, or a matter of fact. Fertility clinics, particularly private ones, are increasingly in competition for patients. Reputations draw patients, and these are built primarily on successfully initiating pregnancies. A patient calling an infertility unit has a right to, and often will, ask what the center's success rates are. Likewise, success rates for each clinic that wants to be certified by the American Society for Reproductive Medicine must be published annually. The number of successful treatment cycles as a ratio of all cycles carried out in a center must exceed minimum rates that currently define competent care for each procedure.

Much energy, then, goes into compiling the statistics and generating success rates. Competitors' rates are viewed with interest and sometimes with suspicion, and ways in which reported rates from center to center might not be comparable are much discussed.[43] An embryologist responsible for the compilation of statistics at one clinic described the open-endedness and anxieties that that gives rise to in the following way:

(Centers) are so competitive . . . they will say, "Okay, well, I'm not going to include this patient, because she has this or that—throw her out." Or do a study where they're just looking at a certain group of patients and report the statistics on that. And centers that are very large will divide their patient populations into all different groups. "We're doing a research study on patients with male factor, so we've taken all those male factor patients out. So when we report our statistics we only report this group over here." . . . The problem is that there is so much dishonesty in reporting things, so that now there are actually going to be programs set up just for that fact.[44]

Statistics are generated, recorded, and manipulated in several places, and a fairly large proportion of the embryologists' time is spent on them. In the laboratory, records of all procedures are kept in binders by date, diagnosis, procedure, and age and identity of the patient. These are handwritten and form the evidential base for statistical claims, and for regulatory checks by outsiders. There are times when statistical policies are developed and modified as part of the self-definition and modification of the clinic as a whole. On these occasions, what to count as a homogeneous group of patients, which cycles to count in the analysis, and whether or not to treat patients who are likely to affect overall statistical results adversely are discussed. Weekly team meetings with the director (these meetings seem to be standard fixtures in clinics) are occasions where the parameters of statistical analysis become negotiable. Pregnancies are listed, and failures are discussed in terms of the reason the procedure might not have worked. Sometimes a reason is suggested that makes it dubious to those present whether the unsuccessful cycle should be included in the statistics.[45]

Some cases can uncontroversially be left out of the statistics, such as those in which the patient drops out of treatment before finishing for a non-treatment-related reason. But other cases raise general points about the clinic's policy. For example, at one meeting a patient over forty with multiple sclerosis had not become pregnant. The staff felt that she should not be counted because most clinics would not even treat a patient like that, making comparisons between clinics unfair. They discussed whether they ought to restrict treatment to patients under a certain age and with specific diagnoses that are associated with good success. This was rejected as being out of line with their clinical as opposed to research orientation. An element of the discussion was whether or not it was ethical to the patient to treat her when success rates for that age group were so low. A consensus was reached that any patient had a right to treatment as long as the success rates were realistically portrayed at the outset. Nonetheless, it was decided to separate off the patients of forty and over in compiling the statistics, so that their decision of whom to treat would not be adversely affected by their desire to maximize success rates. This decision ended up reconciling the two things that defined the pragmatic goals of this clinic: to treat as many patients as possible and present as good success rates as possible. It was also expressed within the predominant ethic of clinical priority based on patient choice.

Results Create Expectations and Expectations Create Statistics: What Happens When the Results Don't Meet Expectations?

In the section on who can be an infertility patient, I discussed some aspects of living with a statistical measure of success from the point of view of the gap between statistics and mechanism when applied to an individual patient. A more radical problem arises for the unit when the statistical rates themselves seem not to be holding up for a given procedure. In this case a double epistemological crisis is experienced: the practitioners no longer have the justificatory standard for initiating treatment and continuing in the face of failure, and, because statistical justificatory standards only say that x works in y percent of the cases, and not why x works when it works, there is no way of knowing what has gone wrong, and so what to correct. This double crisis is further compounded by the nature of statistical reasoning itself. Practitioners are aware that the statistics alone predict that dry runs should occur, but in the short term they have no recourse in the theory of statistics for knowing when local lapses are just statistical dry runs and when they indicate that a procedure has in fact been relevantly changed in a detrimental way. There are of course statistical methods for saying how likely a dry run of a given magnitude and duration is, given sufficient cases, but a small clinic, like most private infertility clinics, cannot quickly amass that number of cases. They must respond to local failures to maintain success rates before they have the relevant data to make this judgment.

While I was working at one of the clinics, such a crisis was being experienced for the IVF results. The clinic had reported their best ever success rates for IVF in the previous year, well above the national average. In the first five months of the current year, however, their success rates for IVF had dropped to half the number for the comparable period of the previous year (their results for other treatments were as good or better than the previous year's results). The numbers of patients having to be told that they were not pregnant, and the sense of backsliding, were taking a toll on the staff, and by the time I was there, much effort was being directed into deciding what was going wrong. This is how one embryologist described the crisis that this represented.[46]

Our IVF program, we had a wonderful pregnancy rate last year, this year our pregnancy rate has dropped drastically. And then the question was, what is different? What has changed? . . . calling around other centers, talking to them, everybody goes through what they call the "dry spell." We had never hit one before, and because we are a small program it hit us much harder. Other centers will do fifty cases in a month, and they can tell, if they do a series of twenty patients and they get no pregnancies, they go, "Okay, what's going on here?" Well, it takes us six months to do twenty [IVF] patients, so we have a very long period of time, and then when we change, we kept trying changing things to see if that was it. Well then, you would have to wait months and months to see if that change had an effect.

Despite this epistemological uncertainty, local action was taken. These are some of the things that were done to try to identify the cause of the drop in success rates, and some of the explanations that were considered. The embryologists looked in the laboratory:

We went through everything—we tried looking at every single chemical we used, every single plastic ware, anything the embryos come in contact with, looking at the gas we used in the incubator, looking at temperatures of everything, checking to see if there could be anything that is different. A few things I found is that one of the tubes that we use, the company changed the way they labeled them, so I contacted the company and discussed with them the changes, got them to give me tubes that were unlabeled and tested those to see if—they said everything else was exactly the same, except the very last step where they put the label on the tubes was a different procedure. So I had them send me the tubes prior to them labeling them, to test it to see if that was the problem. That didn't seem to be the problem. I started calling other centers and asking them, you know, what could be the problem?

One of the physicians found something awry in the operating room while she was doing an egg retrieval for IVF:

One of the things we did find was that there was a problem down in the OR where the heating blocks that we use, for some reason the temperature had gotten changed on us; something had happened to it, and so now we monitor that on a very close basis, checking the temperature the entire procedure to make sure that it doesn't go too hot. And our pregnancy rate has gotten better since we found that.

The nurse coordinator, who keeps track of the treatment protocols and individual characteristics of each patient, thought it might have been partly due to differences in the individuals who had gone through IVF—a slew of older patients for whom you would expect worse results. She wasn't convinced, though:

I could go through them and say, "Oh, this patient had this problem, this one had this one, and this one had this one," but there were a few patients in there that were good patients that should have gotten pregnant and didn't get pregnant. So we felt that maybe it appeared to be more than just coincidence.

After I had been at the clinic a couple of weeks, the June/July figures were processed, and they were much better than the ones obtained earlier in the year. The director was ready for closure and settled on the theory that it was the malfunctioning heating blocks that had been the problem. He informed me both that the June figures had "saved this half year's statistics,"[47] and that the few pregnancies that *had* occurred before the heating block was discovered all "for one reason or another did not involve putting the test tubes in the heater." Both the physicians seemed sure that this was at the root of the problem, expressed anger about it, and appeared confident that with the new checks in place things had been taken care of. The embryologists appeared to be somewhat more ambivalent about this single-cause theory, and one of them

said that she would not regain confidence until the numbers themselves
bore out the theory that the problem was resolved:

We're hoping that was the problem. I'm still not 100% convinced that was the
only problem. I'm hoping that was it and that we've corrected it, but I can't guarantee at this point, we haven't done enough cases for me to regain confidence.

Despite the fact that it is the success of procedures that generates
the statistics, it is the statistics that justify the carrying out of infertility
medicine, the choice of that treatment for this patient. Without the
statistical justificatory system working, all the other repertoires of normalization and making things relevantly the same cannot be calibrated
and validated.

Organizing Privacy and Timing

Privacy

A central organizational problem for infertility medicine is how to deal
with the possible sexuality of the object of study (the patient's body and,
specifically, the reproductive organs) and procedures of diagnosis and
treatment, when timing and locale require that they be seen or done
clinically and relatively publicly. If this boundary between the private
and the public is not negotiated well, the routinization of these procedures as part of infertility medicine will break down. This arises in all
medical practice, and the rituals for establishing this boundary in the
examination room have been described as an "etiquette of touching"
(Young 1989).
Circumstances for blurring the distinction between public and private are so pervasive in infertility clinics that there is a well worked-out
choreography of privacy. Some things cannot be rendered innocuous by
imposing a clinical, scientific semiotics on gestures that might otherwise
be read as private and/or sexual. For these, spaces that are usually occupied by more than one person can be transformed into private spaces.
We are familiar with casual granting of privacy where it is not strictly
demarcated—undressing in shops, public lavatories, respecting library
space—but in this clinical setting the etiquette covers spaces that are
only sometimes private, and the behaviors for marking the transformation are well developed, routinized, and strictly adhered to. The multiple
lives of the examination room at one of the clinics make a good example.
For a regular pelvic exam, the examination room door is closed while
the patient gets undressed, making the room a temporarily private
place. The privacy is marked by the closed door, together with a light

that is lit up indicating that the room is in use. The privacy is broken by a combination of a lapse of time followed by knocking. No answer is required for the knock; it simply registers the physician's imminent entrance. This requirement of privacy stands in contrast to a requirement of accountability that must be met after the physician knocks. The physician announces herself or himself with something like "Can I come in?" as he or she enters the examination room. When I was observing, the patient would be asked at this point if she minded my being in the room. Before the pelvic exam can begin, the physician must have a female professional witness. At some clinics I was considered an adequate witness, but at others I was not, because my impartiality was not institutionally accountable. Typically, a nurse simultaneously helps the physician and witnesses the propriety of the exam.

For "artificial" inseminations and IVF, the male partner's semen must be produced. Collection is not always done on the premises, but the exigencies of timing often necessitate on-site collection.[48] An examination room is used for masturbation by male patients, and a similar protocol to that used for women patients undressing is followed, except that there are mechanisms for enhancing the spatial and experiential privacy of the room. If possible, the examination room furthest away from the nurses' station is assigned for male patients to collect. It is out of the line of sight of any of the offices.[49] A magazine rack holds a magazine for female patients occupying the room. There are also *Playboy*-type magazines in the room for semen collection, but they are not out on open shelves. So that no one need visually register them, these magazines are kept in a drawer. The "in use" light is put on, and no one may break the seal of privacy except the patient himself, which he does by exiting. He is instructed to lock the door from the inside, to avoid error.

When the collection is done, the man exits and hands the sterile and semitransparent container with the semen to one of the laboratory technicians. The technicians fill out forms or use the microscope or heating equipment in a room across the hall. When they hear the door open, they move to the door of their room, to make sure that the man can hand his container straight to somebody who will deal with it technically. The transmission from private and sexual to an appropriate clinical object is thus smoothly assured. Sometimes the man makes a wry comment about the process, and sometimes smiles are exchanged. Patients sometimes joke and commiserate among each other about the process once the man regains the waiting room.

Timing

In an infertility clinic, time is organized around the working day and progresses linearly, just as at any other place of work. All the calendars and other scheduling devices are calibrated to mark an incremental passage of time. Likewise, for the patients, the visits to the clinic must be fitted into working days and coordinated with their own working schedules. Treatment, however, has also to fit into the very different time scale demarcated by the woman's menstrual cycle. To be treatable, then, a woman must be cycling normally, but she has to cycle measurably and on time; the time scale must be reconciled.

For women patients the conflicts between these time scales are salient aspects of their experience of infertility medicine. Each new cycle takes you back to zero in your quest to get pregnant, despite the cumulative treatment process; it also resets one's hopes, frequently only to have them dashed again in a month.[50] Treatment has been successful at that time when the cycling is subverted and the progressive, developmental time scale of a pregnancy begins.

Further complicating the experience of time for many women patients is the so-called "biological clock." As one gets older, the likelihood of pregnancy, as measured statistically, goes down. Thus, although one gets no further along the treatment trajectory, the start of each cycle means a diminished chance for the subsequent cycle. This biological clock pressure is felt mainly by those women who have been told they are at the outside of the normal age range for the procedures to be successful — the statistical drop-off rate is not considered significant until a woman is in her late thirties.

The treatment cycle in infertility medicine is also at odds with the cumulative structure of payment. You pay for all services received, even though many of the procedures are one off: IVF, donor insemination, insemination with husband's sperm, and fertility drugs all work in the cycle they are given in or not at all. There are no hold-over effects.[51] This puts a lot of pressure on staff and patients alike and is a considerable part of the rationale in contemporary infertility medicine for performing surgery, which lasts, if successful, for a much longer time.

These various time scales, bureaucratic, cyclical, and biological, pose several logistical challenges. Appointments have to be made during working hours, but they also have to be made on the right day of the cycle. This external disciplining of the couple is achieved with the help of some simple devices, such as the hand-held device that makes the translation from the day of Mrs. X's cycle to the appropriate date on the linear, shared schedule. Calibrating is done from the reliable visible sign of the first day of a period, which is called Day 1, even though it is the shedding phase from the last cycle.

Where more precise timing is necessary, standardized protocols are at hand. Thus, if the eggs are retrieved in an IVF case at a certain hour, the semen sample must arrive two hours later to be spun down and added to the culture dish. In superovulated cycles, hormones are given towards the end to bring the final maturing process into line with the working hours and to allow the surgeon to schedule insemination or egg retrieval an exact number of hours later. This sometimes means that patients have to have injections in the middle of the night. It also means much communication between the operating room, laboratory, office, and patients. Heavy use is made of the phones and electronic links to achieve this. Finally, the cycle is not completely domesticated; midcycle often falls on a weekend. At most clinics, staff members assume they could be on call on any day of any weekend.

The Aesthetics of the Lab

The laboratories at infertility clinics are the site at which all semen is washed, spun, and separated before inseminations.[52] It is also home to the freezers that contain patient's embryos and semen and donors' semen. Eggs are brought here from the operating room after IVF surgery, and the gametes and embryos are manipulated and incubated and finally frozen or loaded into catheters for transfer all within the labs. There are also several activities that take place on a regular basis to ensure the self-reproduction of the lab, such as the making of new culture media, quality control testing on mouse embryos of each new batch of media, filling of the liquid nitrogen canister, and ordering and receiving new equipment and supplies.

I want to focus on what I came to think of as the aesthetics of the lab in this section. These were a set of standards for dealing with the human embryos being grown and maneuvered in the lab. These standards marked out work with embryos as diffrent from any other work done in the lab, including that done with gametes. They also seemed to enable the embryologists to get on with their work with the embryos in a matter-of-fact way, without having themselves to take time to enact marking of the human potentiality of the embryos, and without being overwhelmed by the responsibility of the preciousness of this potential to the couple from whose gametes the embryo was derived.

IVF surgery is carried out under low levels of lighting. This is supposed to protect the eggs retrieved from potentially harmful exposure to light. All work done in the lab while there are embryos or potential embryos out is done in semidarkness. There is apparently no conclusive evidence that light does harm the eggs or embryos, but the care is felt to be appropriate and to "make sense."[53] This care taken to reproduce what one might think of as the maternal environment stands in stark contrast to the spinning, washing, freezing of sperm and the freezing of surplus embryos. Sperm is very robust and is well known to be capable of fertilizing eggs after these rigors. Freezing embryos is more tricky, but the important thing about freezing is that it puts the life potential on hold, so the practitioners are not responsible for preserving the chain of potentiality while embryos are frozen. As soon as an embryo is unfrozen, however, the same care is once again employed.

At one clinic where the lab was not immediately adjacent to the operating room, the eggs recovered from a woman in the operating room during a cycle of IVF were transported to the lab in an isolette appropriated from the intensive care baby unit. The isolette was originally used to solve the problem of transporting the eggs at the right temperature, and with minimum disturbance, across the distance between the operating room and the lab. Being mobile and having an internal work space where the eggs could be counted, pipetted and mixed with semen, and transported back to the office for embryo transfer were the chief practical assets of the isolette. The serendipitous happening of getting a newborn baby isolette added to the aura of extreme maternal solicitude towards the embryos at this clinic.

Franklin has pointed out that the provision of a maternal environment in the lab for nurturing the embryos is the exact opposite of the entry of science (instruments, techniques, and knowledges) into the woman's body in the earlier parts of the treatment cycle.[54] This crossover of the properties of techniques to the women's body and womanas-mother to the lab creates the matrix in which reproduction can be conceived of and produced medicotechnically.

During egg retrieval, the eggs are sorted by level of maturity as soon as they are retrieved. During the subsequent fertilization and development of embryos in the lab, developmental details are added to the same record sheet. Whether or not the egg was fertilized, whether it was fertilized normally and started to grow normally (specifically, whether more than one sperm fertilized the egg, and whether cell division was progressing normally), and what stage of development the resulting embryo has reached at given times of the next forty-eight hours before transfer are all recorded. The evenness of the cells, the similarity of cell size, and the presence of "blebs" are also recorded. The embryos are given a "grade" to reflect how "pretty"[55] they are.

Round, evenly developing embryos are good, and uneven, "misshapen" embryos with blebs are not good. The "not good" embryos are routinely referred to collectively as "crud." Segregating the embryos in this way turns out to have more to do with managing the disposal or freezing of unused embryos than with the likelihood of a given embryo, whether good or bad, to lead to a successful pregnancy if transferred back to the woman's uterus. When I asked about this means of distinguishing embryos, I was told that IVF doctors are divided as to whether "good" embryos lead to more pregnancies than "bad" embryos if transferred immediately, and that in any case it remains true that most embryos whether good or bad will not implant, and that many "bad" ones do. "Good" embryos apparently survive the thawing process much better than "bad" embryos, however, so only excess "good" ones are frozen.

There are very often more embryos than can safely be transferred in a single cycle, given the risk of multiple pregnancy. Because some embryos were not considered worth the price of being frozen, there were sometimes embryos that were neither transferred nor frozen. A criterion had to be used that justified treating some embryos with the esteem due to their life potential and value to the patients, while enabling the ones for which there is no treatment use to be disposed of without contravening any moral or legal restrictions. Only "bad" embryos were ever disposed of while I was at the unit, and the idea of disposing of a "good" embryo was greeted with moral opprobrium. Taken together, then, the provision of a caring environment for embryo growth, together with morphological criteria for saying "good" (life-sustaining) enables the embryologists to deal clinically with potential life, while also accommodating wastage.

I gratefully acknowledge the help of the following in writing this paper: Adrian Cussins, Michael Dennis, Yrjo Engestrom, Sarah Franklin, Valerie Hartouni, David Kirsh, Martha Lampland, Bruno Latour, Chandra Mukerji, Michael Lynch, Steven Shapin, and Robert Westman. I also thank the members of the Science Studies Program at UCSD, the LCHC group at UCSD, Harry Collins and his students at Bath, Kathryn Henderson and our ASA copanelists, and Sarah Franklin and Helena Ragoné and our AAA copanelists, for listening to and commenting on earlier versions. For the preparation of this updated version I thank Sarah Franklin for characteristically generous and insightful comments and ideas.

Special thanks to the members of the infertility clinics where I worked for their time and for being open to the aims of interdisciplinary studies of science that take practice seriously. Under the conditions of my human subjects clearance, they must remain anonymous.

Finally, I would like to thank Bob Edwards and Sue Avery, of Bourn Hall, Cambridgeshire, for their help during August 1992, and the Science Studies Program of UCSD for supporting this research.

Notes

1. Cf. Adele Clarke's (1990) deft account of using "social worlds theory" in her research. I take social worlds theory's solution to the problem of what unit of analysis to pick—a meaningful grouping recognized by the actors as such and composed of shared temporal and material commitments. Unlike social worlds theorists, I do not attempt to construct my field of inquiry through actors' perspectives, because my political/epistemological interests in the anatomy of routinization do not (or cannot be presupposed to) coincide with any function of the actors' perspectives. I use "socionatural" rather than "social" world to stress that I see no explanatory priority of either the social or the natural.

2. E.g., 1970, preface, xx.

3. E.g., following Lynch (1985), my aim here is to examine the processes of normalization at work in a specific setting. As noted by Sawicki (1991) and others, Foucault usually ignored gender. Contemporary infertility medicine is a locus for the generation and reinforcement of our categories of gender, so gender normalization and other kinds of kinship normalization are non-Foucaultian themes.

4. I have been deeply influenced by Marilyn Strathern's and Sarah Franklin's discussions of the ways in which kinship relations are naturalized in a biological idiom and are simultaneously rendered as bedrock in the kinds of Western culture in which infertility clinics flourish. My debt to these scholars will be evident throughout. See, e.g., Strathern (1992), Strathern and Franklin (1993), and Edwards et al. (1993). For a more detailed discussion of the connections between my ethnographic findings on kinship in infertility clinics and Strathern's and Franklin's pioneering work, see Cussins (forthcoming 1997b).

5. E.g., Wittgenstein (1953).

6. This is particularly true in the United States, where one is studying those of a higher social status than oneself by studying doctors and scientists. It's like cashing in one's rubles for some epistemic yen—who could resist the deal, even at an unfavorable exchange rate?

7. From a rich range, e.g., the early anthology edited by Arditti, Klein, and Minden (1984); Rothman (1986); the sociological collection edited by McNeil et al. (1990); and the collection edited by Stacey (1992).

8. The ethnographic account misses much of the exclusionary work because it only takes one site at one time, rather than following, e.g., women's life trajectories, and seeing what would make someone a candidate or not for calling an infertility program. The same limitation applies to other aspects of this study; I did not follow instruments' or drugs' or practitioners' formations out of the clinic.

9. Letter from director of program to chairman of Human Investigation Committee, May 27, 1992, copied to me.

10. At the second clinic where I worked, the first thing that happened was again that I was given a white coat. My surgery blunders came this time during male infertility surgery, which I had not observed at the first clinic. I inadvertently touched a part of the operating microscope (actually, I didn't realize it was in the "sterile" category) with my "nonsterile" surgery jacket when offered a look through the microscope at the vasectomy site on the patient's exposed vas deferens. I was chided and the nurse showed me how to hold my jacket away with one hand while leaning over and looking through the microscope.

11. I never entered a consultation or examination room at any clinic without one of the doctors having first attained verbal permission from the patients for me to be present. Observing surgery usually requires written permission from the patient beforehand.

12. Robert Westman suggested to me the similarity of this kind of role normalization with black-boxing of technical and scientific facts and artifacts.

13. Sociologists and anthropologists of medicine as well as those involved in technology

transfer have debated the necessity and nature of sterility procedures during surgery—e.g., the articles by Collins (1994), Fox (1994), and Lynch (1994). In my time observing surgery there was debate amongst practitioners, too. Surgeons and nurses agreed that things must be kept as clean as possible to stave off infection, but they also recognized that total sterility was unachievable and unnecessary, and that the precise measures taken could vary from hospital to hospital. So-called "peritoneal fallout" from women staff was discussed as a sexist concept; the concentration of germs under the operating lamp and inside air conditioning ducts was compared unfavorably to the germs around the patient's and practitioners' mouths and noses and the concern taken over the latter but not the former was discussed as rather irrational. The doctor's uncovered nose was evoked as an example of the contingency of the measures. Deciding whether sterility procedures were *either* insider's good sense about sepsis, *or* ritual enactments of such things as hierarchy amongst staff and depersonalization of the patient, would have been the wrong question in this setting. The practitioners themselves did not operate with a ready-made distinction between good sense about sepsis and ritual functions, and occasionally took time to try and mark or create exactly that distinction.

14. The difference between the standards implicitly and explicitly invoked to regulate paying patients and those standards invoked to regulate commercial surrogates and donors is, in my opinion, a particularly sinister application and extension of the norms of the wider society. This differential is mirrored by the physicians' comportment to their "client" patients (commissioning would-be parents) and their "employee" patients (commecial surrogates and donors). There is not room to discuss this here, where the examples are limited to "conventional" infertility treatments involving only patients who contribute the germ plasm to be used for their treatment, but I discuss it elsewhere, e.g., Cussins (1996b).

15. Because of the correlation between socioeconomic status and race (although there are a significant number of couples who do not reflect the stereotype), there is a typical infertility patient couple. The typical patient couple is white, middle-class or higher, and older than the average primiparous age even for their socioeconomic class (to some extent this reflects the ambient demography of the clinic, as I have discovered by working in clinics in very different parts of town). The high age of patients is due in part to economics—older people tend to have more resources—but also to the time taken to discover the inability to conceive, some secondary infertility, and the greater likelihood that one will be infertile if one postpones childbirth. Access to infertility waiting rooms is not this prohibitive in all countries. Whether and how much patients have to pay depends on the country, the patient's nationality, whether the procedure is deemed experimental, what the patient's diagnosis dictates, and so on. For example, Britain has some National Health Service (NHS) clinics, some mixed clinics, and some private ones. The NHS clinics typically have long waiting lists, in the region of two years, and often only treat people who live in the relevant health authority. The wait can be prohibitive, given the decline of fertility with age.

16. Interview, December 1992.

17. Interview, December 1992.

18. *Fertility and Sterility*, the official peer-reviewed journal of the American Society for Reproductive Medicine (ASRM; formerly the American Fertility Society), and its affiliate society, the Society for Assisted Reproductive Technology (SART), reports in the July 1995 issue the statistics for assisted reproduction techniques from 1993. A total of 262 U.S. and five Canadian programs offered assisted reproductive techniques and subsequently reported their statistics to the ASRM that year; the first test-tube baby in the world was only born in 1978.

19. This is based on my impressions from attending conferences and clinic meetings and discussions with practitioners and hospital administrators over the last eight years.

20. Interview, L. B., November 1994.

21. The role of psychologists (the annexation of "caring" to them, their role in moving patients onto alternative treatment options, and their adjudicatory role in patient assessment for access to treatments and in legal contests) and their increasing specialization in infertility medicine represent an intriguing chapter in the professionalization of infertility medicine. I do not have space to touch on it here, but explore it in greater depth in my Ph.D. dissertation, "Technologies of Personhood: Human Reproductive Technologies" (1996b).

22. One of the contested naturalizations of infertility medicine in contemporary culture stems from the view of infertility as a major life crisis. Infertility physicians justify what they do in terms of the *natural* (sometimes explained scientifically, sometimes religiously) drive for biological parenthood, and their role in restoring the miracle of procreation. Critics, including the Catholic Church and some feminists, counter with the *artificiality* of it.

23. Male infertility surgery is performed for vasectomy reversal, retrograde ejaculation, congenital absence of the vas deferens, semen collection in spinal injury victims, varicoceles, and other conditions (conversation with male factor pioneer R. E., August 1992; presentation by urologist/male factor reproductive endocrinologist M. B., June 1994; and observation of male factor surgery, 1995). Problems with sperm are managed outside the man's body (e.g., micromanipulation techniques and zona drilling), and any resultant embryos still need to implant in the woman's uterus, thereby forcing her to become a patient.

24. For a discussion of women patients' active seeking of and collaboration in their own objectification as a means of operationalizing infertility, see Cussins (1996a).

25. I heard this exact wording used by one of the physicians.

26. I. C., World Health Organization Scientific Group on Recent Advances in Medically Assisted Conception, Geneva, 2–6 April 1990.

27. In some clinics it is perhaps the case that natural cycles are discouraged because they do not yield spare embryos and so are not useful for research (e.g., in cryopreservation, micromanipulation, gene therapy, and embryonic development). This more conspiratorial response to the question as to why natural cycles have not taken off is not likely to hold true for predominantly clinical units.

28. Natural cycles have fared a little better in the United Kingdom, where you can start younger because of lower costs, and where medicine in general is a public service and so tolerated as more hit or miss.

29. "Beautiful philosophical object" is an expression used by Bruno Latour to describe a soil-collecting device in a lecture at UCSD in 1992.

30. By "normality" I am referring to the ways in which "nothing wrong here" or "something wrong here" are established and differentiated. This performative notion of normality ("nothing wrong here," or that against which it is decided that "something is wrong here") is itself normative for the practice of infertility medicine.

31. Cf. Latour (1990), Lynch (1985), and Lynch and Woolgar (1990).

32. Hirsutism is associated with high testosterone in women whose ethnicity is usually correlated with small amounts of bodily hair. Hyperandrogenism is in turn associated with infertility.

33. This is what Hirschauer (1991) seems to suggest is the case in surgery.

34. This is in the spirit of Michael Lynch's (1985: 43) fundamental question, "How do graphic properties merge with and come to embody the natural object?"

35. See Cartwright (1992) for an excellent account of the performative relations between seeing and knowing in the introduction of the ultrasound.

36. The characteristic T-shaped uterus of daughters of diethylstilbestrol (DES) users, which can interfere with conception, also shows up.

37. There have been a few superb ethnographic accounts of surgery that treat the operating room as a relatively self-contained, situated activity system with its own enabling practices centered around treatment of a nonsacrificial human body: Goffman's second "encounter" on role distance (1961); Katz (1981), which stresses the importance of sterility rituals in demarcating zones of operation, easing transitions, and neutralizing anomalies; and Hirschauer's enthralling article (1991). Collins (1994) and takes up Hirschauer's notion of "anatomie herstellen" and insists as I want to, that there is always a degree of exploration of unmapped territory in addition to "making a correspondence with an existing map." Where I differ from Collins, however, is in seeing all levels of assimilation to normality as essentially involving exploration, even when the recognitional skills are highly routinized and reliable.

38. Interview with nurse, August 1992.

39. See, e.g., Oreskes's (1995) discussion of Eleanor Lamson, and Martin's excellent (1991) history of women telephone operators for examples of the ways in which presumptions about gender are built into the very nature of the skills required to perform certain jobs.

40. E.g., Hutchins (1989: 16): "The management of the deployment of human resources, the online negotiation of the distribution of labor, is essential to the operation of the system. If the distribution of labor was fixed, the system would surely fail whenever one of its components failed." Hutchins uses the hierarchical nature of skill distributed in teamwork to produce his account of the organic reproduction of overlap of skill through moving up a skill hierarchy, masking other epistemic functions of such role differences, and the boundaries in most workplaces to mobility across the boundaries. It can be argued that Hutchins' Navy work on team navigation is at one extreme for discussing distributed cognition. The Navy takes care institutionally of the enforcement and reproduction of the necessary hierarchies, so that he does not have to confront them in his own fieldwork.

41. Ragoné (1994) provides a fascinating discussion of hierarchical role overlap in American surrogacy, where the commercial surrogate temporarily experiences class mobility as she is disciplined (in terms of diet, drink, substance abuse, and medical surveillance) and pampered (friendship with the commissioning "parents," lavish gifts) across class lines. At the end of the nine months, however, the relationship is over and no permanent mobility was achieved. I have found this in my own work interviewing surrogates, who frequently say that they cannot understand what happened after the baby's birth, cannot understand why they were "dropped" by the socioeconomically privileged commissioning parents.

42. Cf. Knorr-Cetina (1996) for a use of this expression.

43. Many writers have commented on the problematic interpretation of success rates based on statistics in reproductive technologies, e.g., Crowe (1990; 30), Steinberg (1990; 84), Klein and Rowland (1988), and Marcus-Steiff (1991). These accounts focus on how a prospective patient should interpret the published statistics. Which cycles get counted? Do multiple births count as more than one success, inflating the figures? Are only live births considered as successes, or are all pregnancies counted, including perhaps the infamous "biochemical pregnancies" in which no fetus is ever present? Are the figures significantly better than comparable figures for different treatments and figures for no treatment at all?

44. Interview with embryologist, December 1992.

45. Very local success rates, such as the number of pregnancies that week, can have a surprisingly large effect on morale.

46. The embryologists have chief responsibility for the statistics. The following quotes are all from interviews with members of the team in December 1992.

47. This turn of phrase brings out particularly well the fact that the statistics must be produced by the very procedures they are used to justify.

48. Donors usually bring their samples with them to the clinic rather than using the premises. Their semen must be frozen and screened for HIV before use in the donor program, so the timing of collection is not critical.

49. At another clinic where I worked, all the exam rooms were arranged in a square around a central nurses' station. This meant that none of them was sufficiently private for masturbation, and the men's bathroom was used instead. This room boasted an open rack of heterosexual pornographic magazines and sterile collecting pots.

50. These features were commented on by several women in interviews, July 1992 and November 1994. It is often the sheer practicalities of fitting the appointments into one's home and work life, combined with what is sometimes called SOS (sex-on-schedule), that are experienced as particularly arduous.

51. Increasingly, clinics are offering deals where patients pay for a set number of treatment cycles, say three, and then get any additional cycles almost free. If they become pregnant in fewer than three cycles, though, they do not receive a refund, and these deals tie a patient to a given clinic.

52. Some clinics make do with a single laboratory, and other clinics have a suite of rooms, separating diagnostic work from therapeutic work, and separating andrology from embryology.

53. Conversation with embryologist, August 1992.

54. Sarah Franklin, personal communication, commentary on early draft of this paper, 1994.

55. This is the adjective differentiating embryos that I have heard most often in the clinics where I have worked.

References

Arditti, Rita, Renate Duelli Klein, and Shelley Minden, eds. 1984. *Test-Tube Women: What Future for Motherhood?* London, Boston, Sydney, and Wellington: Pandora Press.

Cartwright, Lisa. 1992. "Women, X-Rays, and the Public Culture of Prophylactic Imaging." *camera obscura* 29: 19–56.

Clarke, Adele. 1990. "A Social Worlds Research Adventure: The Case of Reproductive Science." In *Theories of Science in Society*, ed. Susan S. Cozzens and Thomas F. Gieryn. Bloomington and Indianapolis: Indiana University Press.

Collins, H. M. 1994. "Dissecting Surgery: Forms of Life Depersonalized." *Social Studies of Science* 24: 311–33.

Crowe, Christine. 1990. "Whose Mind over Whose Matter? Women, In Vitro Fertilisation and the Development of Scientific Knowledge." In *The New Reproductive Technologies*, ed. Maureen McNeil, Ian Varcoe, and Steven Yearley. New York: St. Martin's Press.

Cussins, Charis. 1995. "Gender as a Means of Distributing Epistemic Virtue: Examples from Infertility Medicine." Paper presented at conference, The Women, Gender and Science Question: What Do Research on the History of Women and Science, and Research on Science and Gender Have To Do with Each Other? University of Minnesota, 12–14 May, 1995.

———. 1996a. "Ontological Choreography: Agency Through Objectification in Infertility Clinics." *Social Studies of Science* 26: 575–610.

————. 1996b. "Technologies of Personhood: Human Reproductive Technologies." Ph.D. dissertation, University of California, San Diego.

————. 1997. "Quit Snivelling, Cryo-Baby; We'll Decide Which One's Your Mama." In *Cyborg Babies: From Techno Tots to Techno Toys*, ed. Robbie E. Floyd-Davis and Joe Dumit. New York: Routledge.

Edwards, Jeanette, Sarah Franklin, Eric Hirsch, Frances Price, and Marilyn Strathern. 1993. *Technologies of Procreation: Kinship in the Age of Assisted Conception*. Manchester and New York: Manchester University Press.

Foucault, Michel. (1966) 1970. *The Order of Things: An Archaeology of the Human Sciences*. New York: Random House.

Fox, N. 1994. "Fabricating Surgery: A Response to Collins." *Social Studies of Science* 24: 347–54.

Goffman, Erving. 1961. *Encounters: Two Studies in the Sociology of Interaction*. Harmondsworth: Penguin.

Haraway, Donna J. 1991. *Simians, Cyborgs and Women: The Reinvention of Nature*. New York: Routledge.

————. 1992. "The Promises of Monsters: A Regenerative Politics for Inappropriate/d Others." In *Cultural Studies*, ed. Lawrence Grossberg, Cary Nelson, and Paula A. Treichler. New York: Routledge.

Hirschauer, Stefan. 1991. "The Manufacture of Bodies in Surgery." *Social Studies of Science* 21: 279–319.

Hutchins, E. 1989. "The Technology of Team Navigation." In *Intellectual Teamwork: Social and Technical Bases of Cooperative Work*, ed. Jolene Galegher, Robert E. Kraut, and Carmen Egido. Hillsdale, N.J.: Lawrence Erlbaum.

Katz, Pearl. 1981. "Ritual in the Operating Room." *Ethnology* 20: 335–50.

Klein, Renate Duelli and Robin Rowland. 1988. "Women as Test Sites for Fertility Drugs: Clomiphene Citrate and Hormonal Cocktails." *Reproductive and Genetic Engineering* 1: 251–374.

Knorr-Cetina, Karen. 1996. "Liminal and Referent Epistemologies." In *The Disunity of Science: Boundaries, Contexts, and Power*, ed. Peter Galison and David J. Stump. Stanford, Calif.: Stanford University Press.

Latour, Bruno. 1990. "Drawing Things Together." In *Representation in Scientific Practice*, ed. Michael Lynch and Steve Woolgar. Cambridge, Mass. and London: MIT Press.

Lynch, Michael. 1985. "Discipline and the Material Form of Images: An Analysis of Scientific Visibility." *Social Studies of Science* 15: 37–66.

————. 1994. "Collins, Hirschauer, and Winch: Ethnography, Exoticism, Surgery, Antisepsis, and Dehorsification." *Social Studies of Science* 24: 354–69.

Lynch, Michael and Steve Woolgar, eds. (1988) 1990. *Representation in Scientific Practice*. Cambridge, Mass. and London: MIT Press.

Marcus-Steiff, J. 1991. "Les taux de 'succès' de FIV—Fausses transparences et vrais mensonges." *La Recherche* 20: 225.

Martin, Michele. 1991. *"Hello Central?" Gender, Technology, and Culture in the Formation of Telephone Systems*. Montreal and Buffalo, N.Y.: McGill-Queen's University Press.

McNeil, Maureen, Ian Varcoe, and Steve Yearley, eds. 1990. *The New Reproductive Technologies*. New York: St. Martin's Press.

Oreskes, Naomi. 1996. "Objectivity or Heroism? On the Invisibility of Women in Science." *Osiris* 11: 87–113.

Ragoné, Helena. 1994. *Surrogate Motherhood: Conception in the Heart*. Boulder, Colo.: Westview Press.

Rothman, Barbara Katz. 1986. *The Tentative Pregnancy: Prenatal Diagnosis and the Future of Motherhood.* New York: Viking Penguin.

Sawicki, Jana. 1991. *Disciplining Foucault: Feminism, Power and the Body.* New York: Routledge.

Stacey, Meg. 1992. *Changing Human Reproduction: Social Science Perspectives.* London, Newbury Park, and New Delhi: Sage.

Steinberg, Deborah Lynn. 1990. "The Depersonalisation of Women Through the Administration of In Vitro Fertilization." In *The New Reproductive Technologies.*, ed. Maureen McNeil, Ian Varcoe, and Steven Yearley. New York: St. Martin's Press.

Strathern, Marilyn. 1992. *Reproducing the Future: Anthropology, Kinship, and the New Reproductive Technologies.* Manchester: Manchester University Press.

Strathern, Marilyn (Project Director) and Sarah Franklin (Research Coordinator). 1993. "Kinship and the New Genetic Technologies: An Assessment of Existing Anthropological Research." Report compiled for the Commission of the European Communities, Medical Research Division, Human Genome Analysis Programme, submitted 1 January.

Wittgenstein, Ludwig. 1953. *Philosophical Investigations.* Trans. G. E. M. Anscombe. New York: Macmillan.

Young, Katharine. 1989. "Disembodiment: The Phenomenology of the Body in Medical Examinations." *Semiotica* 73: 43–66.

Chapter 4
Making Miracles: Scientific Progress and the Facts of Life

Sarah Franklin

As noted in the introduction to this volume, anthropology has long been centrally concerned with the social organization of what are seen as universal natural facts of human regeneration and connectedness. These are the biogenetic facts of human reproduction and heredity, known as the "facts of life." For early anthropologists (such as Tylor 1871; Frazer 1910; McLennan 1865; Hartland 1909) the facts of physical paternity comprised a central point of reference, even an obsession, in theories of social organization (Coward 1983; Weiner 1976; Yanagisako 1985). For Bachofen (1861), Morgan (1871), and Engels (1884) accurate knowledge of physical paternity indexed crucial transitions from one stage of human civilization to another. For Malinowski, the question of physical paternity was no less than "the most exciting and controversial issue in the comparative science of man" (1937: xxxiii).

During the 1980s, as part of the move toward greater disciplinary self-consciousness, and in response to critical challenges from feminist, postcolonial and postmodern perspectives, a series of studies began innovatively to combine the history of anthropology with the problem of both cultural and cross-cultural analysis (e.g., Delaney 1986; Schneider 1984). An emphasis on reflexivity encouraged the integration of ethnographic observation and representation with more critical readings of the unexamined conventions of documentation and analysis present in the development of anthropological perspectives (Clifford 1988; Clifford and Marcus 1986; Marcus and Fisher 1986). In the area of kinship and gender studies, the biological model of reproduction derived from a post-Darwinian universe of consanguinity and sexual selection was critiqued as recent, modernist, ethnocentric, androcentric, and partial in contrast to its presumed self-evidentness and universality (Collier and Yanagisako 1987a).

Schneider, for example, developed the argument that the biological model of the facts of life was a culturally specific symbolic system (1968a, b), as well as a distinctly European one (1984). Yanagisako (1985) argued that this same biological reductionism united the studies of both kinship and gender, an argument that was developed in a range of subsequent publications (Collier and Yanagisako 1987a, b; Yanagisako and Collier 1987; Tsing and Yanagisako 1983; Yanagisako and Delaney 1995). An important series of studies by Mary Bouquet details the cultural specificity of the models of genealogy underlying much of the modern anthropological project and linking it to its European origins (1993, 1995a, b, 1996). Marilyn Strathern's discussion of the significance of ideas of the natural in the formation of Englishness, as well as in anthropological idioms of kinship, is used to analyze Euro-American knowledge practices more widely (1992a, b). The study on which this chapter is based makes a similar refraction, and is responsive to the longstanding dilemma of moving beyond entrenched naturalizations of "the facts of life" in an attempt to retheorize kinship and gender as well as reproduction.

Complementing such studies, the emergence of an anthropology of science and technology offers both theoretical and ethnographic possibilities in the continuing effort to expand anthropological notions of "the field" or "fieldwork."[1] Recent anthropological studies of new reproductive technologies have shown that technology can operate as a defamiliarizing lens, capable of exposing the often invisible givens that have long defined anthropological accounts of kinship, reproduction, parenthood, and social structure (Edwards et al. 1993; Franklin 1997; Ginsburg and Rapp 1991, 1995; and Strathern 1992b). The coherence of the standard (modern biological) model of the facts of life is a good example of the kind of naturalized narrative that is troubled by new technology. Traditionally defined as a natural sequence of biogenetic events, conception in the context of technological assistance is increasingly seen as an *achievement*. The narrative of the facts of life is consequently changed by the advent of assisted conception technologies, or ARTs, as they are often dubbed.

In her witty account of "The Egg and the Sperm," Emily Martin provides a detailed critique of the traditional narrative associated with both scientific and popular representations of conception (1991). Primarily, these narratives are organized around the idiom of a journey, culminating in a rendezvous that begins a new life. Martin argues that the narration of the egg and sperm story reproduces and relies upon conventional gender stereotypes, whereby a division of labor foundational to the determination of sexual difference is inscribed as an essential reproductive telos ensuring human survival. This chapter will develop the approach outlined by Martin by arguing that changes in the causal sequence seen to define the beginnings of life can be indexed to a number of social and cultural factors. By combining analysis of mainstream popular representations of conception in the context of technological assistance and an indicative ethnographic portrait of how these narratives are inhabited by women undergoing IVF, my aim is to reposition a traditional anthropological question (coming into being) within a more recent cultural frame (ARTs).

Several broad changes can be seen to have affected late twentieth-century Euro-American conception accounts as the result of their increasing technologization, commodification, and instrumentalization. The standard conception story, for example, has been lengthened to include not only the journeys of the egg and sperm, but their genetics and their genesis. The lengthening of the conception story familiar through popular accounts of "the birds and the bees" is keyed to its geneticization—oogenesis and spermatogenesis (the production of the germ cells) are now seen as important components in the realization of successful conception, insofar as they may be the source of genetic error compromising reproductive outcome. Similarly, conception is now defined as separate from fertilization. Whereas they are synonymous in older accounts, more recent conception accounts define fertilization as the fusion of the *gametes* (the egg and sperm) and conception as the process of genetic recombination, which occurs over the succeeding thirty-six hours.[2]

A second consequence for conception models post-ARTs is that they are increasingly defined in terms of *reproductive risk*, that is, in terms of what can go wrong. Increasing knowledge of the sources of reproductive failure, from newly discovered genetic diseases to toxicities linked to congenital deformity, has increased public awareness of reproductive risk. Accompanying the specter of *overfertility* (unwanted pregnancy, unwanted multiple pregnancy) are widely publicized accounts of *underfertility* (infertility due to delayed childbearing,[3] venereal disease, exposure to workplace toxicity, etc.). In 1991, *Time* magazine ran a cover story on the "epidemic" of infertility sweeping the United States, in which conception is narrated entirely in terms of "what can go wrong." Preconception has been added to the time frame included in the account of pregnancy, and preconceptive fertility tests are frequently advertised in women's magazines as a new form of reproductive self-monitoring.

These changes recapitulate an emergent isomorphism between fertility and infertility narratives, derivative of the proximity of "what can go wrong" and "how to fix it." In turn, a much-remarked-upon implosion of natural facts and technological assistance blurs the boundary between "natural" and assisted conception.[4] My interest here is in exploring such changes through an ethnographic lens. Though it is possible to chart the reauthorization of the facts of life at the level of mainstream popular cultural representations, scientific texts, or technological procedures, the question of how these new conception stories are lived, embodied, and negotiated remains an ethnographic concern.

Initially, techniques such as in vitro fertilization (IVF) were analogized to nature and described by their provisioners as "just like" natural conception. Terms such as "test-tube babies" were eschewed by clinicians working in the field of assisted reproduction as well as by their clients, who resisted their stigmatizing, made-in-the-lab connotations. Couples I interviewed in Britain about their experiences of IVF strongly stressed the naturalness of the technique, and this finding has been confirmed by other researchers (Sandelowski 1993). Increasingly, so-called "natural" conception is analogized to IVF, in a reverse comparison that stresses their shared high-failure rates. Due to the increasing amount of information available about early human development (as a result of ARTs), it is suggested that "normal" conception fails much more often than was previously thought (Hull 1986). Hence the traffic both ways in comparisons of "normal" and achieved conception stresses their similarity, their vulnerability to failure, and their naturalness.

New Conceptions

This chapter, then, offers an ethnographic perspective on changes affecting the standard model of "the facts of life" in the context of achieved conception (or ARTs). On the basis of fieldwork in an IVF clinic in England and interviews with twenty-two women and couples undergoing this technique, a cultural account of the redefinition of a key set of natural facts is provided using ethnographic data to examine the wider social dimensions of changing conception models. Such a perspective, I argue, not only has consequences in terms of understanding changing definitions of the natural, but also sheds light on the conceptual heritage to which anthropology as a discipline is heir and to which particular conception models have been central. If it is a European folk model of reproduction that underscores the concept of kinship in anthropology (as Schneider, Yanagisako, Delaney, and Strathern all claim), and if in turn that concept has been central to the kind of disciplinary specialization on which anthropology is based (as Bouquet, among others, demonstrates), then ethnographic study of its contemporary redefinition yields a perspective on past epistemic conceptions as well as present organic and cultural ones.

As noted above, "accurate" knowledge of the facts of life has long operated as an important point of reference within anthropology. From late-nineteenth-century speculations about "primitive" paternity to mid-twentieth-century debates about the "virgin birth," Western scientific certainties about the facts of life have stood in sharp contrast to the putative uncertainties of various peoples studied by anthropologists. Specifically, the so-called "primitive ignorance" or "nescience" of physical paternity avowed by Australian aborigines and Trobriand Islanders has fueled repeated controversy among anthropologists.[5] Yet, although the question of "whether they really know or not" was never definitively answered, anthropologists did not debate among themselves the question of whether it takes a sperm and an egg to make a baby. Though many were prepared to acknowledge that this discovery is in fact very recent in European history (e.g., Malinowski 1937, Leach 1967, and Spiro 1968) and that there are scientific grounds to question it (Barnes 1973), noone was prepared to suggest that perhaps the Trobrianders were right, that it does take a spirit-child to make a pregnancy.

It is for this reason highly ironic, and perhaps fortuitously just, that increasing *uncertainty* now characterizes the precise mechanisms occasioning successful conception. The seemingly straightforward and indisputable facticity guaranteeing the assumption that it takes an egg and a sperm to make a baby is increasingly revealed as partial, and even in some cases as false. This explanation works retroactively to explain some of the causal elements necessary to establish a pregnancy. However, an egg and sperm may be present and fail to fertilize, or they may fertilize and fail to develop, or the egg and sperm may fertilize, develop, and then be absorbed by the uterus for no apparent reason. In sum, the facts of life have become more visibly partial and contingent.

More to the point, technological assistance is increasingly part of the production of new persons. This creates unique dilemmas and opportunities. As reproductive success is rendered tentative by increasing knowledge of how much can go wrong with the early stages of embryogenesis, so too is reproductive failure rendered tentative by the increasing number of options available to assist the production of pregnancy. True to the pattern of Euro-American representations of the natural as both within and beyond human control, as so deftly described by Tsing (1995), both "normal" and assisted conception are naturalized *at the same time both are described as miraculous.*

Although IVF has now been practiced for nearly two decades, it continues to have limited success.[6] At the best clinics in the world, the success rate—measured as the take-home-baby ratio—remains between 15 and 20 percent. Four out of five couples who attempt IVF will fail, and probably the one out of five who is successful will fail at least once in the process. IVF is also a very arduous procedure. Even well-informed professionals, such as nurses I interviewed who chose to undertake IVF, often have little appreciation of the extent to which the technique "takes over" their lives. This is not only because of the rigorous scheduling demands of the two-week ovulation cycles necessary to remove enough healthy eggs from a woman's ovaries to maximize the chances of successful in vitro fertilization.[8] It is also because of the emotional intensity of the program. In general, ARTs are expensive, time-consuming, and physically and emotionally taxing. The more expensive, time-consuming, and high-tech they are, the less likely they are to succeed. A question that has guided many studies of IVF is why women and couples are willing to undergo its rigors at such high cost for such an elusive reward.[8] However, the answer is quite simple, for it is often the only way to have a child—not just a *biological* child, but simply a child. Where adoption is unavailable, as it is in many parts of Europe as well as the United States, IVF may be the only option for infertile couples who continue to want to become parents.

At the same time that the rationale for undertaking IVF may be obvious, in spite of its shortcomings, all of the women interviewed for this study were aware of the limited chances of success. Moreover, although they were prone to underestimating both the complexity and intensity of the treatment cycle, none of the couples interviewed assumed IVF would be easy. Instead, women expressed two primary aims in relations to IVF: if they succeeded, they would achieve the ultimate goal of a take-home baby, and if they failed, at least they would know they had tried everything. This pair of alternate resolutions was seen to *guarantee success*—one way or the other, a positive outcome was assured. In what follows, I discuss briefly how this initial assumption unravels in the context of IVF treatment, how this can be seen as a social dimension of changing conception narratives, and why this has implications for understanding high-technology medicine more broadly.

Having to Try

Although ARTs are often celebrated as an expansion of reproductive choice, all the women interviewed for this study described not having any choice—they "had to try" IVF. This is how Frances Keating, the mother of an adopted daughter and a childcare worker, described her decision to opt for IVF:

I mean [my husband] says, "Well, the choice is yours." *Well there wasn't a choice,* I mean I just had, I had to have a go for my own peace of mind, because you never, if you don't you're always saying, "Well, if only I'd had a go, perhaps it would have worked."

Whereas infertility, sterility, or serial reproductive failure may be seen to impose a physical, biological, or "natural" limit to procreative choice, ARTs aim to overcome or transcend such limitations. The whole point of ARTs, of assistance of conception, is to gain greater control over the reproductive process and by so doing to increase reproductive choice. Whereas in the past couples had to suffer the iniquities of nature's lottery in the allocation of progeny, today science can provide an increasing range of options for couples seeking to achieve a successful pregnancy—or so the story goes. Yet for many women who choose IVF, such as Frances Keating, the experience is not one of choice but of necessity. The existence of new technological options takes away the choice simply to accept infertility. In the face of a possible treatment, however unsuccessful, infertility becomes a tentative condition.[9] In turn, there can be no "peace of mind." New technological options produce a forced choice; once a choice exists it must either be pursued or refused.

This cycle of the removal of "natural" limits through technology, and the production of new choices that may feel like nonchoices or forced choices, continues throughout treatment. For example, couples are often told there is "nothing wrong" with them and that their failure to conceive is "unexplained." In this study, half the group interviewed had unexplained, or inadequately explained, infertility. More commonly, about a third of infertility cases are clinically diagnosed as "unexplained infertility." This means that all of the (known) causal requirements for conception and pregnancy are in place, but for unknown reasons the expected developmental sequence fails either to begin at all or to proceed past a certain point. When a cycle reaches a point of failure, it is described as "being abandoned." Paradoxically, some women described a desire for "something to be wrong" in lieu of having to endure the frustration of repeated failure and abandonment in the context of no apparent fault. As one woman described her situation:

You know, in some ways it would have been easier if they had said, "Well, you've got this problem and there is nothing we can do about it, you will never become pregnant." . . . But it's quite frustrating for them to say, "Well, we can't find anything."

Other women interviewed expressed similar frustrations:

Nobody has ever said to me, "The reason you haven't gotten pregnant is . . ." What they've *always* said to me, without fail, is, "I really don't know why you haven't gotten pregnant, but I thought you would . . . , and I'm sure you will." . . . I can't cope with the idea that, you know, there's just some minor adjustment to be made.

The tantalizing feature of IVF is the idea that there *is* just a minor adjustment to be made, just a small gap to be bridged, just a little push in the right direction, just the need for a "helping hand," as the technique is often described. More often than not, several adjustments are needed, and consequently there is a significant component of trial and error in identifying them. As one successful couple put it, "It seemed to be very much trial and error, because nobody ever found anything wrong with either of us."

The feeling that there is always "just some minor adjustment to be made" exacerbates the situation that IVF was undertaken by women or couples to relieve. The assumption that the technique would provide either longed-for offspring or at least peace of mind in having exhausted every avenue of possibility becomes more elusive in the context of having no obvious point of completion of treatment. As failures increase, so do avenues of possibility, as failure often yields diagnostic information of some possible advantage in pinpointing the source of difficulty.

In this sense, a "failed" cycle can even be redefined as a successful one, complicating the identification of an endpoint to treatment. For example, many couples were found to underestimate the complexity of an IVF cycle. This results in part from the naming of the IVF technique for one of the simplest components of the procedure, when the egg and sperm are placed together in a petri dish to achieve fertilization. The initial impression many couples have of IVF, therefore, is that an egg is removed from the woman's body, fertilized in a dish, and then returned to the womb. Although, in essence, this *is* the technique, these three steps or stages all break down into myriad smaller stages or steps, at each of which something can go wrong or fail to proceed, leading the cycle to be abandoned.

As one woman, Meg Flowers, described her initial impression of IVF:

[We just thought] that it would be an administration of a drug and a recovery of an egg and then fertilization, test-tube fertilization, and reimplant, and essentially that *is* the procedure, but that is very much an oversimplification of the procedure.

As each stage is revealed as more complex, consisting instead of several smaller stages, the analogy that came to many women's minds was of an obstacle course. As Meg Flowers continued:

It's like, to me, . . . running the Grand National without a horse and with your legs tied together and with a blindfold on. I don't know how long the Grand National is . . . , it feels like that . . . , but with all the brooks and everything else, and you've got to get over every single hurdle and you can still fall at the finish line.

The sense of being on an obstacle course in which any fall will disqualify you was a frequently encountered image in this study, as in others (Sandelowski 1993). Like athletes seeking a championship performance or a personal best, women undergoing IVF must balance hope for a successful run against awareness of the likelihood of failure and disappointment. Unlike an obstacle course or similar athletic challenge, IVF is described as a disabling experience in which the runner is handicapped by having "your legs tied together and with a blindfold on." Such statements convey the deepening appreciation of the scope of unknown and unknowable factors that may compromise success for many women and couples undergoing IVF. In addition to an elusive goal, those in pursuit of IVF often feel a compromised sense of agency towards the task at hand.

Making Progress

Faith in progress is an essential component of the IVF experience at several levels. For individual women and couples, faith in progress is seen as an important psychological element of preparedness. As one husband described it, "You've got to be totally dedicated." Positive thinking and strategies such as conscious visualization of successful pregnancy were pursued by women and couples who balanced hope for success against preparedness for failure. The media ubiquitously celebrate the advent of ARTs as evidence of progress. As a Sunday feature from the London *Times*, typical of the period under study, asserted:

For . . . an estimated one million . . . couples in Britain striving to overcome childlessness, doctors can now resort to a remarkable and increasing number of treatments. Advances in the use of drugs, surgical techniques and *in vitro* fertilization mean that babies are now being born to couples who until quite recently would have been described as hopeless cases.(Prentice 1986: 10)

Similarly, the Warnock Committee, appointed by the British government to advise on matters of human fertilization and embryology, hailed the development of IVF as "a considerable achievement" that "opened up new horizons in the alleviation of infertility," creating "pride in technological achievement" and affirming the distinguished traditions of scientific progress so esteemed as part of the English national heritage (Warnock 1985). Parliamentarians also frequently cited the need to support scientific progress and development as one of their chief reasons for establishing Britain as one of the most permissive climates in the world for research into ARTs.[10] This emphasis on progress has an overdetermined character in the context of ARTs, in which technological innovation is united with the production of children. Symbolically, both children and scientific progress instantiate ideas about the future. Children born of IVF thus literally embody a potent connection to the next generation—and its potential generativity, which is increasingly both practiced and imagined through new technology. Ethnographically, such symbolic formations can be seen to have specific social manifestations, and one of the tasks in assessing the "implications" of new technology is to identify these effects.

Tentative Futures

The location of women and couples, on what Rayna Rapp describes as the moral frontier of new reproductive and genetic technologies, is one of embodying progress. As Barbara Katz Rothman (1986) so eloquently argued in the first major social scientific study of new reproductive technologies, this position is a tentative one. Couples who seek IVF aim to move out of the situation of confronting tentative futures, in which the issue of having children or remaining childless is unresolved. Women who agree to undergo the intensive procedures involved in IVF often feel they will at least be able to know they left no possibility unattempted. Yet, far from settling these unresolved issues about the future, IVF often renders them *more* tentative. As it becomes increasingly clear that there are always new options to be tried, always more that can be done, and always something to learn from failure that may increase the chances of success, the possibility of finding resolution becomes more remote. Added to this is the problem that IVF may bring a woman closer to pregnancy than she has ever been, thus diminishing her ability to "back off" from the quest for a child. As serial attempts at IVF progress further and further, sometimes to the point of reimplantation, women who have experienced their bodies as an obstacle to procreative progress literally are able to see its fertility "ripening." Through scans that monitor the growth of eggs, through the opportunity to view enlarged projections of fertilized ova before reimplantation, and through the experiences of having a fertilized egg implanted into her uterus, a woman may well feel closer to experiencing pregnancy than she has ever felt before. If IVF then fails at such a stage, the loss is all the more acute.

Many women made statements such as the following by Mavis Norton to describe their initial decision to opt for IVF:

I think you feel you've got to try it. It may not work, but if it's the only thing that's left for you, you've got to try it. . . . I didn't want to feel in a few year's time, "Oh, I wish I had tried that"—you know, I had the opportunity and I didn't take it. I felt as if I'd regret it later on.

Beth Carter put it more succinctly when she said, "I don't want to get to menopause and feel I haven't tried everything." The assumption is that "trying everything" will help to resolve feelings of loss, unhappiness, or grief accompanying unwanted childlessness. As Susan Doyle stated, "To know we've done everything [helps] to come to terms with [infertility]." Other women too said they wanted to dispel any doubt by knowing that at least they'd "given it a shot."

Over the course of IVF treatment, however, this conviction can unravel. Because of the intensity of the program, the unanticipated physical and emotional demands, the greater complexity of the technique, and the momentum that is generated, women's initial sense of a guaranteed positive outcome may dissipate. The if-not-a-baby-at-least-peace-of-mind logic occasioning the initial decision to opt for IVF is discovered to be more elusive than anticipated.

In contrast to the extensive media depiction of women choosing IVF because they are "desperate" for a child,[11] this study found that women were in fact often already resigned to the likelihood of not having children *before* undergoing IVF. Indeed, it was often this ability to live with the prospect of remaining childless that enabled women to undertake IVF, as they felt more protected from emotional overinvestment. Ironically, it is the experience of undertaking IVF that may *produce* the very "desperateness" that it is often represented as helping to relieve. Kate Quigley explains:

When I first attempted to get pregnant [through IVF] . . . I think I was more philosophical about it—just, well, if I do get pregnant I do, and if I don't I don't—and then sort of the longer it went on the more I realized that, you know, I really did want a family, and now I don't know what I'm going to do if I can't become pregnant.

Having believed her career interests would protect her from investing too much hope in a successful outcome from IVF, she found that the intensity of focus on the possibility of pregnancy had made her lose interest in her job. "I decided that I'm not all that interested in my career anymore," she explained, adding, "I'm actually going to give up." Having felt "philosophical" about the idea of not being able to have a child, she was changed by the experience of IVF, to the point where she felt that "if I can't have a family, I really don't know how I'm going to cope."

In sum, the public representation of IVF as a response to a "desperate" desire on the part of infertile women and couples for relief from childlessness can be revealed through ethnographic study to be a misleading justification. To the contrary, the technique can be shown to produce a greater desire for children than existed at the outset. Similarly, the assurance that undergoing IVF will at least bring "peace of mind" unravels over the course of treatment, during which it becomes increasingly clear that there is no such thing as leaving every stone unturned — the greater a couple's involvement in the world of achieved conception defined by the capacities of ARTs, the greater the number of possibilities to try something new. Whereas IVF and other ARTs are sought to relieve the tentative futures produced by infertility, as a result of which couples feel they cannot plan for the future or settle on a shared path forward, the world of achieved conception often only offers more uncertainty, especially in the case where "there is nothing wrong." Each of these dilemmas produces unique challenges for women and couples seeking to make sense of missed conceptions in a context of increasing information but still very limited actual knowledge about "the facts of life."

These dilemmas in turn reflect broader anxieties about risk, technology, and health in the context of high-technology medicine (Stacey, 1992). The paradoxical dimensions of hope, choice, and belief in scientific progress that characterize the experience of IVF have much in common with other situations faced by individuals, friends, and family encountering forms of technological intervention that in turn take them into unfamiliar territory. Understanding the specific vicissitudes of such encounters — for example, through documenting their multiple and contradictory demands — is an essential dimension of the effort better to comprehend and negotiate the unique moral, ethical, and emotional issues of high-technology medicine.

This chapter draws on research conducted in England in 1988–1990 with support from the Wenner-Gren Foundation. The full study is described in Franklin 1992, 1997. All names used in this account are pseudonyms.

Notes

1. For a discussion of the anthropology of science, see Franklin 1995b. For a review of new forms of ethnographic representation, predominantly multisited ethnography, see Marcus 1995. For a discussion of the notion of the field in anthropology, see Gupta and Ferguson 1992.

2. For a more detailed discussion of changes in conception narratives derivative of the world of achieved conception, see Franklin 1992, 1995a, 1997.

3. Susan Faludi provides a thorough critique of the widely publicized Harvard and Yale studies suggesting that delayed childbearing has catastrophic effects on women's fertility in her book *Backlash: the Undeclared War Against American Women* (1991).

4. See Haraway 1992, Rabinow 1992, and Strathern 1992a and 1992b for commentary on the "implosion" of the nature-culture opposition such overlaps manifest.

5. As Delaney notes in her critique of these debates (1986), the obsessive interest in paternity expressed by anthropologists more accurately indexes their own concerns than those of the peoples they studied (see also Coward 1983).

6. The success rates for IVF in England at the time of this study (1988–1989) were less than 10 percent (ILA figures; see also Pfeffer and Quick 1988). Worldwide, they were approximately 2 percent (World Health Organization figures).

7. During the two-week ovulation induction cycle, women are given a steroid to induce chemical menopause, creating a blank slate on which a regulated hormonal cycle can be established. Hormone shots are given once or twice daily in conjunction with oral doses of fertility drugs, including Clomid® (clomiphene citrate), Perganol® (menotropins), and Metrodin® (urofollitropin). Egg development is monitored by ultrasound until the ova are mature. Forty-eight hours before extraction, a dose of follicle stimulating hormone (FSH) is administered to catalyze the surge of luteinizing hormone (LH), after which up to forty eggs can be removed by aspiration.

8. Studies that have addressed this issue include those of Crowe 1985, 1988; Klein 1989; Koch 1990; Lorber 1989; Modell 1989; and Williams 1988a, b.

9. Infertility in the context of ARTs can be considered "tentative" in a manner that is thus similar to the situation described by Rothman (1986) of pregnancy in the context of amniocentesis. In both cases, the introduction of increased technological choice alters significantly the experience of both the desire to reproduce desire and its embodiment (see also Martin 1987).

10. For further discussion of the parliamentary debate on human fertilization and embryology, see Franklin 1993, Morgan and Lee 1991, Riviere 1985, Stacey 1992, and Strathern 1992b. For the importance of progress in the life sciences to definitions of English national heritage, see McNeil 1987. See also Squier 1994 for an intriguing history of the image of the "baby in the bottle" in twentieth-century English scientific and literary culture.

11. I have elsewhere analyzed the media representation of "desperate" infertile couples. See Franklin 1990 and Pfeffer 1987:82.

References

Bachofen, J. J. 1861. *Das Mutterecht.* Trans. as *Myth, Religion, and Mother-Right.* New York: Schocken Books, 1967.

Barnes, John Arundel. 1973. "Genetrix:Genitor::Nature:Culture." In *The Character of Kinship*, ed. Jack Goody. Cambridge: Cambridge University Press.

Bouquet, Mary. 1993. *Reclaiming English Kinship: Portuguese Refractions of British Kinship Theory.* Manchester: Manchester University Press.

———. 1995a. "Strangers in Paradise: An Encounter with Fossil Man at the Dutch National Museum of Natural History." *Science as Culture* 5.

———. 1995b. "Displaying Knowledge: The Trees of Haeckel, DuBois, Jesse and Rivers at the *Pithecanthropus* Centennial Exhibition. In *Shifting Contexts*, ed. Marilyn Strathern. London: Routledge.

———. 1996. "Family Trees and Their Affinities." *Journal of the Royal Anthropological Institute* 2, 1:43–67.

Clifford, James. 1988. *The Predicament of Culture: Twentieth-Century Ethnography, Literature and Art.* Cambridge, Mass.: Harvard University Press.

Clifford, James and George E. Marcus, eds. 1986. *Writing Culture: The Poetics and Politics of Ethnography.* Berkeley: University of California Press.

Collier, Jane F. and Sylvia J. Yanagisako, eds. 1987a. *Gender and Kinship: Essays Toward a Unified Analysis.* Stanford, CA: Stanford University Press.
————. 1987b. "Introduction," in *Gender and Kinship: Toward a Unified Analysis,* ed. Jane Collier and Sylvia Yanagisako.
Coward, Rosalind. 1983. *Patriarchal Precedents: Sexuality and Social Relations.* London: Routledge and Kegan Paul.
Delaney, Carol. 1986. "The Meaning of Paternity and the Virgin Birth Debate." *Man* 21, 3:494–513.
Edwards, Jeanette, Sarah Franklin, Eric Hirsch, Frances Price, and Marilyn Strathern. 1993. *Technologies of Procreation: Kinship in the Age of Assisted Conception.* Manchester: Manchester University Press.
Engels, Friedrich. 1884. *On the Origins of the Family, Private Property, and the State.* New York: International Publishers, 1972.
Faludi, Susan. 1991. *Backlash: The Undeclared War Against American Women.* New York: Crown Publishers.
Franklin, Sarah. 1990. "Deconstructing 'Desperateness': The Social Construction of Infertility in Popular Representations of New Reproductive Technology." In *The New Reproductive Technologies,* ed. Maureen McNeil, Ian Varcoe, and Steven Yearley. London: Macmillan, pp. 200–29.
————. 1992. "Making Sense of Missed Conceptions: Anthropological Perspectives on Unexplained Infertility." In *Changing Human Reproduction: Social Science Perspectives,* ed. Margaret Stacey. London: Sage, pp. 75–91.
————. 1993. "Making Representations: Parliamentary Debate of the Human Fertilisation and Embryology Bill." In Jeanette Edwards et al., *Technologies of Procreation: Kinship in the Age of Assisted Conception.* Manchester: Manchester University Press, pp. 96–131.
————. 1995a. "Postmodern Procreation." In *Conceiving the New World Order: The Global Politics of Reproduction,* ed. Faye Ginsburg and Rayna Rapp. Berkeley: University of California Press, pp. 323–75.
————. 1995b. "Science as Culture, Cultures of Science." *Annual Reviews of Anthropology* 24:163–84.
————. 1997. *Embodied Progress: A Cultural Account of Assisted Conception.* London: Routledge.
Frazer, J. G. 1910. *Totemism and Exogamy: A Treatise on Certain Early Forms of Superstition and Society.* London: Dawsons, 1968.
Ginsburg, Faye and Rayna Rapp. 1991. "The Politics of Reproduction." *Annual Review of Anthropology* 20:311–43.
————, eds. 1995. *Conceiving the New World Order: The Global Politics of Reproduction.* Berkeley: University of California Press.
Gupta, Akhil and James Ferguson. 1992. "Beyond 'Culture': Space, Identity, and the Politics of Difference." *Cultural Anthropology* 7, 1:6–23.
Haraway, Donna. 1992. "The Promises of Monsters: A Regenerative Politics for Inappropriate/d Others." In *Cultural Studies,* ed. Lawrence Grossberg, Cary Nelson, and Paula Treichler. New York: Routledge, pp. 295–337.
Hull, M. G. R. 1986. "Infertility: Nature and Extent of the Problem." In CIBA Foundation, *Human Embryo Research: Yes or No?* London: Tavistock, pp. 24–35.
Interim Licensing Authority. 1989. *IVF Research in the UK: A Report on Research Licensed by the Interim Licensing Authority (ILA) for Human in Vitro Fertilisation and Embryology 1985–9.* London: Interim Licensing Authority.
Klein, R., ed. *Infertility: Women Speak Out About Their Experiences of Reproductive Medicine.* London: Pandora Press.

Koch, Lene. 1990. "IVF: An Irrational Choice?" *Reproductive and Genetic Engineering* 3: 225–32.

Leach, Edmund R. 1967. "Virgin Birth." *Proceedings of the Royal Anthropological Institute*: 39–49. Reprinted in Leach, *The Structural Study of Myth*. London: Jonathan Cape, 1969.

McLennan, John Ferguson. 1865. *Primitive Marriage: An Inquiry into the Origin of the Form of Capture in Marriage Ceremonies*. Ed. Peter Riviere. Chicago: University of Chicago Press, 1970.

McNeil, Maureen. 1987. *Under the Banner of Science: Erasmus Darwin and His Age*. Manchester: Manchester University Press.

Lorber, Judith. 1989. "Choice, Gift or Patriarchal Bargain? Women's Consent to In Vitro Fertilisation in Male Infertility." *Hypatia* 4, 3:23–34.

Malinowski, Bronislaw. 1937. "Foreword" to M. F. Ashley Montagu, *Coming into Being Among the Australian Aborigines: A Study of the Procreative Beliefs of the Native Tribes of Australia*. London: George Routledge & Sons, pp. xix–xxxv.

Marcus, George E. 1995. "Ethnography in/of the World System: The Emergence of Multi-Sited Ethnography." *Annual Reviews of Anthropology* 24: 95–117.

Martin, Emily. 1987. *The Woman in the Body: A Cultural Analysis of Reproduction*. Boston: Beacon.

———. 1991. "The Egg and the Sperm." *Signs* 16, 3: 485–501.

Modell, Judith. 1989. "Last Chance Babies: Interpretations of Parenthood in an IVF Program." *Medical Anthropology Quarterly* 3: 124–38.

Morgan, Derek and Robert Lee. 1991. *Human Fertilisation and Embryology Act 1990: Abortion and Embryo Research, the New Law*. London: Blackstone Press.

Morgan, L. H. 1871. *Systems of Consanguinity and Affinity in the Human Family*. Smithsonian Contributions to Knowledge. Washington, DC: Smithsonian Institution.

Pfeffer, Naomi. 1987. "Artificial Insemination, In Vitro Fertilization, and the Stigma of Infertility." In *Reproductive Technologies: Gender, Motherhood, and Medicine*, ed. Michelle Stanworth. Cambridge: Polity Press.

Pfeffer, Naomi and Allison Quick. 1988. *Infertility Services: A Desperate Case*. London: Greater London Association of Community Health Care.

Prentice, Thomson. 1986. "Living in Limbo, Longing for Life." *Sunday Times* (London), 8 April, p. 13.

Rabinow, Paul. 1992. "Artificiality and Enlightenment." In *Incorporations*, ed. Jonathan Crary and Sanford Kwinter. New York: Zone.

Riviere, Peter. 1985. "Unscrambling Parenthood: The *Warnock Report*." *Anthropology Today* 1, 4:2–6.

Rothman, Barbara Katz. 1986. *The Tentative Pregnancy: Prenatal Diagnosis and the Future of Motherhood*. New York: Viking.

Sandelowski, Margarete. 1993. *With Child in Mind: Studies of the Personal Encounter with Infertility*. Philadelphia: University of Philadelphia Press.

Schneider, David. 1968a. *American Kinship: A Cultural Account*. Englewood Cliffs, N.J.: Prentice–Hall.

———. 1968b. "Virgin Birth" (correspondence). *Man* 3:126–29.

———. 1984. *A Critique of the Study of Kinship*. Ann Arbor: University of Michigan Press.

Spiro, M. E. 1968. "Virgin Birth, Parthenogenesis, and Physiological Paternity: An Essay in Cultural Interpretation." *Man* 3: 242–61.

Squier, Susan Merrill. 1994. *Babies in Bottles: Twentieth-Century Visions of Reproductive Technology*. New Brunswick, N.J.: Rutgers University Press.

Stacey, Margaret, ed. 1992. *Changing Human Reproduction: Social Science Perspectives*. London: Sage.

Strathern, Marilyn. 1992a. *After Nature: English Kinship in the Late Twentieth Century*. Cambridge: Cambridge University Press.

————. 1992b. *Reproducing the Future: Anthropology, Kinship and the New Reproductive Technologies*. Manchester: Manchester University Press.

Tsing, Anna L. 1995. "Empowering Nature, or: Some Gleanings in Bee Culture." In *Naturalizing Power: Essays in Feminist Cultural Analysis*. New York: Routledge. 113–44.

Tsing, Anna L. and Sylvia J. Yanagisako. 1983. "Feminism and Kinship Theory." *Current Anthropology* 24: 511–16.

Warnock, Mary. 1985. *A Question of Life: The Warnock Report on Human Fertilization and Pregnancy*. Oxford: Basil Blackwell.

Weiner, Annette. 1976. *Women of Value, Men of Renown: New Perspectives in Trobriand Exchange*. Austin: University of Texas Press.

Williams, Linda. 1988a. "'It's Going to Work for Me': Responses to Failures of IVF" *Birth* 15, 3:153–56.

————. 1988b. *Wanting Children Badly: An Exploratory Study of the Parenthood Motivation of Couples Seeking In Vitro Fertilization*. Doctoral dissertation, University of Toronto.

Yanagisako, Sylvia J. and Jane F. Collier. 1987. "Toward a Unified Analysis of Gender and Kinship." In *Gender and Kinship: Essays Toward a Unified Analysis*, ed. Collier and Yanagisako. Stanford, Calif.: Stanford University Press. 14–52.

Yanagisako, Sylvia J. and Carol Delaney, eds. 1995. *Naturalizing Power: Essays in Feminist Cultural Analysis*. New York: Routledge.

Chapter 5
Incontestable Motivations

Helena Ragoné

> Previously, I thought the genetic link helped create the bond
> between you and the baby, but it has nothing to do with it.
> —Vicky, an AI surrogate

With the introduction of assisted reproductive technologies (ARTs),
seemingly simple yet nonetheless culturally bound assessments of what
constitutes family, motherhood, and fatherhood, such as the one expressed above, can no longer be taken for granted. ARTs have served
to defamiliarize what was once understood to be the "natural" basis of
human procreation and relatedness. In essence, ARTs have served, as
the Comaroffs so eloquently said of ethnography, "to make the familiar strange and the strange familiar, all the better to understand them
both" (1992).

Although "the family" as it has traditionally been understood in Euro-
American culture continues to be shaped by a number of factors such
as race, class, ethnicity, and sexual orientation, Americans are nonetheless regularly subjected to popular depictions of "the family" as a
monolithic, timeless, universal institution. In spite of well-documented
historical particularities and visibly diverse current practices, definitions
of the family continue to follow fairly predictable trajectories, depicting
families as nuclear, heterosexual, middle-class, white, and in a state of
decline.[1]

Gestational (IVF) Surrogacy

Gestational (IVF) surrogacy was made possible by greatly accelerated
advances in reproductive medicine and by increased consumer demand.

Together, these approaches have contributed to and extended a redefinition of reproduction as a field of technological possibility and greater consumer choice. Resulting shifts in the conceptualization of reproduction and parenthood have been attributed to the "enterprising up" or increased commercialization of reproduction. The first of these shifts occurred in response to the separation of intercourse from reproduction through birth control (Snowden et al. 1983). The second shift occurred in response to the fragmentation of the unity of reproduction, wherein it has become possible for pregnancy to occur without necessarily having been "preceded by sexual intercourse" (Snowden et al. 1983: 5), and the third shift occurred in response to further advances in reproductive medicine so that the "organic unity of fetus and mother can no longer be assumed" (Martin 1987: 20). Not until the emergence of reproductive medicine did the fragmentation of motherhood (or fatherhood, for that matter) become a possibility. As a consequence, the "single figure of the mother is dispersed among several potential figures, as the functions of maternal procreation aspects of her physical parenthood become dispersed" (Strathern 1991: 32).

With the advent of gestational surrogacy, however, reproduction is not only separated from sexual intercourse and motherhood but from pregnancy as well. In addition, gestational surrogacy creates three discernible categories of motherhood where there was previously only one: (1) the biological mother, the woman who contributes the ovum (traditionally assumed to be the "real mother"); (2) the gestational mother, the woman who gestates the embryos but who bears no genetic relationship to the child; and (3) the social mother, the woman who raises or nurtures the child.

Two of these categories can be readily accounted for in established American kinship terminology. The biological mother occupies a position similar to that of a woman who places her child for adoption, although in the two cases the intention is clearly different. A surrogate intentionally conceives a child for the purpose of surrendering that child to its biological father and his wife; she thus creates a "wanted child," who is, however, wanted by someone other than herself. The social mother is similar to the adoptive mother in that her relationship to the child exists not in nature, but in law alone (Schneider 1968). However, the intentionality of the participants makes social motherhood, in the case of surrogacy, different from adoption in that the child is fathered by the adoptive mother's husband during their current relationship, not in a prior relationship, as in the case of a stepchild.

The gestational mother's position is less readily analogized to existing relational precedents, for her relationship to the child does not occur strictly in either nature or in law, that is, it partakes of neither "code for conduct" nor "substance" (Schneider 1968), at least as that relationship has tended to be defined. Of fundamental importance to the understanding of gestational (IVF) surrogacy and ARTs is thus the recognition that cultural domains, e.g., reproduction and family, have been "dialectically formed and transformed in relation with other cultural domains" (Yanagisako and Delaney 1995: 11).

One of the most important contemporary contributions made by feminist anthropologists is an exploration of how inequalities have been made to appear as "logical outgrowths" of the facts of life (Yanagisako and Delaney 1995: 11). This is nowhere made more demonstrably clear than in the area of reproduction, the subject of this and other chapters of this volume, which calls into question many previously held beliefs and ideologies concerning family and parenthood, revealing the ways in which it is "inextricably bound up with the production of culture" (Ginsburg and Rapp 1995: 2). Reproduction is concerned with topics no less central than worldview, cosmology, and culture (Delaney 1986: 495); definitions of personhood; and the production of knowledge (Strathern 1991, 1992).

Of Nonbiological and Other Mothers

When I began my research on surrogate motherhood in 1987, gestational (IVF) surrogacy was a relatively uncommon procedure. I remember, for example, one program director expressing scepticism about the use of procedures such as IVF, Zygote Interfallopian Transfer (ZIFT) and Gamete Interfallopian Transfer (GIFT). She described them as a "rip-off that simply prolongs the couple's infertility while charging them outrageous sums of money per attempt." However, during the six-year period that followed, the practice of gestational surrogacy increased in the United States at a rather remarkable rate, from less than 5 percent of all surrogate arrangements to approximately 50 percent as of 1994 (Ragoné 1994). With gestational (IVF) surrogacy, the surrogate does not contribute an ovum, but instead "gestates" a couple's embryo(s); for this reason, gestational surrogates in general tend to begin the process with different concerns and expectations than traditional surrogates.[2]

Overall, women who elect to become gestational surrogates tend to articulate the belief that traditional surrogacy, even though less medically complicated,[3] is not an acceptable option for them because they are uncomfortable with the prospect of contributing their own ovum (or ova) to the creation of a child. They also cannot readily accept the idea that a child who is genetically related to them would be raised by someone else. In other words, they explicitly articulate the opinion that in traditional surrogacy (where the surrogate contributes an ovum) the surrogate is the mother of the child, whereas in gestational surrogacy (where she does not contribute an ovum) she is not.

Interestingly enough, IVF surrogates' beliefs run contrary to current legal opinion as expressed in the findings of both Britain's Warnock Report and the Australian Waller Commission's report that "when a child is born to a woman following the donation of another's egg the women giving birth should, for all purposes, be regarded in law as the mother of that child" (Shalev 1989: 117). It should be noted that the opinion expressed by the Warnock Report and the Waller Commission not only contradicts Euro-American kinship ideology, specifically the continued emphasis on the centrality of biogenetic relatedness, but it also contradicts the views expressed by IVF surrogates, who choose gestational (IVF) surrogacy precisely because it eliminates the issue of genetic relatedness for them. Of additional interest and concern is why the law should be applied differentially to a gestational surrogate when a sperm donor, for example, bears neither legal rights nor legal duties toward the resulting child and is not regarded as the father of the child (Shalev 1989: 117). However, this effort to expand our definition of biological relatedness, which has until recently depended on a genetic component, runs contrary to the Euro-American emphasis on biogenetic relatedness, in which genetic parents are legally and socially considered the "real" parents. As we can see, the fragmentation or dispersal of parenthood, a byproduct of reproductive technologies, has resulted in what Strathern has described as the "claims of one kind of biological mother against other kinds of biological and nonbiological mothers" (1991: 32) and biological and nonbiological fathers.

How then to account for the gestational surrogate's motivations? Should a gestational surrogate's maternal rights be "modeled on the law of paternity, where proof of genetic parentage establishes . . . parentage, or . . . on the nine month experience of pregnancy as establishing the preponderant interest of . . . parentage" (Hull 1990: 152).

It is of fundamental importance to IVF surrogates to circumvent the biogenetic tie to the child, and they do so in spite of the greatly increased degree of physical discomfort and medical risk they face in IVF procedures as compared to risks associated with traditional surrogacy. Following are some examples of the medical procedures commonly encountered by gestational surrogates. Barbara, age thirty, married with three children, Euro-American, a Mormon, and a two-time gestational surrogate (who is now planning a third pregnancy) discussed the considerable discomfort she experienced during the self-administration of hormonal medications:

After a while, you dread having to do it; I had lumps from all those injections. Two times a day and twice a week three injections a day. If you don't do it, the pregnancy would be lost. Whenever I get pregnant with [babies], you are just [as] concerned with the pregnancy as if it's your own, sometimes more.

Linda, age thirty, Mexican-American, married with three children and six months pregnant with a child for a couple from Japan, described her feelings about the physical discomfort in this way:

At first . . . I broke out. [But] I got past the lumps in my thigh and butt. It was uncomfortable, but it's worth it.

Vicky, age thirty-three, Euro-American, married with three children, who had given birth three weeks earlier, explained how she was able to sustain her motivation and commitment throughout the difficult medical procedures:

It was hard, but it needed to be done for the baby's sake. All the shots [were] on a daily basis. I didn't mind it at all, but it had to be at a certain time. It was like a curfew. Sure it was painful, but it does go away.

The sentiments expressed by Barbara, Linda, and Vicky are similar to those expressed by traditional surrogates who have experienced difficult, sometimes life-threatening pregnancies and deliveries, both cast these experiences in terms of meaningful suffering and heroism (Ragoné 1996). The vastly increased physical discomfort and scheduling difficulties are, however, a price that gestational surrogates are willing to pay in order to circumvent what they regard as the problematized biogenetic tie. Barbara expressed a belief shared by many IVF surrogates about their pregnancies when she said:

I separate AI [artificial insemination] and IVF completely, almost to the point I don't agree with AI. I feel like that person is entering into an agreement to produce a child to give to someone else. I feel it is *her baby* [emphasis mine] she is giving away.

In a similar fashion, Lee, age thirty-one, married with two children, Euro-American, who was waiting for an embryo transfer, discussed the differences between AI and IVF:

Yes, it's [the fetus] inside my body, but as far as I am concerned, I don't have any biological tie. The other way [AI], I would feel that there is some part of me out there.

This view of surrogacy differs in several important ways from the one expressed by traditional surrogates, who advance the idea that the term "parent" should be applied only to individuals who actually choose to become engaged in the process of raising a child (or children), regardless of biogenetic relatedness. They achieve this perspective in part by separating motherhood into two components: biological motherhood and social motherhood. Only social motherhood is viewed by traditional surrogates as "real" motherhood; in other words, nurturance is held to be of greater importance than biological relatedness. In this respect, it is the gestational (IVF) surrogate, not the traditional (AI) surrogate, who tends to subscribe to a decidedly more traditional rendering of relatedness.

Of some concern in the practice of gestational surrogacy is the health of the surrogates. For example, in an attempt to maximize success rates, physicians routinely implant more than one embryo at a time (usually between four and six). The decision to implant several embryos is determined by a number of considerations—for instance, the number of eggs retrieved and fertilized and the quality of the resulting embryos (eggs and embryos from older women are often of an inferior quality). The by now routine practice of implanting multiple embryos produces multiple birth rates among surrogates that are higher than those reported for the general IVF population, since surrogates are usually young, healthy women who are not infertile and have not previously taken infertility drugs. The rates of multiple births among IVF surrogates are so high that a single child is now referred to as a "singleton" in one of the surrogate programs where I conducted research. Further complicating this practice is the fact that many surrogates are opposed to abortion and to the practice of selective reduction (which they view as a form of abortion). In my earlier research on traditional surrogacy, I discovered that, although many traditional surrogates are themselves opposed to abortion, they are often willing to defer to the couple's wishes, since they do not consider the child or children their own and believe that the couple should make such decisions (Ragoné 1994). However, a problem may arise if the surrogate and the couple are both opposed to abortion and to selective reduction. I learned, for example, of a case in which both the gestational surrogate and the couple were opposed to abortion and the surrogate was pregnant with triplets. While the prospect may seem like an exciting and joyful one to couples who have been infertile, the realities of caring for more than one infant at a time can be daunting (Price 1992).

Race and Relatedness

Since IVF is a complicated medical procedure with rates of success that are markedly lower than those for traditional surrogacy (95 percent with AI and 28 percent with IVF as of 1994 at the largest U.S. surrogate-mother program), not all gestational surrogates are able to conceive in this way or able to sustain such a pregnancy. However, once a gestational surrogate has begun to develop a relationship with her couple and has experienced several unsuccessful embryo transfers, she may begin to reformulate or revise her initial beliefs concerning relatedness and family.[4] An unsuccessful gestational surrogate may, for example, opt to become what is referred to in surrogate-mother programs as a "cross-over," someone who chose initially to participate in gestational surrogacy but then decided to become a traditional surrogate.[5] In these cases, the importance of the personal relationship the surrogate develops with her couple cannot be overstated. This shift in perception is of particular importance because women who choose to become gestational surrogates, as previously mentioned, tend not to consider traditional surrogacy a viable option because they are uncomfortable with the idea of having a biogenetic tie to the child. But once a gestational surrogate has developed a bond with her couple and has been unsuccessful with IVF procedures, she may decide to "cross over," and she, like the traditional surrogate, will also tend to play down the significance of the biogenetic tie to the child, embracing instead the idea that parenting is socially rather than biologically constructed. It has become increasingly clear that "biological elements have primarily symbolic significance . . . [whose] meaning is not biology at all" (Schneider 1972: 45).

The gestational surrogate's articulated ideas concerning relatedness (or, more accurately, the presumed lack thereof) also produces a shift in emphasis away from potentially problematic aspects of gestational surrogacy, such as ethnicity and race. Unlike traditional surrogate arrangements, in which both couples and surrogates are largely Euro-American, it is not unusual for gestational surrogates and commissioning couples to come from diverse racial and ethnic backgrounds.[6] In the spring of 1996, for example, I interviewed a Mexican-American gestational surrogate who was carrying a child for a Japanese couple, an African-American gestational surrogate who had attempted several embryo transfers unsuccessfully for both a Japanese couple and a Euro-American couple, and a Euro-American gestational surrogate who had delivered twins for a Japanese couple. During the course of those interviews, I discovered that the issue of race, like that of class among traditional surrogates, is deemphasized.[7] Since surrogacy challenges so many of our shared cultural ideas about the "naturalness" of reproduction, it may be that other differences, such as those of class and race, are consequently of diminished significance to participants. Both surrogates and couples tend to deemphasize those aspects of surrogacy that represent a departure from tradition, a strategy that for some participants carries over to the area of class and race as well. On one occasion, for example, when I questioned Carol, an African-American IVF surrogate (who at twenty-nine was single, with one child, and had yet to sustain an IVF pregnancy) about the issue of racial difference (between herself and her couple), she stated:

I had friends who had a problem because [they thought] I should help blacks. And I told them, "Don't look at the color issue. If a white person offered to help you, you wouldn't turn them down."

Efforts such as these to deemphasize racial and class differences may be interpreted as an attempt by participants (surrogates, commissioning couples, and surrogate-mother programs) to portray surrogacy in a positive light by playing down those aspects of surrogate motherhood that are culturally problematic. Class and race differences also tend to be set aside when infertility and childlessness are at issue. As I discovered in my earlier research (Ragoné 1994), when questioned about class inequities between themselves and their couples, traditional surrogates also tend to describe their own fertility indirectly as a leveling device, because they reason that couples' financial success and privilege cannot provide them with happiness; only children can give them that. For example, when pressed to elaborate on the issue of class, one surrogate said, "I am fertile and she [the adoptive mother] isn't." When I questioned gestational surrogates whose racial backgrounds were different from those of their couples about the issue of racial difference, they responded much as traditional surrogates respond to questions about class difference. However, the following statement by Carol, the African-American gestational surrogate mentioned earlier, reveals that the issue of racial difference is further nuanced as a positive factor, one that facilitates the surrogate/child separation process:

My mom is happy the couple is not black, because she was worried I would want to keep it [the baby]. The first couple I was going to go with was black. I don't want to raise another kid.

When I questioned Linda (a thirty-year-old Mexican-American, married with three children and six months pregnant with a child for a couple from Japan) about this issue, her reasoning illustrated how beliefs concerning racial differences can be used by surrogates (and couples) to resolve any conflicting feelings about the child being related to them because it is being or was carried in their body:

No, I haven't [thought of the child as mine], because she's not mine, she never has been. For one thing, she is totally Japanese. It's a little hard for me. In a way, she will always be my Japanese girl; but she is theirs.

One can see how Linda recapitulates one of the initial motivations cited by gestational surrogates, the desire to bear a child for an infertile couple, while highlighting the lack of biological, physical and racial resemblance, or the lack of a biogenetic tie. Linda added:

> If I was to have a child, it would only be from my husband and me. With AI [traditional surrogacy], the baby would be a part of me. I don't know if I could let a part of me. . . . AI was never for me; I never considered it.

Carol and Linda are aware, of course, as are all gestational surrogates, that they do not share a genetic tie with the children they are producing or have produced as gestational surrogates, but remarks such as Carol's about her previous match with a Euro-American and Japanese couple and her concerns about the prospect of having to raise an African-American couple's child reveal how racial resemblance raises certain questions for her about relatedness even when there is no genetic tie.[8] Here, popular conceptions about the connection between race and genetics deserve further exploration. Although she knows that the child is not genetically hers, certain boundaries become blurred for her when an African-American couple is involved, whereas with a Euro-American couple the distinction between genetic/nongenetic or self/other is, for her, made more clear. Here we can see that the issue of likeness and difference is being played out in unique configurations, similar to those expressed by social fathers in a longitudinal study on Donor Insemination (DI), in which they (social fathers) theorized that "the role of genitor is unimportant compared with that of the nurturing father" (Snowden et al. Snowden 1983: 119). By stressing the social aspect of parenthood, fathers minimize the genetic "facts" (Snowden et al. 1983: 141), a strategy that is remarkably similar to that adopted by AI (traditional) surrogates and adoptive mothers. Once DI children are old enough to exhibit gestures, mannerisms, and characteristics that are similar to their fathers', however, it is not unheard of for a father to speculate that perhaps the child is after all his own biological child; to say, for example, "I keep thinking perhaps he is mine" (Snowden et al. 1983: 141). In traditional surrogate arrangements as well, a statement such as the following from one of the fathers illustrates that perceived likeness plays a very strong part here just as it does in other families: "Seeing Jane [the surrogate mother] in [my son], it's literally a part of herself she gave. . . ." Likeness or resemblance as a symbolic feature signifies more than just biological resemblance. It also signifies a type of identity with the self and separation between all that is a part of oneself and all that is not, although it is nonetheless problematic in families that utilize ARTs.

During a gestational surrogate's initial in-person screening at a surrogate program, the resident program psychologist asks her whether a commissioning couple's racial background is of concern to her. The psychologist also asks the same question of the commissioning couple.[9] My preliminary findings suggest that the majority of gestational surrogates do not object to and may actually find it desirable to be matched with a couple from a different racial background. One of the reasons for this preference, as mentioned earlier, is that racial/ethnic difference provides "more distance" between them, a degree of separation the gestational surrogate is able to place between herself and the child or children she is producing for her couple through her manipulation of existing cultural ideations about racial identity and difference. In this way, we can see that a decision that initially appears to be uninflected by racial difference is, upon closer examination, a means by which surrogates and couples establish or reinforce distance and emotional boundaries between themselves. Many earlier theories about the practice of gestational surrogacy focused somewhat exclusively on its potential for exploitation, failing to take into consideration the fact that both fertility and infertility are best understood as embedded in a series of social, historical, and personal processes, allowing for the complexity of issues such as agency and choice.

The initial motivation of couples who pursue IVF surrogacy is to provide themselves with a child who is genetically related to both of them, not just to the husband, as is the case with AI.[10] In June 1993, in a precedent-setting decision, the California Supreme Court upheld a gestational surrogacy contract (*Anna Johnson v. Mark and Crispina Calvert*, case no. SO 23721), concluding that whereas both the gestational and biological mother could under California law claim maternal rights to the child, a legal decision was not rendered on the basis of genetic relatedness or on the basis of who carried the child to term but rather on the "intent" of the parties involved. The court ruled that gestational surrogacy contracts are legally enforceable and consistent with prevailing public policy. In his decision, Justice Edward Penelli wrote, "It is not the role of the judiciary to inhibit the use of reproductive technology when the Legislature has not seen fit to do so. Any such effort would raise serious questions in light of the fundamental nature of the rights of procreation and privacy." In this case, the gestational surrogate and the commissioning couple both filed custody suits. Under California law, both of the women could, however, claim maternal rights—Johnson by virtue of having gestated and given birth to the child, and the Calverts, who donated the sperm and ovum, as the child's genetic mother. In rendering its decision, however, the court in a sense circumvented the issue of relatedness and focused instead on the intent of the parties as the decisive factor in any determination about parenthood.[11]

Having stated that there are important differences between women who choose traditional surrogacy and those who choose gestational surrogacy, and the importance of not conflating IVF and AI surrogate motivations, it must be acknowledged that there are certain commonalities among surrogates, namely, that both traditional (AI) and gestational (IVF) surrogacy allow women to transcend the limitations of their family roles and to achieve a certain degree of independence and personal fulfillment without appearing to challenge their family and community relationships. As the following statement, which relies on a gender-specific occupational metaphor, reveals, surrogates as a group are not unaware of the potentially radical nature of their behavior:

Not everyone can do it. It's like the steelworkers who walk on beams ten floors up. Not everyone can do it. Not everyone can be a surrogate.

Within a six-year period, advances in conceptive technology, and IVF in particular, have made surrogacy an option for women who found surrogacy in its traditional form (AI) socially unacceptable or physically impossible.[12] Women who choose to become IVF surrogates thus are not required to contribute ova. The shifting nature of the perceived centrality of the blood tie is, however, revealed in the experiences of the IVF surrogate who begins that trek committed to a more traditional rendering of relatedness, and who then experiences a shift in perception so that she begins to view parenthood as comprised of two components (as does the AI surrogate), with social parenthood assuming the more important position. Surrogate motherhood reveals that the perceived importance and symbolic centrality of the blood tie in Euro-American culture remains contested, and is sometimes, as in the case of IVF surrogacy, privileged, while in AI surrogacy it is deemphasized by the surrogate and privileged for the father.

In conclusion, the question remains: what, if any, impact will IVF and AI surrogacy have on existing Euro-American kinship ideology? Although there may never be a definitive answer to this question, perhaps the most prudent conjecture is that AI and IVF surrogacy will continue to be viewed by the participants as consistent with values that uphold the importance of the family.

I would like to express my appreciation to Dr. Sydel Silverman and to Wenner Gren: The Foundation for Anthropological Research for their support of my research on gestational (IVF) surrogacy and to the University of Massachusetts for a Faculty Development Grant. I owe a very special thank you, once again, to the individuals who have made this and earlier research possible—the surrogate mothers and commissioning couples who have so generously shared their experiences with me. I would also like to express my appreciation to the surrogate-mother programs—their directors, psychologists, and staffs—for their generous support of my research.

Notes

1. See Rapp (1978: 279) and Gordon (1988: 3) for a historical analysis of the idea of the demise of the American family.

2. It should, however, be noted that it is not unusual for an applicant to a surrogate program to declare herself willing to serve as either a traditional surrogate or an IVF surrogate, and the standard protocol in these circumstances is to "encourage" her to select the arrangement in which there is currently a shortage of available women.

3. Gestational surrogates often complain about the discomfort they experience due to having to self-inject two to three times per day for as long as three to four months of the pregnancy. They report that progesterone is especially painful, since it is oil-based and has a tendency to pool and lump under the skin. Even though the largest of the surrogate programs claims to inform gestational surrogates about the need to self-administer shots, several gestational surrogates reported that they had not anticipated either the frequency or the discomfort of the injections.

4. The exact number of gestational surrogates who cross over is not available, since the largest surrogate-mother program (where I was conducting my initial research) does not maintain records on this phenomenon. The resident psychologist at the program I studied reported to me that she has found it difficult, if not impossible, to predict which of the gestational surrogates will cross over, and that she continues to be surprised by those who do. I intend to make this phenomenon the subject of further study.

5. With the advent of assisted reproductive technologies, in particular gestational surrogacy, will we, as a culture, be forced to make a distinction between biological and genetic relatedness? The Warnock and Glover reports (British and European commissioned studies; Warnock 1984 and Glover 1990) have concluded that the gestational surrogate should be considered the mother of the child, a position that runs contrary to the Euro-American emphasis on biogenetic relatedness wherein genetic parents are considered the "real" parents. Will Euro-American cultural definitions of biogenetic relatedness be modified by the phenomenon of gestational surrogacy? Specifically, will we as a society come to emphasize biological relatedness over biogenetic relatedness so as to account for the fact that the gestational surrogate provides the physiological/biological environment for the embryo/fetus/child? Or will we instead circumvent this issue by continuing to emphasize the genetic component of parenthood, characterizing the gestational surrogate as the vessel through which another couple's child is born, as is currently the case amongst gestational surrogates and couples who employ their services. As AI and IVF surrogates' and commissioning couples' responses indicate, nearly everyone involved in these processes appears to experience some ambivalence about the relationships created by these technologies.

6. Approximately 30 percent of all IVF surrogacy arrangements at the largest program now involve surrogates and couples matched from different racial and ethnic backgrounds.

7. As I have written elsewhere, differences in class backgrounds are frequently deemphasized by all parties, a response that may be the result of several factors (see Ragoné 1994), not the least of which is the fact that "American discourse lacks a developed vocabulary

of class . . . [and that] class as a social phenomenon is almost never talked *about*" (Ortner 1995: 259).

8. During the course of the interview, I specifically asked her what her feelings and ideas were about having a child for a couple with another racial background. (I also asked this question of all the surrogates who were matched with couples with different racial backgrounds.)

9. I have observed numerous consultations between program staff and prospective commissioning couples and surrogates at the largest program, and the resident psychologist routinely asks gestational surrogates and couples if the race/ethnicity of their future surrogate/couple matters to them. While the program does not compile statistics on this issue, the majority of individuals (both surrogates and couples) appear not to be concerned about race/ethnicity. However, it is important to note that both surrogates and commissioning couples routinely reject the prospect of being matched with an individual from a different racial/ethnic background than themselves when pursuing gestational surrogacy.

10. A newly emerging pattern in the world of surrogacy is that in cases where the wife either has no ova or no viable ova, a couple may elect to pursue egg donation and then enlist the services of a gestational surrogate. The obvious question is why one would not enlist the services of an AI surrogate (who contributes an ovum), with a 95 percent rate of success, since the child produced through egg donation/gestational surrogacy has no more of a genetic tie to the social mother than the child produced through AI surrogacy. I am currently in the process of conducting research into egg donation and gestational surrogacy. The surrogate-mother program psychologist has told me that since the program has over two hundred egg donors on file, a couple has much greater selection than with AI surrogacy. In addition, another situation has arisen in which Asian-American or Asian couples are requesting Asian surrogates, when few, if any, Asian-American women are willing to serve as surrogates, although some are willing to donate ova. When programs report that couples who pursue egg donation/gestational surrogacy do not consider race, they are not allowing for the fact that the gestational surrogate bears no genetic tie to the child, which is not the case with AI surrogacy. Whether or not this is one of the factors involved in these couples' decisions remains to be explored.

11. Surrogate-mother programs screen all surrogates for suitability, and they also supervise and usher participants through the entire process of insemination, pregnancy, and delivery. In the Calvert case, however, the arrangement was a private one, so that the surrogate was not "screened" at all (e.g., for the stability of her marriage, for an unresolved need to have a child, and so on), and the supervision provided by the surrogate-mother program was lacking. In the Calvert arrangement, the gestational surrogate was African-American, the genetic mother Philippino, and the father Euro-American, and although I am arguing here that a gestational surrogate who is matched with a couple from a different racial background may experience this as a means to detach from that child, the Calvert case illustrates that in the presence of unresolved needs to have a child, the manipulation of notions of racial identity is insufficient to prevent her from wanting to keep the child. In addition, the decision of the New Jersey Supreme Court in the infamous "Baby M" case, wherein the surrogate was granted legal visitation rights, has been criticized by feminists for its reinforcement of essentialist ideas about the primacy of biological motherhood (see, for example, Dolgin 1990: 103).

12. This includes cases in which a surrogate has had a tubal ligation. This group of women is now considered a significant pool of available surrogates by surrogate programs, so much so that programs routinely include the phrase "tubal ligation OK" in their advertisements for surrogate mothers.

References

Comaroff, John and Jean Comaroff. 1992. *Ethnography and the Historical Imagination*. Boulder, Colo.: Westview Press.

Delaney, Carol. 1986. "The Meaning of Paternity and the Virgin Birth Debate." *Man* 24, 3: 497–513.

Dolgin, Janet. 1990. "Status and Contract in Feminist Legal Theory of the Family: A Reply to Bartlett." *Women's Rights Law Reporter* 12, 3: 440–53.

Ginsburg, Faye and Rayna Rapp, eds. 1995. *Conceiving the New World Order: The Global Politics of Reproduction*. Berkeley: University of California Press.

Glover, Jonathan. 1990. *Ethics of New Reproductive Technologies: The Glover Report to the European Commission*. DeKalb: Northern Illinois University Press.

Gordon, Linda. 1988. *Heroes of Their Own Lives: The Politics and History of Family Violence*. New York: Viking.

Hull, Richard. 1990. "Gestational Surrogacy and Surrogate Motherhood." In *Ethical Issues in the New Reproductive Technologies*, ed. Richard Hull. Belmont, Calif.: Wadsworth, pp. 150–55.

Martin, Emily. 1987. *The Woman in the Body: A Cultural Analysis of Reproduction*. Boston: Beacon Press.

Ortner, Sherry. 1995. "Ethnography Among the Newark: The Class of '58 of Weequahic High School." In *Naturalizing Power: Essays in Feminist Cultural Analysis*, ed. Sylvia J. Yanagisako and Carol Delaney. New York and London: Routledge, pp. 257–73.

Price, Frances. 1992. "Beyond Expectation: Clinical Practices and Clinical Concerns." In *Technologies of Procreation: Kinship in the Age of Assisted Conception*, ed. Jeanette Edwards et al. Manchester: Manchester University Press, pp. 20–41.

Ragoné, Helena. 1994. *Surrogate Motherhood: Conception in the Heart*. Boulder, Colo. and Oxford: Westview Press.

———. 1996. "Chasing the Blood Tie: Surrogate Mothers, Adoptive Mothers and Fathers." *American Ethnologist* 23, 2: 352–65.

Rapp, Rayna. 1978. "Family and Class in Contemporary America: Notes Toward an Understanding of Ideology." *Science and Society* 42, 3: 278–300.

Schneider, David Murray. 1968. *American Kinship: A Cultural Account*. Englewood Cliffs, N.J.: Prentice-Hall.

———. 1972. "What Is Kinship All About?" In *Kinship Studies in the Morgan Centennial Year*, ed. Priscilla Reining. Washington, D.C.: Anthropological Society of Washington, pp. 32–63.

Shalev, Carmel. 1989. *Birth Power: The Case for Surrogacy*. New Haven, Conn.: Yale University Press.

Snowden, Robert, G. D. Mitchell, and E. M. Snowden. 1983. *Artificial Reproduction: A Social Investigation*. London: Allen and Unwin.

Strathern, Marilyn. 1991. "The Pursuit of Certainty: Investigating Kinship in the Late Twentieth Century." Paper presented at the American Anthropological Association Meetings, Chicago.

———. 1992. *Reproducing the Future: Essays on Anthropology, Kinship, and the New Reproductive Technologies*. New York: Routledge.

Warnock, Mary. 1984. *The Warnock Report: Report of the Committee of Inquiry into Human Fertilisation and Embryology*. London: Her Majesty's Stationery Office.

Yanagisako, Sylvia J. and Carol Delaney, eds. 1995. *Naturalizing Power: Essays in Feminist Cultural Analysis*. New York: Routledge.

Chapter 6
Irishness, Eurocitizens, and Reproductive Rights

Laury Oaks

Thousands of people assembled in Dublin in the pre-spring of 1992 to demand the right to travel of a fourteen-year-old Irish rape survivor who had been forbidden by a court order to have an abortion in England. In attending this mass gathering, people "voted" with their bodies, voices, and placards in an unprecedented public display of support for a woman's right to travel in order to obtain an abortion. Though the pro- and anti-choice struggle is not new to Ireland, the timing of the events associated with the sexual assault case complicated issues of Irish law and Ireland's relationship to Europe, and prompted a rethinking both of the legal status of Irish women's reproductive rights and of definitions of "Irishness." Conflict over the symbolic and legal status of abortion rights for Irish women permeated public discourse, and abortion was figured as an issue central to Ireland's national and political identity.

In this chapter, I explore how abortion politics, which dominated the question of Ireland's relationship to the "New Europe," underscores the importance of reproductive rights to national and cultural identities. The complex and passionate protests over Ireland's membership in the European Union reveal multiple ways in which reproduction is reproduced as a symbolic network conveying core meanings of citizenship, gender, nationalism, ethnicity, and the renegotiation of cultural identities. My analysis centers on pro-choice and pro-life "Vote No" campaigns against the Irish referendum on the Maastricht Treaty for European Union membership, includes an ethnographic account of a pro-life demonstration staged by "Youth Defence" and a pro-choice counter-demonstration.[1] While pro-choice campaigners framed their argument in terms of women's citizenship status in a New Europe, pro-life supporters concentrated on the protection of the "unborn Irish" under

European law. The discourses promoted by either side of the debate reveal that reproduction invokes sensitivities about Irish national identity that are rooted in Ireland's colonial history and postcolonial present.

The rhetoric and action of one pro-life organization, Youth Defence, demonstrates tensions about safeguarding "Irish tradition" against the threat of "European values," and I provide an ethnographic account of a Youth Defence "Vote No to Maastricht" march and rally and a prochoice counterdemonstration held in the streets of Dublin in June of 1992 as an example of how these tensions were publicly expressed. I also present the alternative views of pro-choice activists, who regard women's rights under European law as examples of what Irish law should strive for. As I discuss below, their position is asserted against "cultural traditions" that stand opposed to women's social equality.

In part, Irish abortion rights became central to Ireland's referendum on membership within the European Union due to the coincident timing of increased public attention given abortion rights and the inclusion of a special provision in the Maastricht Treaty that sought to retain Ireland's ban on abortion within the New Europe. The fusion of two discourses that are usually thought of as distinct—one on reproductive rights and the other on Ireland's status within Europe—is not, however, the result of timing alone. The Maastricht Treaty debates made explicit the symbolic power that reproduction obtains in the Irish context, and revealed how facets of reproduction can be mobilized to narrate Ireland's colonial past, postcolonial present, and uncertain future.

Anthropologists Sylvia Yanagisako and Carol Delaney (1995) argue that "origin stories" describe a seemingly natural order of social relations and provide people with an understanding of their positions within that order. In Ireland, reproduction is a medium through which competing national origin stories that focus on Irish national identity and cultural self-determination, indeed visions of "Irishness" itself, are imagined and expressed. An emphasis on women's right to control their bodies invokes narratives of independence struggles that resulted in Irish citizens' self-governance, whereas attention to the "rights of the unborn" perpetuates a literary-mythical image of a natural, innocent Erin or motherland threatened by hostile outsiders and in need of protection (Innes 1993). Although conflict over reproductive rights provides but one social issue that illustrates how definitions of Ireland and Irishness are constructed, during debates over the Maastricht Treaty the abortion issue was a privileged one.

Sites of Contest: Definitional Divisions and Creating Identities

The island of Ireland was legally divided in 1921, ending centuries of British colonial rule and leading to the establishment of two distinct political entities now recognized as the Republic of Ireland and the United Kingdom's province of Northern Ireland. The so-called "Troubles" and violence surrounding the "national question" continue to involve those living in the militarized "Protestant" North and, to a lesser extent, those in the free, "Catholic" South.[2] The continued dispute over possible reunification with the six British-ruled counties of Northern Ireland calls into question the identity of the Irish nation (regarding culture, race, language, and religion) and of the state (regarding law and citizenship; Alcock 1992: 152). The uncertain and contradictory relationship between the Republic of Ireland and the European Union was emphasized during the Maastricht Treaty campaigns, which focused on Ireland's economic status and, moreover, its "moral" position within Europe.

During Ireland's revolutionary period (beginning in the 1880s, and followed by the creation of the Irish Free State [1922], called Eire or Ireland in 1937), competing versions of what Ireland was and what it ought to become were debated in the political sphere, and inconsistency in defining Ireland geographically and culturally continues today. The current constitution, drafted in 1937, states in Articles 2 and 3 that Irish national territory consists of the whole island, yet law administered under this constitution applies only to the Republic. In addition, Gaelic is the primary official language of Ireland, yet it is spoken by few people living outside of small *Gaeltacht* (Irish-speaking) areas. Transformation to a "modern, industrial" Ireland began in the 1950s and was encouraged with economic support from the European Community when Ireland joined as a member in 1972. Subsequent economic advances in the Republic created a situation in which emigration, historically involving large numbers due to high unemployment levels (especially among young adults), has ceased to be an absolute necessity and has become less attractive. The population of Ireland is young, with over 50 percent of the population under age 26 (O'Brien 1993), and while emigration remains an alternative for these young people, many of them are demanding changes within Ireland rather than choosing to leave it. In large part, tensions surrounding the definition of Ireland's identity are related to the question of modernization: can a "traditional, Catholic" identity resist the pull from the more progressive Europe to become modern, less Catholic, and tolerant of diversity?

European involvement in Ireland's social or so-called moral issues has become of increasing concern. Divisive social-political issues, such as high emigration and unemployment rates, abortion, divorce, and the 1986 Single European Act, pointed to areas of Irish legislation that could become subject to European law. In fact, the European Parliament broached the topic of unwanted pregnancies in 1981, urging the European Council to move "to ensure that every woman who finds herself in difficulty can obtain the necessary assistance in her own country" (Northern Ireland Abortion Law Reform Association 1989: 2). Several Irish cases were appealed to the European Court of Human Rights and Court of Justice in the 1980s, including those on the right to information on abortion and abortion counseling (*Society for the Protection of Unborn Children v. The Dublin Well Woman Centre, Open Line Counselling and the Union of Students of Ireland*) and the decriminalization of homosexuality.

Intervention by the European courts in such situations illustrates that Ireland is not isolated economically, politically, or socially from the rest of Europe. For some, Ireland's participation in a united Europe represents a positive move toward social equality within Ireland, for example in terms of women's rights. For others, this move threatens Ireland's "Catholic, traditional" status, and thus increased participation with Europe has been resisted. During debates over the Maastricht Treaty, the passage of which would further consolidate Ireland's relationship with Europe, abortion rights became a powerful symbol of cultural conflict, broadly framed, between "progress" and "tradition." This particular struggle points to the capacity for reproductive issues to emerge as important signifiers of cultural and national identity, and in 1992 several events related to abortion rights highlighted contradictory strands of reproductive, cultural, and identity politics in Ireland.

While mass media and public attention were preoccupied with actions to broaden the legal status and availability of contraceptive devices and contraceptive advertisements in the 1970s (a 1935 constitutional ban on the importation of contraceptives was lifted by the Irish Supreme Court in 1973), public concern in the 1980s and 1990s has focused on abortion and divorce (a referendum to legalize divorce in limited circumstances was defeated in 1986 but passed in 1995; see Dillon 1993). There has been much controversy over the problem of pregnant women's access to medical treatment in relation to abortion, in part due to the Catholic Church hierarchy's approval of abortion only in instances of ectopic pregnancy and cancer of the womb (O'Reilly 1992; Treacy 1992). An estimated 4,000 to 7,000 Irish women travel to England each year to terminate unwanted pregnancies (Francombe 1992; Frankel 1992; Northern Ireland Abortion Law Reform Association 1989: iv), and this number has been steadily increasing (*Irish Times* 1992b). These women must follow what is referred to by both pro-choice and pro-life supporters as the "abortion trail," calling attention to the way both Irelands "export" the contentious problems of unwanted pregnancy and access to legal abortion.

Anxiety about Ireland's identity as part of "modern, unified Europe" served as a backdrop to continued concern over Irish legislation on what were often framed as moral issues. Pro-life activists perceived the New Europe as a danger, fearing, as they did before the 1983 ban on abortion under the Eighth (so-called Pro-Life) Amendment to the Irish Constitution, that blocking the right to legal abortion in Ireland was the "last line of defense against the encroaching moral decadence of Europe" (Hesketh 1990: 6). In 1991, these activists approached a pro-life, conservative Senator, Des Hanafin, who successfully lobbied the Irish Government to include a protocol (number 17) in the Maastricht Treaty that would prohibit European Union interference with the Irish Pro-Life Amendment (Article 40.3.3 of the constitution). The Irish public was unaware of this process, and few within the government voiced opposition, resulting in a Pro-Life Amendment that its supporters assumed to be "copper-fastened," or sealed.

This public silence was broken in early 1992 as the result of the so-called "X Case," in which a young woman was restrained by law from obtaining an abortion in Britain (see Murphy-Lawless 1993; Smyth 1992). A fourteen-year-old Catholic middle-class young woman from a suburb of Dublin alleged that she was sexually assaulted by her classmate's father. The rape survivor's father asked the Irish police whether DNA tests of fetal tissue could be submitted in a court case against the accused man. As a result of this inquiry, the Irish attorney general issued a court injunction to the young woman and her family while they were in England seeking an abortion that forbade termination of the pregnancy. Fearing criminal charges, the surgical procedure was canceled and the family returned to Ireland. The case was taken to the Irish High Court, where, based on the Eighth Amendment ban on abortion, it was ruled that the fourteen-year-old could not leave the country for nine months. However, in subsequent Court decisions, it was decided that she could travel in order to obtain an abortion on the grounds that she was suicidal, indicating a "real and substantial risk to the life, as distinct from the health, of the mother." [3]

Despite enthusiastic public displays of support for the young woman's right to travel and polls indicating that a majority agreed with liberalizing the Irish ban on abortion (Johnson 1992; O'Mara 1992: 5A), exactly how public opinion would guide both the considerations on European unity and the proposed November 1992 national referendum on abortion remained complicated.[4] The unpredictable future of Irish abortion law paralleled uncertainty on the part of many people as to whether or not Ireland should join the rest of Europe in allowing legal abortion, and the X Case emerged in the critical months before the Maastricht Treaty referendum. Following the X Case rulings, pro-life supporters protested the partial lifting of the abortion ban, while pro-choice activists rejected the condition that only women whose lives were "threatened" had the right to information on abortion and the right to travel for the procedure. Further, due to the special provision meant to exempt Ireland from European jurisdiction over abortion law (Protocol 17), it appeared that Irish women would be denied a significant aspect of Eurocitizenship if the Maastricht Treaty passed: the right to freely travel between member states.

Hence both pro-choice and pro-life organizations campaigned for a "no" vote to the Maastricht Treaty. This was neither comfortable nor an alliance. Procuring "no" votes from citizens was only one aim; the *reasons* people gave for voting against European unity demonstrated a range of understandings of Irishness and were equally important in shaping the meanings of Irish rights. The broad implications that the Treaty had for Ireland meant that differing arguments were aligned with the "Vote No" message, and the charge against the Treaty was not a unified one. In short, pro-choice supporters concentrated on Irish women's rights within the "New Europe," while pro-life supporters expressed greater concern for the rights of the unborn.

It is understandable that sexual politics, inherently dealing with women's position and social and reproductive roles, emerged explicitly at a time when a new level of consolidation and reorganization within the European Community is being negotiated. Relying on varied versions of Ireland's past, activists brought social visions into public discourse with an urgent sense that current action would gravely influence the future direction of Irish society. Pro-choice and pro-life imaginations parted on the way this future was to be construed. On the pro-choice side, it was predicted that the status of Irish women's rights would improve due to progressive European influences and changes in Irish reproductive and family law that are occurring at a time of increasing cultural openness and tolerance. On the pro-life side, a contrasting theme of unique "traditional" Irishness was foregrounded alongside an emphasis on the protection of Irish unborn citizens in the constitution, even to the extent that "the recognition of the humanity of the unborn child could be Ireland's most distinctive contribution to the soul of Europe" (Coughlan 1992b: 12). The abortion debate thus acquired multi-valent meanings and shaped the interwoven definitions of reproduction, nation, culture, race/ethnicity, and Irishness. In the following sections, I examine these facets of abortion through arguments put forth by the pro-choice, pro-life, and pro-European Union movements.

Envisioning Eurocitizens

The referendum on the Maastricht Treaty was a locus of public contestation over numerous social issues, including women's citizenship rights and reproductive responsibilities, employment opportunities, monetary support from Europe, neutrality, the role of Catholic ideology in Irish politics, and recognition and respect for diverse cultural histories. The subject of abortion rights, a politically and symbolically charged issue, was most directly entangled in discourses on Irish women's status/rights, Eurocitizenship, and Irish national identity. Pro- and anti–Maastricht Treaty campaigns illustrated the crucial link between reproduction and Irish understandings of both national and gendered identities.

Ongoing, competing political and social narratives emerged with greater visibility during the Maastricht debates. For example, the confluence of reproductive rights and national identity discourses brought to the fore the questions of Irish women's status in the New Europe and women's responsibility to the Irish nation. During the months before the June 18 referendum, Dublin was deluged with contradictory information about what the Treaty would mean for the future of abortion rights for Irish women. The Irish government and European unity supporters attempted to disengage the Treaty from abortion politics, while others focused on this as the Treaty's most significant component.

Women were asked by their government to vote for Maastricht despite the unclear consequences this would have for women's right to appeal to European courts on questions of reproductive rights. Echoing the calls of the leaders of the predominantly Catholic Irish independence movement in the late nineteenth and early twentieth centuries, a pro-European Union narrative developed in 1992 in which women's issues were to be subordinated to the interests of the nation. This scenario, in which so-called "nationalist politics" overshadows the political agendas asserted by women's rights organizations, has been documented in many countries at the moment when colonialism is resisted and overthrown and when new nations or national identities are created (Anthias and Yuval-Davis 1989; Chatterjee 1989; Jayawardena 1986; Radhakrishnan 1992; Rose 1974: 46–51; Ward 1983). In the Ireland of 1992, this political logic of national priorities was articulated by those campaigning for a "yes" vote and rejected by those campaigning for women's equal rights as Eurocitizens. Pro-European unity supporters made obvious attempts to subordinate competing or dissenting social and political agendas to the government's concerns (presented as unified) about the economic risks if Ireland were to forego European Union membership.

The Irish government vigorously attempted to dissociate abortion politics from the Maastricht Treaty, and arguments for a "yes" vote contended that European Union participation by Ireland was necessary for the national interest. Before the June 1992 referendum, the Government Publications Office distributed a "Short Guide to the Maastricht Treaty" to all residences. The first pages consisted of an address by then-Taoiseach (Prime Minister) Albert Reynolds on "What Maastricht is about—and not about." Over half of the address is devoted to the abortion issue, defending the government's decision to wait until after the Treaty referendum to hold a separate referendum on abortion rights (made necessary by the X Case). He concluded that "all Irish People can vote in the Maastricht referendum *solely* on the issues affecting European Union. They may do so safe in the knowledge that all matters relating to abortion will be resolved later in the year, through further referendum and legislation" (Government Publications Office 1992: 3, original emphasis).

An interview with Jacques Delors, then President of the European Community, illustrates a romantic, nationalist-yet-international spirit with which Irish voters were asked to approach the Treaty. When asked by an Irish journalist, "If you met an Irish voter en route to the polling station, why would you advise him or her to vote Yes to Maastricht?" Delors responded "I would tell them to vote Yes if they wanted to be *real Irish patriots* and if they wanted their country to be strengthened immeasurably. Full participation in Europe is the only way" (Flynn 1992a: 7, emphasis added). It is notable that this line of reasoning would be used in a nation that struggled for its *independence* as a nation. This message implies that it would be "unpatriotic" for Ireland to remain independent of Europe, and instead patriotic for Irish people to vote for their national economic growth. More to the point, then, Delors could have said that a "yes" vote would mean that a person was a patriotic "Irish-Eurocitizen."

For those concerned with the legal status of abortion, Protocol 17 and its implications for Irish women as Eurocitizens was central to whether or not to vote for the Maastricht Treaty. The issue of Irish women's right to travel was brought to the fore of Ireland's political sphere during the X Case. The Supreme Court, however, did not ensure a woman's unqualified right to travel for an abortion due to the fact that its decision focused narrowly on the young woman's suicide threat. It therefore seems ironic that pro-European Union forces emphasized that people living in the New Europe would have rights as national citizens and Eurocitizens and would have the right to freely cross national borders.

This did not appear to be the case for Irish women, and it was pointed out that voting for the Maastricht Treaty would eliminate recourse to European law in cases of constraints on women's rights, such as the right to travel for an abortion and the right to information on abortion services. In February 1992, pro-choice activists staged a dramatic protest at Dublin Airport, where an "X-ray machine" was used to screen female "passengers" to England. Those found to be pregnant were not allowed to board the planes and were "taken into State custody" (*Irish Times* 1992c).

Discourse on women's rights was not limited to explicitly feminist or pro-choice groups, and other "Vote No" campaigns emphasized the inextricable link between reproductive rights, citizenship rights, and Ireland's national identity. Progressive political organizations and a major trade union urged a vote against Maastricht, arguing that with European unity (due to Protocol 17) Irish women would be "second-class Eurocitizens." Posters were plastered around Dublin by the Democratic Left Party, with a picture of a male judge wearing a wig and the statement:

With Maastricht, women will have to deal with a new kind of travel agent.
With Maastricht, Irish women will not have the same rights that men have to information, travel, and access to European justice. We have to let them know, with our vote, that Europe must include Irish women as equals.

The meaning of reproductive rights was often debated with reference to representations of an Irish, Catholic national identity. The most explicit comment on this connection was found on a flyer reading:

The Workers Party wants legislation that will allow women to travel freely and control their own fertility. By voting NO you reject second class status for Irish women and a religious fundamentalist style state.

This statement combines support for women's right to travel for abortion with criticism of the Irish law as governed by Catholic ideology. The equation of Irish government with Catholic dominance is often made by politically and socially progressive organizations; however, it obscures a complex political environment in which some legislators are backed by the Church while others speak against the "legislation of Catholic morals." What is most interesting about the Workers Party position is that it reveals a split with pro-life arguments along religious lines. The Workers Party seeks a "no" vote as a gesture against Catholic governmental power, whereas pro-life supporters criticize the Irish state as being anti-Catholic on two counts: disregarding the views of its citizens (the majority of whom are Catholic) by not calling an immediate referendum on abortion, and accepting abortion in an instance not justified by the Church hierarchy (suicide intent). For these opposing activists, then, both abortion rights and the form of Irish catholicity in relation to governmental power are disputed.

Anti-abortion supporters rejected the Maastricht Treaty, contending that the government was intent on liberalizing Irish law, and refuted the Irish government's "Vote Yes" campaign on very different grounds than pro-choice activists. Eye-catching "Don't be Maastricked" posters and flyers were plastered around Dublin, carrying the message of the Pro-Life Campaign, "Vote 'No' now, and make them get it right!" The Pro-Life Campaign predicted that, due to the Supreme Court ruling on the X Case, Protocol 17 now could be interpreted as allowing abortion when suicide threats were made by a pregnant woman. Their flyers touted that:

A "NO" vote in the Maastricht referendum will help prevent abortion being foisted on us by Europe. It says that we must retain the right to make our own abortion laws in Ireland, and to make sure that these laws cannot be overturned by Europe.

In my reading, this statement reveals greater anxiety about Irish self-governance than it does about abortion, and indicates that the abortion question stood for concern over Irish national identity. Further, the possibility of overturning laws from within Ireland is not raised. The Pro-Life Campaign appeared confident that a majority of Irish voters would be against liberalized abortion legislation despite opinion polls to the contrary.

Women voters were particularly caught in the confusion over the implications of the Maastricht Treaty for their rights as Irish-Eurocitizens. Women's ambivalence toward European unity was evident in polls taken the day before the referendum, when 28 percent of women voters were still undecided, and women appeared much more hesitant to support the Treaty than men (Coughlan 1992a: 8). In a move opposed by many grassroots pro-choice activists, the state-supported but generally liberal umbrella group for ninety organizations called the Council for the Status of Women (CSW) campaigned for a "yes" vote but simultaneously lambasted the Irish government for supporting Protocol 17, which would continue the ban on Irish abortion rights. The Council contended that Ireland's membership in the European Union was essential if progressive changes were to be made in Irish law: "a pluralist and confident society, where women are respected and included equally, will only emerge within a European context" (*Irish Times* 1992a). This position was harshly criticized by ("Vote No") pro-life supporters on the grounds that the CSW could not profess to speak for all Irish women. The Pro-Life

Campaign's *Right-to-Life News* commented, "Sorry Sisters!! Obviously, Mna na hEireann [women of Ireland] are now beginning to realise that the title of CSW would more appropriately read 'Council for the Status of SOME Women'" (Anon. 1992: 4). In short, Irish women were not expected to "Vote No" as women, but as pro-choice or pro-life women.

Struggles over political representation, as witnessed between the CSW and the Pro-Life Campaign, are characteristic of politicized abortion discourse that contrasts "women's interests" with "fetal interests." Yanagisako and Delaney (1995) argue that notions of reproduction are particularly crucial components of (Western) gender-identity politics in that the procreative differences between men and women have been construed as natural, thus justifying political, social, and economic inequalities. Faye Ginsburg's (1989) ethnographic analysis of the abortion debate among white, middle-class women in the midwestern United States illustrates how reproductive politics stands as a symbol for competing notions of "womanliness" and women's reproductive responsibilities and mobilizes core values associated with American culture. The vastly different definitions of woman's nature held by pro-choice and pro-life women, both in the United States and in Ireland, challenge essentialist perspectives that see women's experiences and interests as unified or commonly shared.

Discussions of reproductive rights in the Irish context self-consciously referred simultaneously to gender politics and national identity or cultural politics more vividly than in the American case. I would argue that this was made possible by the "distinctly Irish" version of abortion politics given Ireland's historical, social, economic, and demographic trends. In both places, abortion (its legal status and its incidence) is taken as a measure of national well-being. For pro-choice activists, abortion rights show respect for women as capable, complex actors with equally important productive and reproductive roles. For pro-life activists, abortion is an indicator of the seriousness of other related social issues, such as sexuality, divorce, religious faith, unemployment, the commodification of life, and the place of the vulnerable in society. In Ireland, however, the "protection" of the nation and Irish culture in the face of abortion and other so-called social ills has maintained heightened urgency due to its postcolonial identity and the prospect of a more consolidated political-social relationship with a "pro-choice" Europe.

Unlike pro-choice supporters, Irish and American pro-life activists resist cultural change, with attendant shifts in women's status. While in both contexts the pro-life movements take a romanticized, unified national past as their desired national imaginary, representations of national cultural identity are impeded in the U.S. context. To speak of "American culture" is more difficult than to invoke "Irish culture," despite the fact that both are clearly open to constant reinterpretation. American racial/ethnic politics, economic restructuring, downward mobility, and the continued visibility of post-Vietnam era social divisiveness all make the dominant pro-life vision of U.S. national culture—white, middle-class, and Christian—unattainable.[5] In Ireland, pro-life activists point to the population's racial/ethnic and religious homogeneity as representative of an enduring Irish national culture and identity and believe that sustaining this vision is contingent on keeping abortion illegal.

In short, the entanglement of the questions of European Union membership and legal abortion in the Irish context provided a forum that visibly exposed how unstable and mutually defining the concepts of reproduction, gender, cultural and national identity, and citizenship rights indeed are. During the Maastricht debates, despite the fact that pro- and antiabortion-rights activists campaigned for a "no" vote, they did so with contrasting sets of justifications and assumptions. Activists mobilized distinct components of these multivalent concepts and drew varied connections between them in line with their divergent visions of the Irish nation and Irishness.

Opposing Visions of Citizenship and New Citizens

One key difference between the Irish pro-life and pro-choice organizations' campaigns for a "no" vote was that instead of focusing on the rights of Irish women under European Union law, the pro-life contingent concentrated on the rights of the unborn. The subjects of reproduction and citizenship were inevitably discussed simultaneously, as the Maastricht Treaty indeed had the power to create "new" Irish-Eurocitizens and women have the capacity to procreate future citizens, or, as some pro-life activists would have it, to produce "unborn citizens." The conceptual separation of woman from fetus is common in medical discourses and practices involving pregnancy and childbirth.[6] This view is correlated with the argument that "unborn babies" have personhood and thus deserve human rights, a basic tenet of the right-to-life movement and an ideology that facilitates and necessitates a struggle between the "rights" of the fetus and the "rights" of the pregnant woman. With increased medicalization of pregnancy, as Petchesky (1987) illustrates, visualization of the fetus through technology such as ultrasound further provides a personalized context in which women and men view and think about a fetus as distinct from a woman and her body. Pro-life activists exploit this, appropriating it in their arguments for fetal human rights and citizenship.

Images of fetuses were seen regularly in Dublin during the months previous to the Maastricht Treaty referendum. Posters of "the reality of abortion" in the form of dissected, bloody fetuses were common at pro-life rallies and literature tables, and several letters to the editor of the *Irish Times* stated opposition to these displays. The language used by pro-life advocates supports the visual images that create fetuses as persons and assumes that fetal personhood, from conception, is a scientific and natural fact. The phrase "the unborn" itself is an assertion of a collective "imagined community," to employ Benedict Anderson's (1983) concept. In one pro-life organization's literature, this community is envisioned as "Ireland's unborn citizens," illustrating how what is embraced as a universal, natural concept can be used to promote the social concepts of citizenship and nation. At a rally before the referendum, the Irish Right to Life of Cork and Westmeath distributed flyers that urged a "no" vote because "Ireland must protect her unborn citizens." Their message plays on the idea of basic human rights, arguing that rights of living people must be extended to the unborn:

ABORTION MEANS NO JUDGE, NO JURY NO TRIAL NO APPEAL AND NO STAY OF EXE-CUTION. . . . Only the Irish people have stood firm, demanding legal protection for all citizens—born and unborn. The Maastricht Treaty threatens Ireland's right to protect her unborn citizens.

This reference to unborn Irish citizens shows that pro-life activists have established a powerful vocabulary through which symbolic forms are articulated. The defense of unborn Irish lives has become an expression of patriotism in the name of the preservation of an Irish ethnicity/race, a unique Irish moral order, and national self-determination. Each of these concerns can be traced to colonial conditions. As literary critic Catherine Innes (1993) discusses, the relation between political power and land tenure attributed great meaning to racial purity and cultural identity such that only those who could prove true Irishness were deserving of being Mother Ireland's heirs. While the theme of protection of dependents (the unborn, children, and lesser abled) is also evident in pro-life discourses in the United States (Ginsburg 1989, Fernández-Kelly 1992, Taylor 1992), Irish activists' messages contain the additional element of postcolonial concern over protection of the nation and of its dependent citizens, encapsulated in attention to "Ireland's right to protect her unborn citizens."

A pro-life organization comprised of teenagers and young people, Youth Defence, has gained much media attention due to its activism on behalf of unborn Irish citizens. This group has been considered "radical" both by other pro-life activists and by pro-choice activists.[7] The following account illustrates how Youth Defence is unique in that it reveals tensions between "youth" and "tradition" in Ireland in ways that are not articulated by other pro-life groups.

New Enactments: A Young Social Movement and Old Visions of Ireland

Youth Defence has been one of the most publicly visible and active pro-life organizations since it was organized in February 1992. In the wake of the X Case, formation of Youth Defence was "necessary," its public relations (PR) officer informed me, because the mass media (Irish and international) were portraying young people as "a new generation with new ideals." Seven organizers, teenage women and men, promoted Youth Defence membership during an FM radio program hosted by the Rev. Michael Cleary (Cummins 1992). In a nation with nearly half of its population below the age of twenty-six, the attitudes and actions of youths immediately and directly influence the direction it takes. Although its members are "young" (only those between the ages of eighteen and thirty-five are eligible), Youth Defence is concerned with Irish history and tradition and with maintaining a narrative about Ireland's past as its generation looks toward the future. Claiming a membership of 5,000 (of which 800 are "active members") and offices throughout Ireland, Youth Defence is dedicated first and foremost to the "right to life of the unborn." Second, according to members I interviewed, they are prepared "to defend against attacks on the social fabric of traditional Irish culture and faith." The connection between the two aims is clear: to allow abortion would tear that social fabric.

The rhetoric that the Youth Defence PR officer and other members employ when speaking at rallies or in their office constantly interweaves Ireland's Catholic and Gaelic "dominant" cultural traditions, its unfair and violent colonial past ("we were a cultured nation way before Britain was") and the need to protect the unborn ("human beings have human nature. It's very simple. Respect them"). It is a conservative call back to a perceived natural, thus privileged, balance between environment, population, and social roles. Youth Defence posits that Ireland's natural resources can support a population three times the size it does now, and that the family, and women's role in it, are central to society. One Youth Defence member was quick to point out in reference to fertility and childbearing that "Nature shouldn't be tampered with," and explained that while France offers financial incentives to women to encourage them to bear children, Ireland does not have to resort to that due to its "traditional Irish society and religion."

For these pro-life activists, abortion and the protection of the unborn become the main signifiers of anxiety about the preservation of a distinctly Irish society. The naturalization of reproduction and of women's reproductive and social roles lies at the heart of their envisioned society. Youth Defence's language is saturated with references to "nature" and "traditional," revealing a specific version of a social order worth promoting on the grounds that it represents the truly natural Irish social order. Their emphasis on social institutions such as family, nation, church, and even the environment, as Carol Delaney discusses in the context of Turkey, conceals "the internal stratifications and the gendered hierarchies in these institutions" (1995: 178). Youth Defence's ideology clearly illustrates how reproduction is naturalized in keeping with the promulgation of a certain nationalist logic: the Irish nation is Catholic, Irish Catholics have large families as part of a "national tradition," and women primarily define themselves as mothers and housewives.

Youth Defence's character—infused with youthful energy backed by adult financial support (through the "Friends of Youth Defence") and representative of an anger "fierce and intense against almost everybody" (Cummins 1992)—is apparent in their public appearances at rallies, marches, and weekend informational activities in central Dublin in front of the General Post Office, where they hand out literature and "show posters of aborted children" in order to "reveal reality." On Saturday, June 6, 1992, I attended a Youth Defence "March Against Maastricht" and simultaneous counterdemonstration.[8] Dublin was plastered with posters publicizing both actions, some of them torn or defaced. In a convergence of youthfulness and Irish tradition under the theme of protecting the unborn, this event enacted Youth Defence's political positions. People of all ages joined the march. Children carried Youth Defence balloons while adults raised handmade banners, placards, or commonly seen posters of bloody fetuses. The more creative slogans included "Government to Grab Maastricht Shilling and Allow the Dirty Killing" and "Stay with God and Country, Vote No to Maastricht." Nearly everyone wore a sticker reading "Vote NO, Maastricht = Abortion."

Large male "stewards" formed the front line of the march, followed by a huge Irish tricolor flag and young boys playing traditional Irish instruments. A priest blessed the marchers, a boy cried out, "Right, let's rock and roll!" and the stream of supporters began to walk while singing the rewritten lyrics of Pink Floyd's "Another Brick in the Wall":

We don't need your legislation.
We don't need no birth control.
We don't want your referendum.
Hey! *Taoiseach* [Prime Minister]! Leave our kids alone!
All in all you're just another dick in the Dáil [Parliament].

As the marchers reached the location of the counterdemonstration, composed mainly of young women and men waving pro-choice banners and placards, the tune faded away amid deafening chants of "SPUC

Figure 6.1. Youth Defence supporters of all ages assemble for the "March Against Maastricht" in central Dublin, June 6, 1992. One side of the girl's placard cites the "Pope's Plea to Ireland," which reads in part, "May Ireland never weaken in her witness before Europe and the world to the dignity and sacredness of all human life—from conception until death." The other side displays a drawing of a child and a baby picture and reads, "I know I'm somebody 'cause God don't make no junk!" Photo: author.

Off!" [in reference to the Society for the Protection of Unborn Children] and "Not the Church, not the State, women must decide their fate," against "Abortion is Murder! Baby killers!" The *Irish Times* gave the story front page coverage and reported that "the intensity of the mutual hatred on display, and the use of apparently hired muscle to defend the march, suggested the street politics of another era" (O'Loughlin 1992).

Such reference to colonial struggles for Irish independence and comments about the past's view of the future were prominent at the Youth Defence rally following the march, where the young women and men leaders shared the podium. In several statements indicative of postcolonial national self-consciousness, the protection of the unborn and protection of Ireland's independent status were specifically linked. One speaker claimed that the "founders of our Nation are turning in their graves" as the Irish government now stood silent on the protectin of the unborn. A woman hailed as "a real woman of Ireland" concluded her remarks by saying, "Abortion is unacceptable to Irish people. Say no to abortion being forced on our Nation." She further urged the audience to "let Ireland be an example to the rest of the world" through having an antiabortion constitution. The highlight of the rally was an appearance by Michael Ahern, an actor in the film "The Commitments." Ahern introduced himself as being Irish, a democrat, and pro-life and called for a "no" vote to the Maastricht Treaty. He concluded with a rebellious, reworded "Commitments" motto: "Say it now, say it loud, I'm pro-life and I'm proud." Here, a shift from Youth Defence's view back on a traditional Irish past to a modern, optimistic, youthful Ireland is enacted.

What is it these young women and men are reacting to, motivating them to mobilize as they have? How is this intolerance of women's decisions to have abortions and the assertion of the primacy of Ireland's identity as a "Catholic nation" to be seen regarding conflict over the making of a New Europe? Along with the economic instability the prospect of a New Europe has caused, resurgent nationalism has been witnessed in various European countries, with that in France and Germany most publicized recently. Whereas in Germany and France unemployed youth "activists" and rightist social movements have targeted "foreigners," in Ireland, unemployed youths and students have mobilized around abortion and the "defense of culture and tradition." Youth Defence's identification of the truly Irish nation as Catholic provides the organization some institutional backing from the Church and allows the group to emphasize emotive references to Ireland's colonial past and its nationalist, Catholic, and Gaelic identities. This social movement's activities and discourses reveal how, given the prospect of European Union, nationalist concerns became inextricably interwoven with reproductive politics.

Irish National Identity in the New Europe

Whereas Ireland's national identity has generally been viewed within the contexts of postcolonialism, Catholic dominance, and the ongoing border dispute between the North and the South, the extreme publicity of the interrelationship between abortion politics and the meanings of Irish membership within the European Union created a different space for the presentation of competing sorts of Irishness at a time when "nation" itself is being transformed within the New Europe. As changes have transformed the meaning of Irishness, so too "European" identities are being explicitly reformulated within and across the European Union, evidenced by a Euro-flag, Euro-currency, Euro-anthem, and hyphenated Eurocitizenship (Fulbrook 1993). At issue during the Maastricht Treaty debates was whether Ireland—and, moreover, what *sort* of Ireland and of Irish-Eurocitizens—would join the New Europe.

Part of what people in Ireland reacted to when forming opinions about European unity was Ireland's colonial past. Ireland's move to "Go with Europe, Grow with Europe," in the words of a pro-European Union slogan, was seen by some as a betrayal of Ireland's nationalist struggles against Britain in the early twentieth century. In 1992, the Maastricht Treaty provided a forum for public dispute and negotiation of what the New Europe should entail, thus raising questions about the definitions of "nation" as being founded in "belonging," ethnicity, or citizen responsibility (Borneman 1992; Verdery 1993). While in France and Germany debates focused on the citizenship status of immigrants (Brubaker 1992), in Ireland the most salient subject during this turbulent period was legal abortion, which exposed the fact that citizenship and Irishness could not be separated from the symbolic and material implications of reproduction (Taylor 1995). European Union membership involved a shift in legal identity from Irish citizen to Irish-Eurocitizen, and the content of Eurocitizenship differed greatly for men and (pregnant) women due to Protocol 17 and the occurrence of the X Case.

While much literature on national identity and nationalism has marginalized women, interdisciplinary feminist scholarship has revealed that women are central to the material (biological reproduction) and symbolic dimensions of "nation" and "citizen" (Anthias and Yuval-Davis 1989; Bock and James 1992; Mosse 1985; Parker et al. 1992). Pateman (1992) argues that the paradox around the meaning of women's citizenship and political status lies in the way that women have been included *and* excluded from these concepts on the basis of sexual difference. In various countries, women's reproductive capacities have both excluded them from sharing full citizenship rights and been crucial to the nation-state, because only women can bear future citizens. The involvement of abortion in the Maastricht debates in Ireland illustrates the way that this paradox is enacted in public discourse. Pro-choice activists' messages highlighted and rejected the way in which "childbirth and motherhood have symbolized the natural capacities that set women apart from politics and citizenship" (Pateman 1992: 18). At the same time, pro-life messages focused on the inclusive aspect of citizenship with claims that reproduction and motherhood represent women's service and duty to the state.

Writing in the *Irish Times*, journalist Nuala O'Faolain's comments (1992) echo Catherine MacKinnon's (1989) scholarship on the "maleness of the state." O'Faolain notes that Protocol 17 "takes the Irish people and divides them in two: men and women. Men are given all the rights there are. Women are given lesser rights, because they are women . . . the protocol applies no sanctions to the male citizens without whose partnership no baby is made." She further asserts that women have been excluded from recourse to the European courts simply because they are women, and that therefore a vote for Maastricht would mean that "women are to be punished with second-class citizenship for having wombs—all women—because a minority of women take the option of terminating the pregnancies that they and men have brought about." Indeed, the Protocol represented a case in which law would be established on the grounds that women and men are *not* equal, in a reversal of the liberal "gender-neutral myth" of equality under the law. The Irish abortion debates highlight not only legal tensions, but divergent cultural meanings that surround several components of national identity, including personhood, citizenship rights, and society.

The constant reviewing of Ireland's identity is, I posit, due to the country's rather recent colonial past, its relationship to the New Europe, the inability to resolve the political and cultural "Troubles" on the island, and deeply embedded religious/"ethnic" tensions. Different aspects of such identity politics witnessed in Ireland, particularly symbolic and material concerns with reproduction and national identity, were conflated under the rubric of the Maastricht Treaty. The prominence given abortion politics, due to the X Case and Protocol 17 of the Maastricht Treaty, guided dialogues on national identity toward the problem of locating citizens both within Ireland and within the New Europe and led pro-choice and pro-life movements to oppose the Treaty with different justifications. While pro-choice activists focused on the future of Irish women's citizenship rights within the European Union and looked to the New Europe for further progress in recognizing Irish women's decisions to have legal abortions, pro-life campaigners concentrated on the idea of protecting Ireland's unborn citizens and portraying Ireland as an example of a model, traditionally Catholic, moral country. Most visibly, images of Ireland as a tolerant, pluralist nation or as an essentially Catholic society directly clashed.

Abortion rights became the major issue through which the Maastricht Treaty was framed in Ireland. This reveals that reproduction is crucial to the definitions of citizenship, gender, and (post)colonialism, and invokes notions of the continuity of national, ethnic, and cultural identities. Within the New Europe, reproduction has further implications for the creation of transnational "European" identities. While anthropologist Thomas Wilson writes that currently, "most Europeans identify themselves as members of a nation . . . but many are not so sure of their identity as 'EC Europeans'" (1993: 11), future generations of Eurocitizens may attach entirely new meanings to European identity. What sorts of individuals and what cultural meanings will be reproduced in the future? Pro-European Union literature contends that "a genuine sense of European identity is gradually being forged—a shared identity, at the heart of European citizenship, preserving the diversity of our separate heritages but adding a further dimension that Europeans have never had before" (ECSC-EEC-EAEC 1992). The debates in Ireland over Irish-Eurocitizen's reproductive rights indicates that reproduction is likely to remain a site of symbolic contestation not only in struggles that continually recreate national identities, but also at the location of the problematic intersections of reproductive rights, cultural self-definition, gender equity, and citizenship rights.

This chapter is based on fieldwork conducted over two summers, and was supported by the Program in Atlantic History, Culture and Society and the Women's Studies Program at Johns Hopkins University (1992–1993) and the Council for European Studies (1993–1994). Valuable comments have been provided by too many people to list by name; however, I particularly thank Doug English, Jo Murphy-Lawless, and Sarah Franklin for their close readings of several drafts, suggestions, and encouragement. I also thank Helena Ragoné and Sarah Franklin for their organizational and editorial perseverance in putting this volume together.

Notes

1. The Maastricht Treaty, which Irish voters approved in 1992, has transformed the European Community into the European Union, which established European citizenship, less restricted movement across borders, integrated markets, a common currency, a more powerful European Parliament, and a common foreign and security policy.

2. The "unique" identity of the South is generally traced to either Gaelic culture or Catholicism, and different groups emphasize opposing definitions of national identity. Ireland has the highest rate of "practicing" Catholics (86 percent) in Europe. Recently,

however, the declining role of the Church in everyday life has been noted and/or lamented (see Peillon 1982: 89–99; Whyte 1980: 3–8).

3. Reports state that the young woman miscarried during an amniocentesis procedure in England, and that DNA tests legitimated the sexual assault claim against the accused man. He pleaded guilty and was given a one-year prison sentence (O'Loughlin 1994; O'Neill 1994).

4. Referenda were held in 1993, and the proposition of legal abortion in Ireland in order to "save the life, as distinct from the health, of the mother" failed by a margin of 2:1. Pro-life campaigned for a "no" vote on the grounds that it was too liberal, whereas pro-choice activists advocated a "no" vote on the grounds that it did not respect all women's right to choose. However, the right to information on abortion, including referral addresses, pre- and postabortion counseling, and the release of medical records to clinic doctors abroad was approved in 1993 and legislated in 1995. This move has been hailed by one pro-choice activist as indicative of "the New Ireland" (Barbash 1995).

5. This argument is consciously overly generalized to highlight U.S.-Ireland contrasts. Further scholarship on the subject of U.S. cultural/abortion politics is needed (see Fernández-Kelly 1992).

6. For example, in 1982 the Royal College of Obstetrics and Gynecologists in Britain argued for a division in obstetrics between "reproductive" and "fetal" medicine (Oakley 1984: 280). Jo Murphy-Lawless describes the control male medicine has exerted over Irish women's bodies historically (1991) and the power that institutionalized male medicine has today (1992). Emily Martin's (1987) ethnography discusses American women's fragmentation and alienation from their bodies and bodily processes in relation to medical discourses.

7. Youth Defence has become less marginalized by other pro-life groups, however, and the Youth Defence public relations officer is now the director of the Irish branch of Human Life International (HLI), established in 1994. Three new political organizations serve on HLI-Ireland's board, the right-wing Catholic movement Solidarity, political party Muintir na hEireann, and the Christian Solidarity Party.

8. The Garda (Irish Police) and the *Irish Times* estimated 1,000–1,200 Youth Defence marchers, while Youth Defence claimed 5,000. The counterdemonstration was comprised of 150–200 pro-choice activists from various organizations (O'Loughlin 1992).

References

Alcock, Anthony. 1992. "Northern Ireland: Some European Comparisons." In *Northern Ireland: Politics and the Constitution*, ed. Brigid Hadfield. Buckingham: Open University Press, pp. 148–64.

Anderson, Benedict. (1983) 1991. *Imagined Communities: Reflections on the Origins and Spread of Nationalism*. London: Verso.

Anthias, Floya and Niva Yuval-Davis, eds. 1989. *Woman-Nation-State*. New York: St. Martin's Press.

Barbash, Fred. 1995. "Abortion Information Law Is Latest Landmark in 'New Ireland.'" *Washington Post*, May 20, p. A16.

Bock, Gisela and Susan James, eds. 1992. *Beyond Equality and Difference: Citizenship, Feminist Politics, and Female Subjectivity*. London and New York: Routledge.

Borneman, John. 1992. *Belonging in the Two Berlins: Kin, State, Nation*. Cambridge: Cambridge University Press.

Brubaker, Rogers. 1992. *Citizenship and Nationhood in France and Germany*. Cambridge, Mass.: Harvard University Press.

Chatterjee, Partha. 1989. "Colonialism, Nationalism, and Colonialized Women: The Contest in India." *American Ethnologist* 16, 4: 622–33.

Coughlan, Denis. 1992a. "Poll Indicates 28% of Women Still Have to Make Up Their Minds About How They Will Vote." *Irish Times,* June 17, p. 8.

———. 1992b. "Government Sees Church Statement as Support for Maastricht Treaty; Hierarchy Seeks Vote on Abortion." *Irish Times,* May 27, pp. 1 and 12.

Cummins, Mary. 1992. "Mobilising Youth as a Weapon to Crusade Against Abortion." *Irish Times,* May 4, p. 16.

Delaney, Carol. 1995. "Father State, Motherland, and the Birth of Modern Turkey." In *Naturalizing Power: Essays in Feminist Cultural Analysis,* ed. Sylvia J. Yanagisako and Carol Delaney. New York: Routledge, pp. 177–200.

Dillon, Michele. 1993. *Debating Divorce: Moral Conflict in Ireland.* Lexington: University of Kentucky Press.

ECSC-EEC-EAEC. 1992. *A People's Europe.* Commission of the European Communities European File Series Pamphlet.

Fernández-Kelly, M. Patricia. 1992. "A Chill Wind Blows: Class, Ideology, and the Reproductive Dilemma." In *Challenging Times: The Women's Movement in Canada and the United States,* ed. Constance Backhouse and David H. Flaherty. Montreal and Kingston: McGill-Queen's University Press, pp. 252–67.

Flynn, Sean. 1992. "Sean Flynn Interviews Jacques Delors." *Irish Times,* June 13, p. 7.

Francombe, Colin. 1992. "Irish Women Who Seek Abortions in England." *Family Planning Perspectives* 24, 6: 265–68.

Frankel, Glenn. 1992. "Irish Supreme Court Allows Teenager to Seek Abortion." *Washington Post,* February 27, p. A27.

Fulbrook, Mary, ed. 1993. *National Histories and European History.* London: UCL Press.

Ginsburg, Faye D. 1989. *Contested Lives: The Abortion Debate in an American Community.* Berkeley: University of California Press.

Government Publications Office. 1992. *A Short Guide to the Maastricht Treaty.* Dublin: Cahill Printers, April.

Hesketh, Tom. 1990. *The Second Partitioning of Ireland? The Abortion Referendum of 1983.* Dun Laoghaire: Brandsma Books.

Innes, Catherine L. 1993. *Woman and Nation in Irish Literature and Society, 1880–1935.* New York and London: Harvester Wheatsheaf.

Irish Times. 1992a. "Council for Women Favours a 'Yes' Vote." June 10, p. 8.

———. 1992b. "Abortion Figures Up." April 2, p. 1.

———. 1992c. "Airport Abortion Screening." February 17.

Irish Women's Abortion Support Group. 1988. "Across the Water." *Feminist Review* 29, 1: 64–71.

Jayawardena, Kumari. 1986. *Feminism and Nationalism in the Third World.* London: Zed Books.

Johnson, Rebecca. 1992. "The X Case and Rights: An Analysis of Letters to the Press on the Abortion Debate in Ireland, February–March, 1992." M. Phil. dissertation, Trinity College, Dublin.

MacCurtain, Margaret. 1983. *Unmanageable Revolutionaries: Women and Irish Nationalism.* Dingle, Ireland: Brandon Book Publishers.

MacKinnon, Catharine A. 1989. *Toward a Feminist Theory of the State.* Cambridge, Mass.: Harvard University Press.

Martin, Emily. 1987. *The Woman in the Body: A Cultural Analysis of Reproduction.* Boston: Beacon Press.

Mosse, George. 1985. *Nationalism and Sexuality: Respectability and Abnormal Sexuality in Modern Europe.* New York: Howard Fertig.

Murphy-Lawless, Jo. 1991. "Images of 'Poor' Women in the Writings of Irish Men Midwives." In *Women in Early Modern Ireland,* ed. Margaret MacCurtain and Mary O'Dowd. Edinburgh: Edinburgh University Press, pp. 291–303.

———. 1992. "Reading Birth and Death Through Obstetric Practice." *Canadian Journal of Irish Studies* 18, 1: 129–45.

———. 1993. "Fertility, Bodies and Politics: The Irish Case." *Reproductive Health Matters* 2: 53–64.

Northern Ireland Abortion Law Reform Association. 1989. *Abortion in Northern Ireland: The Report of an International Tribunal.* Belfast: Beyond the Pale Publications.

Oakley, Ann. 1984. *The Captured Womb: A History of Antenatal Care in Britain.* New York: Basil Blackwell.

O'Brien, Jon. 1993. "Adolescent Pregnancy Prevention Needs and Services: Constraints and How to Overcome Them." In *Progress Postponed: Abortion in Europe in the 1990s,* ed. Karen Newman. London: International Planned Parenthood Federation, pp. 157–65.

———. 1992. "How Women Can Vote 'Yes' and Achieve Inferior Status." *Irish Times,* June 1, p. 10.

O'Loughlin, Edward. 1992. "Hatred Is Displayed on Both Sides at Youth Anti-Abortion Rally in Dublin." *Irish Times,* June 8, p. 3.

———. 1994. "Silent Court Told of Devastation of Two Families." *Irish Times,* June 3, p. 1.

O'Mara, Richard. 1992. "Ireland in Anguish over Teen Rape Victim's Pregnancy." *Baltimore Sun,* February 24, pp. 1, 5A.

O'Neill, Paul. 1994. "DNA Tests Show Genetic Link." *Irish Times,* June 3, p. 9.

O'Reilly, Emily. 1992. *Masterminds of the Right.* Dublin: Attic Press.

Parker, Andrew, Mary Russo, Doris Sommer, and Patricia Yaeger, eds. 1992. *Nationalisms & Sexualities.* New York and London: Routledge.

Pateman, Carole. 1992. "Equality, Difference, Subordination: The Politics of Motherhood and Women's Citizenship." In *Beyond Equality and Difference: Citizenship, Feminist Politics, and Female Subjectivity,* ed. Gisela Bock and Susan James. London and New York: Routledge, pp. 17–31.

Peillon, Michel. 1982. *Contemporary Irish Society: An Introduction.* Dublin: Gill and MacMillan.

Petchesky, Rosalind Pollack. 1987. "Fetal Images: The Power of Visual Culture in the Politics of Reproduction." *Feminist Studies* 13, 2: 263–91.

Radhakrishnan, R. 1992. "Nationalism, Gender, and the Narrative of Identity." In Parker et al. (1992), pp. 77–95.

Riddick, Ruth. 1990. *The Right to Choose: Questions of Feminist Morality.* Lip pamphlets. Dublin: Attic Press.

Right to Life News 1, 2 (June 12): 4.

Rose, Catherine. 1974. *The Female Experience: The Story of the Woman Movement in Ireland.* Galway: Arlen House.

Smyth, Ailbhe, ed. 1992. *The Abortion Papers—Ireland.* Dublin: Attic Press.

Taylor, Janelle S. 1992. "The Public Fetus and the Family Car: From Abortion Politics to a Volvo Advertisement." *Public Culture* 4, 2: 67–80.

Taylor, Lawrence J. 1995. *Occasions of Faith: An Anthropology of Irish Catholics.* Philadelphia: University of Pennsylvania Press.

Treacy, Bernard, ed. 1992. "Abortion, Law and Conscience." Special issue of *Doctrine and Life* 42, 5.

Verdery, Katherine. 1993. "Whither 'Nation' and 'Nationalism'?" *Daedalus* 122: 37–46.

Ward, Margaret. 1983. *Unmanageable Revolutionaries: Women and Irish Nationalism.* London: Pluto Press.

Women's Coalition. 1992. Press Release, June 12.

Whyte, J. H. 1980. *Church and State in Modern Ireland: 1923–1979.* Second edition. Dublin: Gill and MacMillan.

Wilson, Thomas M., and M. Estellie Smith, eds. 1993. *Cultural Change and the New Europe: Perspectives on the European Community.* Boulder, CO: Westview Press.

Yanagisako, Sylvia J. and Carol Delaney. 1995. "Naturalizing Power." In *Naturalizing Power: Essays in Feminist Cultural Analysis,* ed. Sylvia Yanagisako and Carol Delaney. New York: Routledge, pp. 1–25.

Chapter 7
Rights to the Children: Foster Care and Social Reproduction in Hawai'i

Judith Modell

In the summer of 1991, I spent an afternoon with my friend Debra at her house in a Hawaiian area of Oahu. We talked about the latest crisis in her family, which involved the possibly permanent removal of her sister's child from her sister's care and from the household in general.

Debra's story and situation are not uncommon. I am going to use that afternoon's conversation as the core of my argument in this paper. But the subject is a broader one, having to do with the "politics" of child placement in the state of Hawai'i and the conflictual interpretations of family, kinship, and reproduction those politics expose. The story is one of struggle over the child, and it reveals the myriad ways in which a debate about child placement elicits the constituents of a culture's commitment to survival and integrity.

My focus is on foster care, and specifically on the intersection of an American child welfare system with Hawaiian cultural interpretations of moving children from household to household. The situation I describe differs from accounts of fosterage in which people choose to "give" or "take" children outside the regulations imposed by a state bureaucracy (e.g., Goody 1982; Bledsoe 1990). In Hawai'i, the act of moving a child does not occur independently of American principles and policies. Even if an individual moves a child "casually" and "informally," the American legal system is the background against which the action takes place.

Like Caroline Bledsoe, I consider foster care a mode of reproduction. As such, it is a valuable resource and thus subject to the competing interests of various parties. In the Hawaiian context, as I show, the competition expresses itself in contrasting discourses about kinship, family, and, in the words of American child placement policy, "the best interests of a child." Moreover, these discourses are highly politicized; competition over a mode of reproduction reflects and impinges upon the structure of inequality in the wider setting. In what follows, I suggest that foster care is an especially politicized mode of reproduction, since it deals with the *distribution* and not just the "production" of children. The person (or group) who controls foster care is in a position of power, able not only to place and replace children but also to determine the terms of continuity from one generation to the next.

Such power increases, I argue, when a foster care arrangement takes place in the public domain—and more so when the public domain is characterized by a history of struggle over the "proper" condition of children. By now fully embroiled in the institutions and ideologies of an American state, people of Hawaiian ancestry confront the possibility of "losing" their children to a non-Hawaiian placement system. Gaining control over foster care, then, becomes part of the much larger debate over Hawaiian cultural identity and national sovereignty. This debate has as one of its central points a claim to distinct interpretations of kinship and family that, as symbolic and as social structural elements, stand for the wider realm of control over their own affairs Hawaiian people are demanding in response to two centuries of subjection to an alien state.

With Debra as my principal collaborator, if not coauthor, I will describe the competition over child placement that occurs between Hawaiian people and the personnel in the child welfare system, virtually all of whom are non-Hawaiian. In conversations with me, Debra effectively conveyed the parameters of this competition. She knew that the contest was not limited to the physical movement of a child but had equally to do with the reasons and rationale for such movement. Winning control of fosterage was a matter of imposing Hawaiian meanings on the practice—of bringing the "native" discourse to bear on the "foreign" categories that dominate child placement in Hawai'i.

Before I substantiate my assertion that foster care is profoundly implicated in a political system, I ought briefly to say what I mean by "Hawaiian." I use the term to refer to people of Hawaiian ancestry, calculated either by percentage of Hawaiian blood or through kinship connections; equally important, the people I work with identify themselves as culturally Hawaiian.[1]

The data I draw on for my argument come from fieldwork on Oahu in three areas of high Hawaiian population density: a neighborhood of Honolulu and two outlying communities, Waimanalo and Waianae. In the course of my fieldwork, I have spent time not only with Hawaiian families but also with the social workers, public health nurses, and Family Court personnel who are the "gatekeepers" of an American child welfare system. Interviews with professionals tended to be more structured and formal than those with individuals like Debra, where casual talk was the norm.[2] My conversations with Debra went on over several summers and took place in various settings, including her household. Observations supplement what I learned in talking with her. In this paper, my conversations with Debra are supplemented with several other stories, elicited in the same informal way. Debra's case is central, proving my point, but it is by no means unique.

Debra is in her mid-thirties and lives on the Waianae Coast. I have known her for over five years. Her family, and her reports of recent contact with state agencies, provide the framework for my discussion of foster care in a late twentieth-century Hawaiian context.

Debra's Story

I want to start by summarizing the conversation I had with Debra that August day in 1991. Behind this summary lie several key issues:

1. The interpretations of foster care by Hawaiians and by the state personnel who handle child placement issues—social workers and court officers who operate under American state guidelines.
2. The conditions under which Hawaiians and non-Hawaiians are likely to move a child from one household to another.
3. The impact of these interventions in "reproduction" on notions of care and kinship.
4. The significance of competing discourses about child placement in the broader negotiation of cultural identity, power, and autonomy in contemporaneous Hawaii.

Here, first, is what happened in Debra's family.

By the time I spoke with Debra, much of the story lay in the past. It began with Debra's younger sister, a drug user who could not care for her four-year-old daughter. Debra and her mother had taken the child into their shared household, only to be told by Family Court, when they petitioned for permanent guardianship, that they were not "fit." In the eyes of the court, they had been "incompetent and irresponsible" in caring for the child—"Because," Debra explained to me, "we had not had her vaccinations updated." The little girl, Precious, was returned to her biological parent "despite the fact that she and her boyfriend were both using drugs," Debra continued.

Some time later, Debra's sister and her boyfriend took the girl on a trip to downtown Honolulu. The sister went off to "earn some money"— probably through prostitution, according to Debra—and the boyfriend walked around town with Precious. He was picked up by two men from a rehabilitation clinic, because, Debra said, he was a black man with a "Hawaiian-looking child." They in turn (and quickly) called the police, who took the girl to the station and called Child Protective Services (CPS). Fortunately, the CPS worker was able to find an "emergency bed" for the child in a shelter.

Eventually Debra and her family were notified of what had happened; meanwhile, the sister and her boyfriend disappeared. The child had been placed in a foster home by CPS. Debra and her mother were invited to meet with Precious and her social worker. The conversation about the future of Precious took place in a local McDonald's—the site of many such fateful transactions. As Debra reported the meeting to me, the child begged to "come home," and the social worker insisted she would be better off in a foster home. Debra, of course, did not know where the girl was living, but she speculated to me that the family was probably "far away" and "different from us." The distance referred to the other side of the island—the Windward side, which tended to be more prosperous and middle-class than the Leeward side of Oahu. Debra's guess about the placement was not unreasonable.

Debra was not happy with the situation, and she was determined to bring Precious back home. By the time of our conversation, she had decided to petition Family Court to become legal guardian of the child. Her hearing was to be the day after we talked. Debra was scared, and not at all optimistic about the likely outcome. She explained why she was both frightened and pessimistic. The court, she said, "does not understand Hawaiian ways. They do not know what *hanai* is or the *'ohana*." Those were crucial words for her. *Hanai* refers to the practice of informal adoption—one person giving a child to another without the necessity of going to court.[3] *Hanai* represents a continuity from one generation to another that does not depend on genealogy but on generosity, not on biology but on belonging. The *'ohana* refers to a group of coresiding individuals who consider themselves kin; like *hanai*, *'ohana* emphasizes the coming together of people who assume responsibility for and loyalty to one another (Pukui et al. 1972: 166–67). That the concepts of *hanai* and *'ohana* have become crucial public symbols in Hawaiian struggles for cultural autonomy and national sovereignty is not irrelevant to the point Debra was making to me.

Hanai was the way to take care of children in trouble, she told me; "Children belong with the family." She also knew that court officials were unlikely to appreciate her family. From *their* point of view, she claimed, the household would seem chaotic and crowded. Debra lived with her five children, her mother, the children of one brother, and a cousin. Moreover, as she told me, her sister "would always be welcome." The social worker had already expressed concern about the boys in the house—Debra had three sons. "How can I help it if I have boys?" she asked me, recognizing the vast cultural gulf that separated her from the concerned social worker. Debra was clearly offended by the implication that her niece would be "at risk" from anyone in the household.

Talking with me, almost as if in rehearsal, Debra began to construct the interpretations of child care, of family, and of responses to a child in trouble that she would bring to court. She was intending to present these interpretations herself. I tried to persuade her to accept the services of a lawyer, but she refused. She wanted to tell the court about Hawaiian-style family and insist that her case for guardianship was a good one. She wanted, in effect, to speak in her own words—to establish her own discourse in the courtroom.

The Significance of Debra's Story

When Debra Miller decided to appear in court, she was confronting head-on the competition over child placement in Hawai'i. Moreover, in insisting on bringing the case herself, Debra recognized the importance of her discourse—and of Hawaiian formulations about kinship—to the satisfactory resolution of a placement debate. The hearing, as she anticipated, would set at odds two distinct versions of foster care, each turning around the connotations of concepts such as parent, child, household, and family. If Debra could control the discourse and force the decision to be made in her terms, she would gain more than a child. She would gain leverage in a state-controlled system of child distribution.

This may sound like an extreme phrasing of the competition Debra faced, but it is accurate to her sense that only when child placement was decided in Hawaiian cultural terms would control over this mode of reproduction truly belong to Hawaiian people. Leverage, then, means making an impact on the articulated principle of "best interests" as the first step in influencing the *practices* of child placement. Behind this, as I have implied, lay a second sense: that loss of control over where and how children live threatens the social and cultural survival of Hawaiians in the state. Debra certainly wanted Precious to come home. She also wanted to appropriate the position of "resource gatekeeper" (Handwerker 1990: 2) from those who held such positions—mainly *haole* (Caucasian) and Japanese professionals.

The phrase is Penn Handwerker's. A "resource gatekeeper," he writes, controls the moral as well as the material conditions of resource allocation. I take him to mean by "moral" that a resource gatekeeper evaluates the material conditions under which resources are *rightly* (or justly) to be distributed. When children constitute the resource, the moral dimension is likely to be especially freighted and jealously contested. Moreover, if children are to be distinguished from a commodity, the conditions under which they are distributed must be couched in the language of well-being—a concept that instantly draws in value judgments. That a child is (presumably) moved for "her own sake," not to satisfy the interests of other parties, does not provide a straightforward prescription, even in contexts of cultural homogeneity, which Hawai'i does not have.

This was the situation Debra faced. Precious had been defined as "at risk" by CPS workers, a designation that for them brought with it the necessity of acting. When I talked with her, Debra was about to question the whole framework, from the category to the resulting action.

Debra's experiences are part of a longer story in Hawai'i, in which the connections between the moral dimension and the material conditions for moving a child have been both intricate and volatile. In this long story, Precious loses her personal distinctiveness and becomes a member of a category: Hawaiian and part-Hawaiian children who are neglected, abused, or living in an unsafe environment. For the past several decades, a disproportionate number of the children in the CPS caseload have been Hawaiian or part-Hawaiian; they appear in the records far more than the population of Hawaiians and part-Hawaiians in the state would warrant. For example, according to the 1988 Department of Human Services report (the most recent one I have), Hawaiian children account for 30 percent of the confirmed abuse and neglect cases, while Hawaiians and part-Hawaiians form approximately 20 percent of the total population.

A consequence of poverty, the increase in drug and alcohol use, and a lack of opportunity and leverage in the social and economic structures of the state, this disproportion may also be a consequence of enforced hegemonic judgments of a child's behavior and circumstances. In no state is the determination of "risk" easy, and in every state child welfare workers tread a knotty path through cultural norms about child rearing, confusing indicators of danger, and uncertainty about the outcome of a placement. In Hawaii, as not only Debra but also social workers and judges complained, the problem was compounded by a strict "mandated reporting" law. The law specifies individuals who are required to report to Child Protective Services any sign that a child is at risk. These individuals include health professionals, school teachers and principals, police, and social workers. It is, then, against the law *not* to report immediately any suspected neglect, abuse, or harm.

The burden falls heavily but not solely on the schools. Along the Waianae Coast, as well as in the other areas of my fieldwork, I frequently heard stories of a child "disappearing" one day—a parent or caretaker coming home to find an empty house and no sign of the child. What had happened was that sometime during the day a social worker or official had removed the "at-risk" child and brought her to a shelter without (immediately) notifying anyone.

Teachers, for their part, confessed to me how constrained they felt by the pressure on them not to be delinquent in acting in what was presumably the child's best interest. CPS figures show that the largest number of reports do come from teachers and, moreover, that in only 64 percent of cases "are families notified of the outcome." That means, of course, that in 36 percent of cases families are *not* notified of the outcome (State of Hawai'i 1986: 84). Due partly to overwork and understaffing, such failure to notify families creates a context in which Hawaiian parents come to feel their children can simply be taken away and placed somewhere else—in a household "far away and different from us," as Debra put it.

Precious was fortunate in that CPS found her first a bed and then a home to live in. Many children have to stay in detention centers before they can be fostered or, when feasible, returned home. Once placed in a foster family, a child is increasingly unlikely to return to her or his original household. As a state agency reported in 1990, if a child is fostered for three months or more, the chances are she or he will remain permanently away (State of Hawai'i 1990: 38). This effect of foster care occurs in all states, but Hawai'i is distinguished by having one of the highest rates of removal of any state in the union—in 1988, nearly 30 percent of children reported to be "at risk" were placed elsewhere. "Hawai'i uses foster care nearly two times more than any other state" (State of Hawai'i 1990: 38).[4]

Furthermore, for children of Hawaiian ancestry, as Debra knew, the probable outcome was placement in a non-Hawaiian family. Foster families in the state tend to be middle-class and conventional in their living arrangements; they are not likely to be Hawaiian. "More Hawaiian children are placed out," a social worker told me, "than there are Hawaiian families who qualify as foster parents." Though a small stipend is paid to foster parents, this apparently does not "qualify" individuals whose incomes are initially low. The real issue is that Hawaiian households tend not to be composed of the mother, father, and child unit social workers assume is "safe" and secure.

Another problem arose as well about qualifying Hawaiian families for foster care. Often, the person who volunteered to be a foster parent defined himself or herself as "related" to the child.[5] And though this perfectly suited Hawaiian cultural interpretations of caring for and nurturing a child—evoking the concept of *hanai* that Debra planned to present in her court hearing—an emphasis on kinship did not at all suit CPS workers. For one thing, they did not want to pay relatives for taking in a child; paying a relative violates an ideology that assumes money is incompatible with the love provided by kin. To simplify, I am not examining the diversity of interpretations that exist within CPS. By and large, most social workers I met operated according to the principles set by an American child welfare system regardless of their own cultural backgrounds.

For another, placing the child with relatives was considered to be a less than safe placement. This, too, was based on a view of Hawaiian families filtered through an American understanding of kinship and household. The fluidity of the *'ohana*, its permeable boundaries, suggested a constant danger to the child not only, I think, because "anyone" could come in, but also because the ebb and flow of people itself seems to pose a risk to a child. The risk posed by nonpermanent adults, from an American perspective, is either neglect of the child or failure of the adults to reach a consensus on what is good for (or harmful to) the child. And of course Debra did say that not only her sister but also her sister's boyfriend always had a place in her home.

Social workers in Hawai'i faced another constraint on their willingness to respect *'ohana* arrangements. The 1983 Hawai'i Child Protective Act states that a child is at risk when there exists the *possibility* of "imminent" or "threatened" harm. Obedient to the law, a social worker would rightly be reluctant to leave a child at home when home has (apparently) so few limits and virtually no closed doors. When new members are so easily welcomed, the chances of someone "possibly" being a threat to a child increases, at least in the eyes of professionals who accept an American standard of safety. At the same time, a person like Debra is equally right in finding the law destructive of the very essence of Hawaiian family and household. Strict construction of the law has the potential of separating a younger from an older generation in living arrangements and in the imposition of new understandings of "family." The impact of the law, as Debra feared, could well be the permanent removal of a child from her cultural as well as her physical setting.

I met a few Hawaiian individuals who had qualified as foster parents. Mrs. K., for instance, a woman in her 60s, had a six-year-old foster child in her household. After I got to know her, she confessed to me that the child was actually her grandson; the boy had been removed from her son, who was a drug addict. Mrs. K. did not tell me this right away since she suspected that I, a *haole* after all, might be critical of her for accepting the monetary support an "official" guardian received from the state. She also may initially have assumed I shared the general non-Hawaiian sense that relatives were not proper caretakers for a child at risk; it was *her* son who abused drugs. Once she told me the situation, however, she went on to express her discomforts with the system she had accepted — particularly the need to go to court to legitimize an arrangement she recognized as "traditional." Hawaiian grandparents took in their grandchildren without having to call on outside authorities to make this acceptable. In the course of our conversations, she complained bitterly about the paperwork legalization involved. For though she had won one side of the issue—gaining permission to foster a relative—she had lost another. "There are too many papers to sign," she told me. She worried out loud about her husband's persistent refusal to sign the required documents each year. He announced that "papers" violated the traditional Hawaiian way, and perhaps beneath her worry she envied his resistance to the hegemonic system of child placement.

"Papers" thus bring the discussion back to my point about conflicting discourses regarding child placement in Hawai'i. During my fieldwork I was to hear the word "papers" so often I came to treat it as symbolic as much as literal. Papers stood for the whole panoply of verbalization and writing that came along with an American regime. Hawaiian people considered the presence of papers in a foster care arrangement an especially cold-blooded *haole* custom. People I met claimed that composing a formal contract to ensure that someone would care for, nurture, and love a child was far more unnatural than giving people money to help support a child. (Many appreciated the monthly payments or additional welfare they received for fostering a child and did not view having resources as antithetical to providing loving care.) Fully prepared to go to court, Debra complained about the paperwork her appearance at the hearing entailed. In the old days, she told me, "there was no need for papers. We just *hanai* the child."

The symbolism of papers condensed complex disagreements over the meaning of foster care, bringing forward the moral evaluation that is inseparable from the distribution of children in any society. For the Hawaiians I talked with, papers indicated how bizarre American notions of foster care were, transforming a "caring" into a "contracted" relationship. More than that, on a practical level that supported the cultural critique, Hawaiians were convinced that papers "messed up" the understanding between those who gave and those who took a child. Early in my fieldwork, a woman named Melody West told me the story of her child's placement, an illustration of the damage papers did.

Melody had become pregnant at 14 and recognized she could not take care of her baby. Following Hawaiian custom, she gave the baby to her mother to *hanai*. Mother and daughter each knew who had parental rights to the child; by the terms of *hanai*, Melody's mother gained these rights. Sixteen years later, Melody was working for a social service agency and her colleagues advised her to formalize the delegation of parenthood. Specifically, they suggested she reclaim her "own" child. Melody brought the case to court and was given the papers that designated her as "rightful" parent of the now-adolescent boy. In the process, she destroyed the relationship with her mother, who felt herself to have been betrayed by her own daughter. When Melody talked to me two years after the event, she was still deeply unhappy. She had been caught in the crunch of two systems and suffered personally from a confrontation between two distinctly different conceptualizations of placing children. That Melody did not blame any one person for the tragedy only indicates how profoundly *cultural* it was. Two ways of thinking about the "good" of a child had clashed, and she bore the brunt.

While fully determined to go to court on her own, Debra too worried about the impact papers would have on kinship arrangements that were mutually understood (and accepted) by the participants. She wanted the court to legalize her guardianship of Precious. At the same time, she confessed to me her concern that this would ruin her relationship with her mother, who also had a claim to parenthood, and with her sister, who was biologically the child's mother. More pressing than that concern, however, was Debra's fear that Precious would "disappear" on the "other side of the island" if she did not gain legal guardianship. And for Debra, in the end, the possibility that Precious would live with her foster family forever was the worst-case scenario. Leaving Precious in a foster home would mean depriving the child of her affiliation with her Hawaiian family. Under those circumstances, Precious would effectively cease to be Hawaiian.

Debra confronted her dilemma out loud, tormented by (and angry at) the necessity of going to American Family Court in order to keep a Hawaiian child in a Hawaiian family. As she considered her decision, with me as audience, she revealed how thoroughly complicated the intersection of the two systems was. The situation was not a simple matter of hegemony and resistance, though it had some of those qualities, but rather of turning the hegemonic structures to one's own advantage. Debra would succeed in doing this if she could persuade the judge and social workers genuinely to "hear" her case by listening to her formulation of the best interests of the child. In making plans for her appearance in court the next day, Debra fully recognized that not only where a child lived but also the terms in which the decision was made were items in the contest between competing parties. She intended to go to court and, with equal firmness, she intended *not* to have a lawyer represent her case. The lawyer's language would not be hers; the opinion given by the court, even if favorable to Debra, would not reflect Hawaiian concepts of the *'ohana* and of *hanai*. "They don't know Hawaiian custom," she said.

Foster Care and Culture

Like other people I met, Debra was attempting to reconcile Hawaiian-style foster care with the urgencies brought by new circumstances—drugs, unemployment, and disruption of kin-based sources of support.

This effort was most apparent when she insisted that of course she would *hanai* her sister's child and, simultaneously, that inevitably she would go to court to legitimize the arrangement. In the process of negotiating two modes of fosterage, Debra modified the meanings of each—such, at least, would be the effect of her appearance in court. Moreover, she would encounter in the American courtroom a definition of foster care that was narrow and restrictive compared with the one she brought, which was diffuse and noncategorical. I will clarify this distinction by referring briefly to Esther Goody's study of foster care in West Africa.

In her 1982 book, *Parenthood and Social Reproduction,* Goody distinguishes between "crisis" and "voluntary" fostering. She claims that crisis fostering occurs when a family has collapsed, whereas voluntary or purposive fostering accomplishes a particular purpose: cementing kin ties, giving the child an otherwise unavailable opportunity, adding to a family's resources (1982: 43 and passim. See also Bledsoe 1990). Crisis fostering, she continues, is "functionally specific," and voluntary fostering is "functionally diffuse." Positive emotions and motivations surround the latter, while the former is a pragmatic action taken to rescue a child. Pushing Goody's distinction one step further, one might say that crisis fostering allows no choice, whereas in voluntary fostering individuals choose to create a relationship. The transactions, then, are totally different in spirit.

The distinction makes sense in the West African context of Goody's fieldwork and also mirrors the viewpoint Debra would hear in an American court. In that context, too, crisis fostering was not the same as "caring for" a child. But for Debra there was no distinction, and this was the point she planned to bring before the judge and other experts at the hearing. By framing her plea in the language of *hanai* and *'ohana,* she did more than remind her audience of Hawaiian cultural concepts. She also rejected the categories through which they appropriated the placement of children. Or, to put it another way, Debra was not merely arguing that she was a "fit" parent or her household a secure place; she was demonstrating that her interpretation of fostering a child was divergent from the one promoted by an American legal system.

In a public forum she would present the case that, if superficially similar in that parenthood was redelegated, foster care was fundamentally different for Hawaiians and non-Hawaiians. Moreover, by drawing upon concepts that had accrued significance in a wider struggle for rights and autonomy, Debra was not letting the courtroom forget the complexities of what was really at stake in a debate over child placement. The "stake" was cultural survival.

Debra did not deny that a crisis existed. Precious had been neglected and then "taken away" by CPS workers. She resisted, however, the definitive criteria for crisis that the state required in order to support a judgment for removal. According to Debra's interpretation of Hawaiian ways, fostering a child was not premised on the child's need for shelter, food, or safety, though those factors could affect the timing of the actual transfer of a child from one household to another. Taking in a child or, as Melody had, giving away a child was an act of generosity that reflected a more diffuse recognition of a child's needs than either "crisis fostering" or "purposive fostering" allowed. Drawing on cultural assumptions, Debra constructed a definition of foster care that was both more amorphous and more powerful than the categorical notions upheld by an American legal system. Her task, the day after I saw her, would be to make this discourse dominant at the hearing.

She was walking into an intricate encounter. The contending parties had the same stated interest: the well-being of the child. The social worker was as much concerned about Precious's future as was Debra. That the two sides shared a common goal made it more difficult and more imperative that each establish a claim to the means of achieving that goal. And they had to do this in a setting that, as Sally Merry has pointed out, severely constrains the "performance" of those who appear (Merry 1991). I would argue that in this very setting, somewhat paradoxically, Debra had the advantage. Unlike the social worker defending her action, Debra was not obliged to follow a script or to obey the mandates of a bureaucratic institution. Debra could speak in her own words, argue her own case, and adapt the proceedings to Precious's particular experiences. The social worker could not operate with similar freedom. Her expert testimony was framed by a system in which statutes pay close and scrupulous attention to suspected abuse and neglect and to the ways these are described. The social worker's discourse was effectively limited by the open-ended quality of the legal phrase, "the possibility of threatened or imminent harm."

But that is not the total picture, nor does it predict the end of the story. Debra's hearing itself is not an isolated event; rather, it constitutes a moment in the ongoing transactions between Hawaiian families and an American state. The performance *inside* Family Court reflects and reinforces the inequalities *outside*, in the surrounding society. And perhaps this is no more evident than in the use of language. Debra could argue in her own words—she did not have to have counsel—but she was arguing against a discourse that represented powerful interests in the state. And, as she indicated to me, at bottom the two languages were mutually incomprehensible. Debra anticipated that she would not "get" what the judge was saying and that no one in the court would "really" understand her presentation of Hawaiian customs. In the end, the imbalance and noncomprehensibility mattered more for her than for them.

In the courtroom setting, talk had consequences and the terms of a decision had a direct impact on behaviors. For Debra, losing the battle at the hearing would mean relinquishing Precious to a foster family "different from us" and "on the other side of the island." Given the stakes, Debra made an interesting choice. She could have accepted a court-appointed lawyer and had her case argued in the terms of the "official transcript" (Scott 1990). She refused that option, instead creating a countertranscript in which Hawaiian concepts were the core of the text. Her staunch refusal in the face of the odds made me realize how thoroughly intertwined issues of child placement are with the movement for Hawaiian cultural autonomy and self-determination.

The Politics of Foster Care: A Conclusion

The circumstances Debra confronted, and the way she was confronting them, show that foster care is not "just" a matter of placing children. As both Esther Goody and Caroline Bledsoe have argued, fostering cannot be regarded solely in terms of the micro-movement of children, but must rather be looked at in terms of the (replication and) reproduction of a society and culture. This is especially evident in late twentieth-century Hawai'i, where an increase in the number of fostered Hawaiian children coincides with an increased emphasis on kinship and family as markers of Hawaiian cultural identity.

Rephrasing the argument Debra made to me, the child who is fostered "disappears" to the "other side" not simply in a geographical sense. What Debra meant, it is fair to say, is that the child will vanish in a cultural sense; she will no longer belong to the *'ohana* or—significantly—be a Hawaiian child. The perception that a child can vanish is devastating and ramifying; without children, the survival of the whole social fabric is threatened. If fostering protects the child in the eyes of the state, in the view of Hawaiian people I met, fostering may well "disappear" the child forever.

If where a child lives determines who the child *is*, then control over child placement becomes control over the next generation. True everywhere, in Hawai'i the contest over foster care is intensified by the wording of the child protective statute, in which the investigator is to look for the "possibility of threatened or imminent harm." The phrase allows for myriad interpretations of a family context. At the same time, the phrase reduces foster care to a response to crisis, a description of the arrangement that is antithetical to the concept of *hanai* embraced by Hawaiians like Debra. Regarding foster care as a set of meanings as well as a collection of practices indicates that the experts who regulate child placement in Hawai'i have an enormous power. Not only can they move a child who is by *their definition* at risk, but they can also place her in a household where the notion of fostering, and thus of care, is driven by non-Hawaiian values. Debra feared this outcome along with the disappearance of Precious "somewhere else."

The power of child welfare workers in these circumstances, if not always exercised, is always available—whether during a court hearing or over a hamburger at McDonald's. In effect, in the role of resource gatekeepers, trained experts can deprive people of Hawaiian ancestry of access to one major strategy of social reproduction—the right, or moral, distribution of children.

"The birth of a child," Penn Handwerker begins his book *Births and Power*, is "a political event" (Handwerker 1990: 1). Until recently, discussions of the control of social reproduction have tended to focus on birth—a limited view of "having children"—and, as if a necessary consequence, on women's sexual behavior and fertility patterns. Throughout this paper I have tried to show that foster care is a highly politicized event, one that has ramifications at least equivalent to those of birth. In fact, foster care may have greater political ramifications than the birth of a child, for two reasons. One, foster care occurs in a public arena. For the transfer of a child to be acknowledged, and informally or formally legitimated, others must notice; the transaction needs an audience of more than the immediately involved parties.

A second reason is the never-ending possibility of *re-placing* a child. Let me explain this statement. In virtually every society in which it occurs, foster care has the characteristic of nonclosure. Strictly construed, fostering does not replicate the absolute and enduring commitment of legal (whether biological or not) parenthood. Theoretically, a child can be moved from one foster arrangement to another, re-placed whenever she seems to be in danger. Though this does not, or ideally ought not, happen in practice, temporariness remains a conceptual aspect of foster care. Hypothetically, the gatekeepers could keep managing the resources and thus continually intervene in reproduction broadly defined as the nurturing of a new generation. A reaction to the characteristic of foster care that it can potentially occur at any time has been the move toward permanency in American child placement policy. Instituting foster care as a lasting arrangement, however, has its own complications, as Debra Miller knew. Under such a principle, Precious could become a lifelong member of the household into which she had been placed by a social worker.

My insertion of foster care into a discussion of reproducing reproduction accomplishes three important ends. For one, it forces us to redefine reproduction, so as not simply to equate the word with "having a child," but rather to recognize its meaning as "raising a generation." Second, a

focus on foster care demonstrates how thoroughly politicized *all* reproductive strategies are. Moving a child from one parent to another is necessarily a public act, which in turn points to the political significance of
any "placement" of a child, including by birth. Third, my discussion of
foster care teaches us that reproduction does not belong to one (or two)
individuals, but to households, however constituted. As Debra would
claim at her hearing, who is "fit" to have a child ought not be considered in individualistic terms, but in terms of a wider cultural institution
like the *'ohana*.

Child placement is subject to the hegemonic ideologies and practices
of a state, and Debra feared she did not have the armaments to battle
the dominant perspective on child welfare in the state of Hawai'i. Foster
care is often considered the most benign aspect of family policy by social
workers who see it as helping a child to a better future. Yet, in actual
practice, state-supervised foster care may be the most incendiary aspect
of family policy, with its potential to "blow up" a household by extracting one of its members and keeping her (or his) whereabouts secret. The
composition and the solidarity of a household unit is severely weakened,
if not destroyed, when a child is removed by outsiders who promise no
assurance of a return.

Debra intended to argue on her own that Precious should remain "at
home," cared for by the members of a household. She went to court as
the representative of an *'ohana*, and she meant by the concept not only a
domestic unit but also an ideology of kinship and a symbol of Hawaiian
cultural identity.

The next time I saw Debra, a year and a half later, she had won legal
guardianship of Precious. I heard only her report on the case, and it was
startingly mild. And I took Debra at her word, since that had been the
position she claimed before she went to court and, I assume, that she
argued in court. The language she chose to use, not a court transcript,
carried the burden of the case. By the time Debra told me the final outcome, she had reconceptualized placement in terms of having Precious
at home, to be raised Hawaiian-style.

I did have to think about why Debra was so casual about the case,
after she had so emphasized its implications for Hawaiian cultural integrity in an American state. After considering all the factors, I came
up with several explanations: the obvious rightness for Debra of the decision to place Precious in the *'ohana* where she "naturally" belonged, so
that Debra forgot the struggle for which she had prepared herself in our
earlier conversation; the demands of childrearing, as Debra added Precious to the five children she already had, so that daily toil dominated
her view of household composition; and, saddest of all, the sense that
she had been lucky and that luck did not bear a great deal of analysis or

probing. Saddest, because the contest over foster care goes on, a test of wit and of wealth between Hawaiians and non-Hawaiians in a "modern" world in which reproduction is rarely without ramifications.

Debra had won an elegant victory. She had the child in her *'ohana* and she had argued the case in her own words. In this instance, the court acknowledged her reliability as a parent and, one hopes, trusted her interpretation of the integrity, trust, and love essential to the *'ohana*, as symbol and as structure. Whether Debra's case can set a precedent is another matter entirely. Given the volatile nature of politics in Hawai'i, it is perfectly—and distressingly—possible that under the guise of the child's best interests and the protection of vulnerable members of society, the state will deny the welfare of the Hawaiian people and "disappear" a generation of Hawaiian children. For a moment, I let Debra's story stand instead as a sign of the leverage that can be achieved by bringing *hanai* and the *'ohana* into courtroom settings.

The leverage is limited, a symbolic gesture that only slowly makes its way into the domain of practice. Yet the gesture is not to be discounted. Debra's case serves as a reminder that discrete domestic struggles constitute the resources for larger political arguments about sovereignty, human rights, and justice. Forms of reproduction and distribution of children are the nodes of wider networks of relationship, whose supervision by the state contains the seeds for reconstructing the state. Whether or not Hawaiians are victorious in their demands for recognition of a cultural and a sovereign identity, efforts to reclaim kinship provide a uniquely clear and cogent agenda for an enduring society and "citizenry." In this respect, too, Debra's case teaches a lesson that is applicable beyond Hawai'i: victory at a contested hearth is a crucial step in the battle for a contested homeland.

I would like to express gratitude to a number of people who have helped me with this work. Debra is the first person to be thanked, since without her generosity and constant offers of talk I could not have written this chapter at all. I also thank the many Hawaiian people who shared their views of children, family, and child placement with me, as well as the professionals who took time from incredibly busy days to talk with me, explain the system, and comment on their own experiences. Fellow panelists at the 1994 Annual Meetings of the American Anthropological Association provided good thoughts, and two commentators shed light on arguments I had just begun to formulate. Helena Ragoné and Sarah Franklin have been remarkable throughout, both in organizing the panel and in editing the essay for publication. They deserve special appreciation. The interpretations are my own.

Notes

1. Determining who is "Hawaiian" has not been consistent; different state agencies make the calculation in different ways, and not every agency accepts the Federal Census figures. I depend on self-identification, residence in a Hawaiian Homelands area, and the designation made by Child Protective Services and the Department of Health.

2. My method of doing interviews fits nicely with Hawaiian-style conversation, which generally consists of the casual exchange of narratives that is called "talk story" in the literature; see, for example, Boggs 1985.

3. Informal child exchange, or *hanai*, continues among Hawaiians, a strategy that is adaptive to the stringent circumstances in which many Hawaiian people find themselves; see Modell 1995.

4. The situation reflects both a complicated history of state intervention in Hawaiian family life and the presence of an active family justice system in the state.

5. I put "related" into quotation marks to remind readers that how the word is defined may vary. In the Hawaiian context it is as likely to refer to a fictive as a blood tie.

References

Bledsoe, Caroline. 1990. "The Politics of Children: Fosterage and the Social Management of Fertility Among the Mende of Sierra Leone." In *Births and Power*, ed. W. Penn Handwerker. Boulder, Colo.: Westview Press, pp. 81–100.

Boggs, Stephen. 1985. *Speaking, Relating, and Learning*. Norwood, N.J.: Ablex.

Goody, Esther N. 1982. *Parenthood and Social Reproduction*. New York: Cambridge University Press.

Handwerker, W. Penn, ed. 1990. *Births and Power: Social Change and the Politics of Reproduction*. Boulder, Colo.: Westview Press.

Merry, Sally Engle. 1991. "Courts as Performances." Paper delivered at 1991 Anthropological Association Meetings, San Francisco.

Modell, Judith. 1995. "Nowadays Everyone is Hanai: Child Exchange in the Construction of Hawaiian Urban Culture." *Journal de la Société des Océanistes* (Winter).

Pukui, M. K., E. W. Haertig, and C. A. Lee. 1972. *Nana I Ke Kumu (Look to the Source)*. Honolulu: Queen Lili'uokalani Children's Center.

Scott, James. 1990. *Domination and the Arts of Resistance*. New Haven, Conn.: Yale University Press.

State of Hawai'i. 1986. *Child Protective Services Report*. Honolulu: Department of Social Services and Housing.

———. 1990. *1990 State of the Children*. Honolulu: Office of Children and Youth.

Chapter 8
A Biodiversity Sampler for the Millennium

Corinne P. Hayden

In May 1995, Dr. Raul Cano, a molecular biologist at California Polytechnic State University, claimed to have revived dormant bacteria that had been preserved in amber for thirty million years. Extraordinary as this feat may be, it is also, in some sense, simply a logical extension of Cano's previous work using DNA from extinct species to recreate evolutionary relationships. Rather than merely recreate past relationships, however, he has apparently extended them into the present/future. If confirmed, Cano's findings could, at least according to the *New York Times*, "force scientists to re-examine long-held notions about the temporal limits of life." But, as is increasingly the case in the world of genetic science, the value of this reputed miracle lies not only in its potential for ontological revolution. Cano has founded a biotechnology company—Ambergene Corporation—to develop pharmaceutical products derived from these ancient organisms; he has already applied for patents on three antibiotics derived from his amber-encrusted bacteria (Browne 1995: A1, A9).

This story, replete with the promise of technoscience to redraw the lines between life and extinction, the intertwined projects of the re-creation of the (evolutionary) past and the projection of life into the future, and the inseparability of such genetic manipulations of life from biotechnological fortunes, lends itself to a rich array of possible readings. As an anthropologist with an abiding interest in kinship theory and the thickness of "biology" as a cultural symbol, I am drawn quite readily to the negotiations of generation, reproduction, and kinship that are called up so vividly in Cano's property-infused (re)production of once-defunct natural lineages. It is along these lines that Cano's discovery sets the stage for the concerns addressed in this chapter. My interest here lies not in the fate of thirty-million-year-old bacteria per se, but more generally in the cultural shape of "nature"—and kinship—in particular late–twentieth-century technoscientific efforts to stave off species extinction and reproduce evolutionary lineages. Much like Cano's regenerative feat, 1990s endeavors to save "biological diversity" provide suggestive avenues for a cultural analysis of current, technoscientific negotiations of ideas about genealogy and origins, nature and culture, and reproductive process and kinship, all of which have long been foundational anthropological concerns.

The field of possibilities through which one might concretize these concerns is vast. I offer here a selected set of two examples, placed in productive dialogue with one another. Both were chosen as much for their singularity as for what they might tell us, together, about the status of nature, culture, and kinship in certain domains of scientific discourse and practice. The first of these examples is the Human Genome Diversity Project (HGDP), a proposed international endeavor to collect and catalogue genetic material from "isolated" or "ancient" human populations. Briefly, the goal of the project is to create a database of human genetic diversity before this diversity becomes extinct, to use this information to trace the evolutionary past, and to investigate the mechanisms and histories of disease. I will place the HGDP in conversation with the practice of biodiversity prospecting, exemplified in a 1991 agreement between the transnational pharmaceutical corporation, Merck and Co., and INBio, a nonprofit biodiversity institute in Costa Rica. The agreement marks a key moment in an ostensibly new era of private, contractual approaches to nature conservation that bank on the value of plant and animal species as raw material for the pharmaceutical industry. As a resource that "pays for itself," biodiversity is thus constructed as the instrument of its own salvation.

Both sets of projects are implicated in the production of knowledges and stories about biologized diversity as a rich site of informational, biotechnological, and/or ecological value. And, I would argue, biodiversity itself emerges in these projects as a cultural value, in many ways standing in as the "West"'s emblem of late twentieth-century nature, and, at times, symbolizing culture as well. The thickness, and contradictions, of these notions of diversity—expressed in the recently-coined and now uniquitous term, "biodiversity,"[1] or in the HGDP's construction of human genetic diversity—are themselves central concerns of this chapter. Much like "nature" itself, the potency of the idea of biodiversity is, in large part, manifest in the term's accumulated contradictory and flexible sets of meanings.[2] To paraphrase Paul Steinberg, a colleague working on biodiversity policy at the University of California at Santa Cruz, the term "biodiversity" hardly makes sense; it is everywhere and nowhere at once.[3] In its most general sense, the term can refer to the sum total of "nature." In formulations that strive for a bit more par-ticularity, biodiversity is commonly constructed on a hierarchy of scale encompassing landscapes, ecosystems, populations, species, and genes. In its various and sometimes contradictory guises, biodiversity is an essential resource for biotechnology industries, a source of evolutionary information, an intrinsically and aesthetically important part of nature, an ecological workhorse, and the raw material for natural selection. It is often injected into ideas about human populations and cultures, whether as inextricable from cultural diversity, as a casualty of human population growth, or as shorthand for human genetic diversity (that is, "human biodiversity").[4] It is also a site of contest in struggles over First World exploitation of Third World and indigenous peoples' "biological resources," which increasingly are defined not only as plant, animal, and mineral substance but human tissue, blood, and genetic material as well.

The complexity of the discursive fields inhabited by the idea of bio-logical diversity appears in high relief when the HGDP and biodiver-sity prospecting are placed on an analytical collision course with one another. As I will discuss throughout this essay, there is heavy traffic between these two initiatives. Yet, for many population geneticists con-cerned with human variability, or conservation biologists interested in the domain of nonhuman nature, the two projects would not necessarily make a well-matched set. To place these two sets of interventions in conversation with each other is to foreground and interrogate the pro-duction of certain commensurabilities within and between them. These commensurabilities, between ideas about nature and culture, between the domains of biology and technology, between nature and humans, are my primary objects of inquiry and fascination.

My attention to the production of meaning across domains contrib-utes to the project of analyzing the kinds of cultural production that occur through knowledge practices and representational strategies, or what Marilyn Strathern calls "domaining" (1992a,b; see also Yanagisako and Delaney 1995). For Strathern, cultural meanings are evident in the work of analogies: "You can tell a culture by what it can and cannot bring together" (1992b: 2). Moreover, if "culture consists in established ways of bringing ideas from different domains together," then new com-binations will engender a "ricochet effect, [so] that shifts of empha-sis, dissolutions, and anticipations will bounce off one area of life into another" (1992b: 3).[5]

It is no accident that this attention to ever-regenerating analogies originates in contemporary feminist kinship theory. Kinship has long been ground zero for anthropologists' interrogations of the relationship between nature and culture. From the evolutionary anthropology of L. H. Morgan ([1871] 1970) to Lévi-Strauss's *The Elementary Structures of*

Kinship (1969), many anthropologists have held kinship as the cultural arbiter of "natural," physical relationships, and thus as the threshold domain through which culture and nature become differentiable orders (see Lévi-Strauss 1969: xxix). In the past two decades, many feminist anthropologists, building on Schneider's analysis (1968), have taken up kinship studies as a vehicle for interrogating the taken-for-grantedness of nature and the biological facts of life in European and U.S. American epistemologies. Several recent anthologies, moreover, have made the argument that reproduction and kinship can profitably be placed at the very center of cultural theory and social analysis (see Yanagisako and Delaney 1995; Ginsburg and Rapp 1995). One of the key interventions of this work has been the suggestion that ideas about reproductive process and natural relatedness are implicated in potent ricochets across analytical domains and identity categories—including race, gender, religion, sexuality, and nationalism—and that these ricochets have concrete material effects (Yanagisako and Delaney 1995).[6] Further expanding the field of possible ricochet points, Haraway (1995), Franklin (1995b), and Strathern (1992a,b) have suggested the utility of defining kinship in a broad sense, as a classificatory technology that produces naturalized categories from race, gender, and sexuality to notions of the past and future, individuality and diversity, the "Great Family of Man," and the Linnaean taxonomic tree.

I would suggest that the HGDP and biodiversity prospecting should be considered as part of this expansive field of (re)productive kinship narratives. How do biodiversity initiatives become implicated in renegotiations of reproductive process? The necessary prelude to answering this question is to note the countless ways in which scientific discourses on diversity are quite literally wrapped up in managing reproduction and tracing genealogies (or, in Darwin's term, "communities of descent"). Take, for example, conservation biologists' explicit mission to ensure the continued reproduction of endangered species,[7] not to mention the definition of the "biological species" that came into prominence in the 1940s, which suggested that species are communities of organisms whose members can reproduce viable offspring. Or consider, on a different but related branch of the taxonomic tree, population geneticists' concern with the loss of human genetic diversity through interbreeding. Moreover, one might point to the thick connections between human reproductive management and that practiced on the nonhuman living world. From the nineteenth-century bovine-oriented origins of insemination techniques to current initiatives to freeze the embryos of endangered species (the so-called "frozen zoo" approach to conservation), one can see the heavy traffic of knowledge and technology between the management of nonhuman reproduction and the ever-expanding technoscientific toolbox available for "assisting" human reproduction.[8]

But these examples of the literal convergence of biological diversity and reproduction discourses are symptoms of, and not explanations for, the kinds of intersections that interest me in this essay. A broader argument can be made that, from the late nineteenth century on, biologized European and U.S. understandings of human kinship and reproduction have shared discursive parentage with Darwinian notions of the genealogical unity and diversity of all forms of life, and with a particular conception of the nature of the natural world. Strathern has suggested that the very separation of natural facts and social facts that has so dominated anthropological discussions of kinship had its origins in a potent series of late nineteenth-century borrowings between the not-yet-biologized domain of human kinship and ideas about the natural world. Nicely complementing Foucault's account of the nineteenth-century emergence of the autonomous, biologized realm of "life" (1990), Strathern locates the genesis of the ostensibly separate domains of (biologized) nature and (artifactual) culture at a moment when Darwin borrowed familiar, decidedly nonbiological metaphors for human kinship to help make sense of his quite radical claim that all forms of life are united by a common, descent-based connection. While the idea of descent was already available to Darwin, its usual sense in nineteenth-century England was as pedigree, a class-imbued narrative that established claims to property and social rank. Thickening the borrowings at work here, the notion of pedigree also deeply infused animal breeders' work, which Darwin used extensively in constructing his theory of natural selection ([1859] 1936).

Yet "genealogy" itself was not seen as a natural artifact; rather, it signalled a means of establishing lines of succession, based very much on the Biblical notion of the genealogical tree (see Bouquet 1994; Franklin 1995b). Making use of this already well-used notion of pedigree or the family tree, Darwin expanded and shifted the range of the metaphor, posing genealogy itself as a materialized narrative, an autonomous fact, "an underlying logic," that can explain both the unity and diversity of all forms of life. Since "all true classification [is] genealogical," he wrote ([1859] 1936: 323), "the innumerable species, genera and families with which this world is peopled, are all descended . . . from common parents, and have all been modified in the course of descent" ([1859] 1936: 352). His injection of these human kinship metaphors into the natural world also naturalized, and indeed *biologized*, human kinship. If biological facts became an autonomous domain, in this epistemological "moment," then too social facts became intelligible as precisely that domain of culture that was not natural (Strathern 1992b: 16), and kinship (or "reproduction") could be seen as the hybrid zone bridging these autonomous domains.

Much current anthropological work on (human) reproductive technologies focuses on the ways in which people continually negotiate these supposedly autonomous domains of social facts and natural facts, bouncing them off one another, denaturalizing once taken-for-granted natural elements of reproduction (such as the link between gestational and genetic motherhood), and renaturalizing them through conventional kinship idioms; or, conversely, naturalizing ostensibly "social" facts.[9] It is precisely these malleable lines and regenerative analogies between nature and culture that are at stake in the HGDP and the Merck/INBio prospecting agreement's particular brands of reproductive management. Here, we see practices rife with ricocheting (re)definitions of instrumentalized nature and naturalized culture, mediated by the now-familiar but hardly stable idioms of cross-species kinship, pan-human consanguinity, and the importance of diversity to the reproductive future of life itself. These projects are thus implicated in negotiations of peculiarly biologized versions of the nature-culture split, which, in turn, are inextricably intertwined with the discursive field in which "reproductive process" can sensibly unfold.

The next two sections of the paper offer provisional accounts of the HGDP and biodiversity prospecting. These accounts have been framed with an eye toward the kinds of knowledges and stories produced in and about the two projects, and towards the institutional and technological conditions of their possibility. In the third section, I address the negotiations of nature, property, and innovation that circulate around, and in many ways link, these two projects. Throughout, my attention will be focused on the conjunctures, analogies, and commensurabilities identifiable across these peculiarly late–twentieth-century constructions of the value of biological diversity.

Genealogy and Culture: Sampling the World, Part I

Our genetic differences are at the heart of our evolution as a species. One of the most fascinating paradoxes of the human condition is that *we are all different, yet we are all the same* (King 1993a: 36, original emphasis).

Thus notes Mary-Claire King, University of California at Berkeley geneticist and a founding proponent of the Human Genome Diversity Project. The HGDP was instigated in 1991 by researchers interested in the science of human genetic variation, including King, Stanford University population geneticist Luca Cavalli-Sforza, and the late University of California, Berkeley evolutionary biologist Allan Wilson. The project is, on one level, an attempt to broaden the vision of the human gene pool that undergirds the Human Genome Project (HGP), a $3 billion international effort to create a single reference map of the genetic code of "the" human species. Arguing that there is no such thing as *the* human genome, HGDP proponents have asserted that the HGDP is a necessary complement to the much larger, well-underway, and well-funded HGP. A statement issued by the North American Committee of the HGDP reads, in part:

Without this Project, science will largely define "the" human genome, with its historical and medical implications, as that carried by a small number of individuals of European ancestry. . . . At a time when we are increasingly concerned with preserving information about the diversity of the many species with which we share the Earth, surely we cannot ignore the diversity of our own species (Human Genome Diversity Project 1994: 3).

HGDP proponents thus envision a constructive, complementary relationship with the HGP. Noting that one of the goals of the HGP is to create the "biological tools that will permit access to any region of a human genome," Cavalli-Sforza and colleagues have argued that one of the more important applications for such a toolkit is, indeed, the investigation of human genetic diversity (1991: 490).

In a 1991 "Call for a Worldwide Survey of Human Genetic Diversity," Cavalli-Sforza and colleagues argue that diverse genomes, located in the bodies of isolated peoples, are invaluable and endangered resources of information about the common human evolutionary past (1991: 490–91). The HGDP goals are to collect DNA samples from individuals in indigenous populations (with priority going to those most endangered), to immortalize cell lines when possible (and thereby provide an endless supply of sampled genetic material), and to analyze the samples for evidence of migration history, mechanisms of mutation, and variation. HGDP proponents are also interested in the medical importance of genetic variation. Pointing to the centrality of studying African "ancestral populations" in past research on sickle-cell anemia among modern African-Americans, King has argued that the HGDP may well enable similar breakthroughs in understanding the genetic mechanisms at work in susceptibility to breast cancer, high blood pressure, and other diseases (1993: 36–37). Medically and historically useful DNA samples (from blood, hair, and cheek tissue) have been or will be collected in collaboration with cultural anthropologists familiar with the "targeted" groups. The samples will be stored in the American Type Culture Collection in Rockville, MD, used for medical research, and entered into a systematic and comprehensive database of human genetic variation.

The HGDP's attention to difference, and the particular form that this difference takes, functions simultaneously as its key to legitimation and a lightning rod for critique from several points of view. Most notably, HGDP proponents' construction of the salient unit of analysis—the isolated, endangered population, or ethnic group—is caught up in a geneticization of (endangered) cultural identity that serves as both a strategic appeal to urgency and a scientific and political Achilles' heel. In the rhetoric of project proponents, the threat of endangered cultural diversity and the logic of evolutionary population genetics intersect to make sense of the claim that the DNA of indigenous groups should be sampled before the "information" contained therein is lost. Cavalli-Sforza and colleagues note:

Isolated human populations contain much more informative genetic records than more recent, urban ones. Such isolated human populations are being rapidly merged with their neighbors, however, destroying irrevocably the information needed to reconstruct our evolutionary history. Population growth, famine, war, and improvements in transportation and communication are encroaching on once stable populations. It would be tragically ironic if, during the same decade that biological tools for understanding our species were created, major opportunities for applying them were squandered (1991: 490).

In this genealogical construction of history, population isolation presupposes endogamy, or, reproductive isolation, and thus the preservation of a pure gene pool. It is specifically as repositories of unmixed DNA that isolated groups become marked as "ancient," or "ancestral" populations (see King 1993b). By identifying the frequencies of certain genes in these populations and comparing them to other populations, HGDP scientists (and population geneticists in general) aim to better "root" the human family tree and trace patterns of human migration.[10]

The HGDP's location of meaningful information about the past in isolated human populations, or cultures, cannot help but recall (among other things) the cultural evolutionism of anthropologists such as L. H. Morgan, for whom so-called "primitive" cultures were invaluable repositories of information about the origins of, and historical relationship among, the different "races of mankind" (Morgan [1871] 1970). Of course, the HGDP is trafficking in gene frequencies and not cultural survivals, and its proponents are invested in creating the most inclusive picture of human genetic variability possible, and not a hiearchy of cultures, or races, along a civilization-barbarism continuum. Nonetheless, the HGDP's interest in a matrix of endangered genetic/cultural isolation inescapably breathes (yet more) life into the multipurpose, recurring image of the disappearing primitive—an image that is mobilized to strategic effect in many representations of the project.[11]

Indeed, at the level of definitions of "disappearance," cultural and genetic diversity work in quite similar ways. Much as the loss of cultural diversity is often registered in terms of literal extinction or homogenization (i.e., the loss of uniqueness), so too is the loss of genetic diversity expressed either as literal extinction or as the sullying of an ostensibly pure gene pool through "interbreeding." As an HGDP study group notes:

Of the roughly 5000 languages in the world, 90% are expected to be lost or doomed to extinction by the twenty-first century. Genetically distinct populations could disappear with them, some by physical extinction *but most by admixture with other groups.* (cited in Gillis 1994: 8, emphasis added)

If the privileging of genetic distinctiveness makes for a somewhat unnerving notion of disappearance here (death by reproduction?), this discursive turn is also taken one metonymic step further, so that *humans in general* become "an endangered species in terms of genetic diversity" (Cavalli-Sforza in Roberts 1991: 1614). If nothing else, this strategic turn of phrase marks the ways in which interventions to preserve genetic diversity are narrated as matters of direct importance to all of humanity. Cavalli-Sforza's statement might be read as both a literal affirmation of the Darwinian idea that genetic diversity is necessary for the survival of any given species, and a modernist, humanist nod to the place of linguistic, genetic, and cultural diversity in the cumulative "heritage" of humankind (see Cavalli-Sforza et al. 1991: 490).

Either way, such universalizing notions of the evolutionary/historical importance of diversity do not go uncontested. A particularly scathing critique has been leveled at the project's preservationist imperative, which, according to one writer, is seen to proceed at the expense of attention to the lives of its "targeted" subjects. In the *Abya Yala News,* Daniela Spiwak writes,

. . . the money could be spent on helping the groups that are facing 'extinction' to overcome the various forces that have placed them in this critical predicament so that they can lead healthy, productive, and self-directed lives now, rather than being recreated and 'immortalized' in laboratories for future science projects. (1993: 13)

The insensitivity gauged in such preservation talk is seen to be mirrored in the terminology used in an HGDP draft report, in which targeted groups (another phrase that often draws fire) are referred to as "Isolates of Historical Interest." (Ironically, the term was chosen precisely to get around the delicate issue of marking groups by their ostensible, impending "extinction.")[12]

This question of the definition of the HGDP's unit of analysis (and the terminology used to describe it) is fraught in more ways than one. The proposed project is rife with contradictions on the question of genetic purity; whether identified as a population, indigenous group, ethnic group, culture, or isolate of historic interest, the target of intervention is marked in most discussions as genetically isolated or genetically distinct. For many people, such a designation calls up all too clearly the scientific reifications of genetic/group identity that have undergirded, among other things, the eugenics campaigns mobilized in the early half of the twentieth century in the United States and in Nazi Germany. Pointing to the HGDP's apparent tendency to conflate cultural, ethnic, and genetic identity, one physical anthropologist and critic has argued that the project is "twenty-first-century technology applied to nineteenth-century biology" (Swedlund in Lewin 1993: 25[13]). Leaders of the European contingent of the project, particularly wary of the ways in which the term "diversity" might suggest a preoccupation with the biological foundations of "race," tend to use "genetic variability" instead (Lewin 1993: 29). And, calling up a differently materialized notion of the danger of geneticizing group identity, some critics have posed the possibility of ethnic-group-based biological warfare, given the availability of information about targeted groups' "genetic makeup" (see Spiwak 1993).

In response to such critiques and anxieties, many participating scientists have argued that, in fact, population genetics has consistently shown that genetic variation is greater within groups than between them, and thus that the data gathered under the auspices of the HGDP will debunk racism rather than fuel it (see King 1993a; Human Genome Diversity Project, North American Committee 1994). Anthropologist Ken Weiss ardently defends Cavalli-Sforza on this front: "No one has done more than Cavalli-Sforza to reveal that genetic variation between groups is continuous, not discrete. This has undermined typological thinking, not supported it" (in Lewin 1993: 29). There is an insistent tension here between population geneticists' desire to locate missing links in the human species genomic database by sampling the DNA of genetically isolated peoples and their argument that groups are not, in fact, defined genetically.

Interestingly, there was some question early in the genesis of the HGDP about sampling strategy that, had it been resolved otherwise, might have made this question, and the project, look quite different. At a meeting held at Stanford University early in the project's planning stages, Luca Cavalli-Sforza argued for sampling "aboriginal populations" that were both isolated and linguistically discrete. Evolutionary biologist Allan Wilson and several colleagues, on the other hand, argued for a geographic grid strategy, sampling individuals every 50 or 100 miles. Effectively eschewing Cavalli-Sforza's notion of what constitutes an ethnic group, Wilson argued that participating scientists should "abandon previous concepts of what populations are and go by geography" (in Roberts 1991: 1615). The Stanford workshop ended with a rather uneven compromise, in which participants agreed that the population-based approach would prevail, though sampling would be done "between ethnic groups, wherever feasible" (Lewin 1993: 28). The designation of "populations" as the salient unit of analysis was thus not self-evident in the design of the HGDP sampling strategy, nor, by implication, was the location of meaningful genetic difference at the level of the cultural/ethnic/indigenous group.

Shaky as its start may have been within the HGDP, and contested as it may be within certain communities, the notion of the "genetically distinct population" nonetheless carries a great deal of weight in remarkably malleable ways. As noted above, it shows up in the ways in which the project's goals are pitched to European and U.S. audiences presumably sympathetic to the value of preserving endangered cultural/genetic diversity. But this expansive genetic reductionism is also taken up by indigenous/ist organizations, for whom the problem with the HGDP is not necessarily its geneticization of cultural identity, but rather its piracy of the very essence of indigenous groups' (genetic) distinctiveness. As I will discuss below, several recent property disputes over the ownership of "indigenous" cell lines illustrate the multidirectional potency of such reductionist narratives.

Whether banking on the informational, evolutionary, or medical value of diversity, King's claim that "we are all different, yet we are all the same" comes irrevocably attached to an interventionist mandate— assertions of "common genetic heritage" are both statements of evolutionary fact and claims to right of access to genetic material. And, as Haraway has noted on the subject, "sampling blood is never an innocent symbolic act" (1995: 31). Opposition to the project has in large part revolved around claims that the project is yet another instance of the piracy of Third World and indigenous peoples' resources on the part of profiteering First World scientists and industry; Latin American indigenous activists have termed the HGDP "the Vampire Project" (Krasny 1995). The recent transformation of human DNA into "the raw material for the next wave of therapeutic discoveries" (Carey et al. 1995: 72) has added fuel to such fears about the material implications for indigenous people targeted by the HGDP. Indeed, in 1993 the U.S. government filed a patent application on the immortalized cell line of a twenty-six-year-old Guaymi woman with leukemia. This particular research was not connected to the HGDP, and Henry Greely, head of the HGDP's North American ethics committee, maintains that the project will not in any way profit from collected material.[14] Yet such assurances have not quelled allegations that the HGDP is simply a "human" version of longstanding plant genetic exploitation (Rural Advancement Foundation International 1993; Spiwak 1993).

Enriching the viscosity of this accusatory analogy between different domains of biological resources, Isidro Acosta, lawyer and president of the Guaymi General Congress, flew to Geneva to protest the Guaymi claim under the terms of the United Nations Convention on Biological Diversity (CBD), which was drafted to protect flora and fauna. In the absence of established international mechanisms for regulating the flow of human DNA (the GATT does not offer definitive guidelines for this particular resource either), the CBD looked like the best option. The patent claim was subsequently dropped, although the cell line remains on deposit in the American Type Culture Collection, outside of Washington, D.C. Acosta and others continue to fight for its "repatriation" to the Guaymi people (Rural Advancement Foundation International 1993; *geneWATCH* 1994: 6–7).

The strategic appeal to the CBD is a complicated maneuver that in many ways reifies rather than contests the construction of human DNA as a biological resource. The language of repatriation fits in nicely with this reification, here calling upon the idea of DNA as a form of cultural property. In the particular brand of possessive individualism (mutated into "possessive collectivism") that informs UNESCO's definition of cultural property, material objects (such as religious and artistic artifacts) become a "basic element of a people's identity" (Coombe 1993: 264).[15] This formulation seems to lend itself particularly well to genetic material and anxieties about its piracy. The Rural Advancement Foundation International (RAFI), known for its vocal opposition to the HGDP and biodiversity prospecting, certainly banks on these connections in publishing the statement of a member of the Central Australian Aboriginal Congress. Referring to two U.S. patent applications on cell lines from individuals from the Solomon Islands and Papua New Guinea, RAFI quotes John Liddle as saying, "Over the last 200 years, non-Aboriginal people have taken our land, language, culture, health—even our children. Now they want to take the genetic material which makes us Aboriginal people as well" (Rural Advancement Foundation International 1994: 9). When applied to human DNA, the language of repatriation and allegations of the theft of material that "makes us what we are" constitute a vividly literal example—and extension—of UN-mediated discourses on the convergence of property and identity (see Coombe 1993: 263–65). Alongside the DNA fingerprint and some geneticists' claims of the vast importance residing in "our common genetic heritage," this geneticized nod to the idea of cultural property suggests one more possible expression of the literalizing power of the "gene" as the ultimate mark of identity.

Geneticizing the discourse of cultural property is clearly a strategic move, as was the deployment of the CBD to contest a patent claim on human genetic material. Yet this strategic analogy can also become a matter of biotechnology-mediated "truth"; genetic material is increasingly instrumentalized as the informational raw material for pharmaceutical development. As will become clear in the following section, this construction of biological resources sometimes engenders quite a different spin on the relationship between genes and identity than that implied in discourses revolving around genetic/cultural distinctiveness and cultural property. In the expansive field of meanings attributed to DNA, genetic material can easily lose its species- and culture-specific associations in its transformation into valuable commodities.

Biodiversity Prospecting: Sampling the World, Part II

The accusation that the HGDP is simply an extension of well-established histories of genetic exploitation is a reference to what some commentators have called the "seed wars," or botanical imperialism—the extraction of the non-Western world's plant resources that has been an inextricable element of European colonial expansion since at least the sixteenth century.[16] Several historians of colonialism and science have pointed to the particular centrality of colonial botanical gardens—as centers of accumulation and points of transfer for exotic(ized) tropical plants and botanical knowledge—to the development of Western medicine and agriculture.[17] The mid- to late twentieth-century version of such genetic colonialism has been perhaps most visible in the transnational (but largely United States-, Japanese-, and European-based) pharmaceutical and agricultural industries, in which plant germplasm has been extracted from the gene-rich regions of the Third World, stored in First World seed banks (in the case of agriculture), and used as the raw material for high-stakes biotechnological enhancement, mass production, and profitable consumption.

One of the key issues in this long history of collecting, classifying, extracting, improving, and commodifying plant material is the Enlightenment construction of intellectual property that has mediated these rather unequal exchanges. Natural genetic material has long been constructed, in international law and in industrial practices, as an ownerless good, or part of the international commons, unless and until subjected to technoscientific manipulation or modification, at which point it becomes thinkable as private property. This construction of property

is very much based on Locke's masculinist notion of possessive individualism that assumes an intrinsic relationship among the individual,
(his) creative labor—which Delaney and Rose have both tied to notions
of paternity and authorship—and the property created by mixing this
potent labor with forms of nature.[18] One of the oft-cited stumbling
blocks to creating effective regulatory mechanisms for granting nations
and indigenous peoples' rights in their biological resources, and therefore asserting that they should at least be compensated for the extraction and use of these resources, has been the inadequacy of this notion
of "property in the self" for granting *collective* rights over so-called "un-
improved" or "wild" forms of nature (see Greaves 1994; Brush 1993).

The idea of biodiversity (or chemical) "prospecting,"[19] largely attributed to Cornell entomologist Thomas Eisner, is an approach to international conservation that stems directly from these kinds of property
dilemmas. In the late 1980s, Eisner began promoting prospecting as
a means for ensuring conservation by transforming biological diversity into a sustainable resource that can pay for itself, thus providing
"gene-rich" but financially poor countries with an incentive to conserve
the biological resources that fall within their boundaries. Prospecting
involves screening natural organisms for useful chemical compounds
and then isolating and characterizing those compounds for analysis
and possible development into marketable drugs. This particular kind
of resource extraction is described as relatively low-impact, insofar as
it involves the small-scale collection of specimens and then synthetic
production of promising compounds rather than wholesale harvest
of "source organisms" (Eisner 1989–1990: 33). Large-scale taxonomic
projects are seen as the necessary foundation for biodiversity prospecting. As University of Pennsylvania-trained biologist and prospecting proponent Daniel Janzen notes, "You've got to know what is in your green-
house if you put it up for sale" (quoted in Roberts 1992: 1142).

Current rapid rates of species extinction (often cited as four thousand
per year, conservatively), coupled with the argument that one out of four
prescription drugs is derived from plants, together provide a calculus
of endangerment and value that Eisner and others frequently mobilize
in their advocacy of prospecting (see Eisner and Beiring 1994: 95–97).
The gravity of potential loss—not only of biodiversity for biodiversity's
sake, but of a resource of immense medical value to "all of humanity"—
is magnified by the fact that standard intellectual property protection is
not available for biological diversity in the wild, and, therefore, nations
have little economic incentive to protect the land that houses these so-
called genetic resources. The solution, Eisner and others have argued,
is to promote private, contractual agreements whereby pharmaceutical
companies and other interested parties (such as the U.S. National Can-

cer Institute) will purchase continued access to biological material and thus share the cost of its upkeep and contribute to its continued survival.

In 1991, the same year that marked the genesis of the HGDP, Eisner helped mediate a now famous prospecting agreement between the pharmaceutical giant, Merck and Co., and INBio, a private, nonprofit Costa Rican biodiversity institute. In the agreement, Merck agreed to pay a $1 million collector's fee for access to plant and insect type specimens collected and identified by INBio staff and by local people trained as "parataxonomists." In return, INBio will receive between 3 and 5 percent of Merck's royalties should any profitable, patentable drugs result from specimens found in Costa Rica. In addition to generating funds for conservation in Costa Rica, the agreement is intended to help build an economic sector and technological infrastructure through which Costa Ricans can increase their "bioliteracy" and become skilled in taxonomy and natural products screening.

For some people, perhaps most vocally Rodrigio Gámez, director of INBio, the Merck/INBio contract constitutes a reassertion of Costa Rican national sovereignty and a reversal of the history of biopiracy that has long marked such transnational traffic in genetic material. Yet critics within Costa Rica and in North America argue that, as a private institute, INBio has itself pirated Costa Rican "national biological patrimony." Others have argued that the agreement elides the stewardship of Costa Rica's indigenous peoples over the resources in question.

The question of the place of indigenous people in the Merck/INBio agreement is in many ways wrapped up in conflicting prospecting methodologies. INBio, following Eisner's preferred route, relies primarily on what has been termed an "ecorationalist" method of drug discovery, in which natural kinship/taxonomic categories provide the clues about what types of specimens might contain useful compounds. (Thus, for example, if a certain species is a known source of a particular enzyme, then others closely related to it are likely to produce similar chemical compounds). In contrast, many ethnobotanists (several of whom have been critical of the Merck agreement) and others interested in natural-products chemistry promote the use of "indigenous knowledge" of species as a more efficient avenue for the discovery of useful compounds.[20] "Traditional" knowledge or information, understood as a cultural resource, thus becomes part of the pool of resources to be mined, conserved, and paid for. As one ethnobotanist has noted, "The knowledge of medicinal plants preserved by indigenous specialists is priceless information. As with genetic diversity, once lost, it cannot be recovered" (Elisabetsky 1991: 10). Yet, as with the controversy around INBio's "appropriation" of national resources, the designation of indigenous knowledge as a good to be conserved and as a remunerable resource raises equally problematic notions of (cultural) sovereignty, group identity, and legitimate claims to stewardship of resources (see Brush 1993; Greaves 1994; Escobar 1994a).

The Merck/INBio agreement—and attendant controversies over the legitimate stewardship of biological resources—is only one instance of the many prospecting agreements that have proliferated in the 1990s.[21] The 1992 CBD, to which Isidro Acosta appealed to contest the U.S. patent claim on a Guaymi woman's cell line, has been a crucial engine in the spawning of such agreements. In many ways, the Convention might be seen as a mandate to create prospecting collaborations, insofar as it asserts the necessity of biodiversity conservation, recognizes states' sovereignty over their biological resources, promotes sustainable development of genetic resources, and requires the judicious distribution of resulting benefits (Gollin 1993: 290).[22]

The 1992 Convention, with its emphasis on the fusion of conservation and economic development, is also part of a trend within influential international conservation circles in which development-oriented conservation has become a relatively mainstream battle cry. Since 1980, three key texts have been published under the auspices of several United Nations organizations, including the United Nations Environmental Program and the Food and Agriculture Organization, in collaboration with several nongovernmental organizations, such as the International Union for Conservation (IUCN) and the World Resources Institute (WRI). These three texts, *World Conservation Strategy* (1980), *Conserving the World's Biological Diversity* (1990), and *Global Biodiversity Strategy* (1992), together constitute a series of policy statements and consensus-building works that fuse an economic-development paradigm with conservationism.[23]

Nicely complementing this de facto trilogy is a work devoted entirely to prospecting, published in 1993 by the WRI in collaboration with INBio, the Rainforest Alliance, and the African Centre for Technology Studies. The volume, entitled *Biodiversity Prospecting: Using Genetic Resources for Sustainable Development*, is billed as a contribution to the 1992 *Global Biodiversity Strategy*. Designed to help fill the "policy vacuum" around the new twin mandates of compensation and conservation, the collection tackles many of the practical, policy, and property issues that arise in establishing prospecting agreements. The authors, who include Rodrigio Gámez, director of INBio, and Walter Reid, president of WRI, provide an in-depth discussion of the history and goals of INBio and its agreement with Merck, an exploration of a variety of legal mechanisms for ensuring proper compensation to genetic source countries, lists of pharmaceutical companies that currently screen natural products collected from "tropical" countries, and a detailed argument for the importance of stepped-up taxonomic enterprises in conservation activities. The appendix includes a sample prospecting contract and an analysis of, and excerpts from, the CBD.

If the Merck/INBio agreement is embedded in this particular international network of development-minded conservationism, it is also part of a larger narrative of the pharmaceutical industry's "return to nature." Merck was, as one story goes, among the few pharmaceutical companies to continue using natural sources (such as plants and microbes) in its drug development process even in the midst of the biotechnology revolution that swept the industry in the 1960s and 1970s (Roberts 1992; Joyce 1991 and 1992). In that period, new molecular understandings of disease and the ability to synthesize chemical compounds of pharmaceutical promise changed the focus of drug research from "ecorationalism," or following "nature's lead," to the complete synthesis of chemical compounds in laboratories. Yet the biotechnological techniques that seemingly made natural-products screening irrelevant have apparently contributed to its resurgence. In particular, new bioassays allow researchers to screen hundreds of plant extracts at a time. Meanwhile, natural chemist Charles McChesney notes that synthetic chemists have already "made the easy molecules"; they must now synthesize and investigate between five and ten thousand chemicals to get one new drug lead. Companies are thus "increasingly inclined to let plants and other organisms do the synthetic work" (in Joyce 1991: 39). Prospecting agreements have become one avenue for collecting the source material that gives biochemists a jump start in manufacturing pharmaceutical products.

This shift towards a particular brand of enterprised-up conservation practice raises important questions about the kinds of nature being produced, conserved, and consumed through prospecting agreements and the technologies that are built into them. The construction of biodiversity as a resource to be mined for its pharmaceutical value suggests noteworthy parallels to the ways in which human genetic diversity is being conceived of, in the shadows and the center of the HGDP. In the discursive practices of biodiversity prospectors and the HGDP's population geneticists and anthropologists, the endangerment of "diversity" is, in many ways, an information management problem. To quote Haraway, the loss of human genetic diversity signals a "biodiversity information loss in the lifeworld of the genome. Like the vanishing of a rainforest fungus or fern before pharmaceutical companies could survey the species for promising drugs, the vanishing of human gene pools is a blow to technoscience" (1995: 27). Indeed, those making a claim to the importance of prospecting often enlist biologist E. O. Wilson's estimate that, while the earth contains between five and thirty million species, less than 1.4 million of those species have been "scientifically described" (Eisner and Beiring 1994: 95; Blum 1993: 17). The impending depletion of species is magnified by the ironic sense that science has yet to capture or know what, precisely, is about to be lost.

Biodiversity prospectors such as Thomas Eisner attempt to ward off this impending blow to technoscience by constituting the endangerment of (biological) species as a taxonomic call to arms.[24] Fittingly, INBio's first claim to fame was not its Merck agreement, but its bid to establish a fully computerized, complete inventory of Costa Rica's biologically diverse resources (Tangley 1990: 633). Taxonomic knowledge and information retrieval are key to the success of biodiversity prospecting, insofar as the only valuable storehouse of biological resources is a properly inventoried one. In fact, prospecting is often constructed as a form of (instrumentalized) taxonomy itself, insofar as it generates an inventory of species marked by their useful properties.

In quite a literal sense, then, scientific knowledge here takes on the promise of forestalling extinction.[24] In the HGDP, this promise is fulfilled by translating cultural/genetic diversity into an informational code that can—and therefore must—be preserved in a database. For biodiversity prospectors, scientific knowledge of species diversity is the foundational step towards putting off the finality of extinction, precisely because classification will make a nation's plants and animals more accessible to researchers and thus more appealing as an investment. This unabashedly instrumentalized construction of the value of biodiversity does not sit well with all researchers interested in the science of diversity. According to Rodrigio Gámez, the commodification of classificatory knowledge has met with some resistance in Costa Rica: "The people we dealt with, like the national museum, were horrified at the idea of chemical prospecting . . . their interest was purely in taxonomy" (quoted in Joyce 1991: 38).

Of course, as noted above, scientific efforts to collect and classify species have never been innocent of property relations. But the form in which taxonomy meets commodity takes on a suggestive, late twentieth-century cast in the methods for collecting, granting access to, and enforcing compensation for natural species in biodiversity prospecting. In what has become relatively standard prospecting practice, researchers often bar code the material extracted from collected specimens before sending it off to be screened by pharmaceutical companies. The goal is to conceal the identity of the organism, so that pharmaceutical companies cannot collect samples on their own in order to bypass the collecting parties with whom they are collaborating. INBio's much-maligned effort to register its name as a trademark was a bid to take this protective move one step further, making its collected specimens property of INBio™ (Kloppenburg 1992).

Such property-mediated transformations in forms of nature—from "wild" organisms, to collected specimens, to chemical extracts, to bar-coded and possibly tradmarked substances, to mass-produced pharmaceutical products (and then back again to funds for conservation?)—constitute a suggestive example of what Haraway has called a shift from "kind" to "brand" within contemporary, technoscientific notions of nature and capital (Haraway 1995: 13). The idea that biological entities (kinds) have themselves become imaginable as forms of intellectual property (such as the trademark, brand, or patent) is graphically literalized in the philosophy of biodiversity prospecting—"classify it so you can sell it"—and the taxonomizing, bar-coding labors that mediate this exchange. Moreover, what is being "sold" here is not only the chemical extract from the natural specimen itself, but a kind of intellectual labor that becomes inextricably intertwined with the (value of the) substance itself. According to Rodrigio Gámez of INBio, the collecting and classifying services of Costa Ricans "add value to the *products*" made available to Merck and other contracting organizations (in Joyce 1992: 400, emphasis added).[26]

This implosion of natural kind and commercial brand provides a fruitful opening through which to reinject the HGDP into this conversation. Like biodiversity prospecting, the HGDP is deeply caught up in the convergence of intersecting claims to property and taxonomic relatedness. As I argued above, the HGDP is undergirded by an evolutionary understanding of natural kinship categories (that is, the human family, mediated by genealogical connectedness), in which the DNA of isolated (ancient) populations provides the historical clues to modern mysteries, from human migration patterns and phylogenetic branching points to disease susceptibility. As both a taxonomic exercise (building a better human family tree) and a project with tangible medical benefits, the HGDP reinvigorates the evolutionary, genealogical metaphor of a germinal relationship between aspects of "ancient societies" and "our own." Through the impetus and ability to collect, immortalize, catalogue, and commodify the so-called essence of temporal kinship connectedness, the familiar trope takes on a new, literalized twist.

This materialization of the evolutionary narrative cannot be separated from recent developments in genetic technologies that make human genes, ancient or not, into objects of immense biotechnological value. Patent applications on human genes and gene fragments have become extraordinarily ordinary in the last five years or so. These property claims in one way are inseparable from the proliferation of genetic code that has been generated as part of, and in tandem with, the Human Genome Project (HGP), and from the increasing facility with which such information can be mined for pharmaceutical value. Automated gene-sequencing machines are in large part responsible for the proliferation of the genetic information that is available to be mined. First developed by University of Washington molecular biologist Leroy Hood in 1986, and later put to service in laboratories across the world participating in the HGP, these sequencing machines are able to perform the tedious task of "reading" the order of genetic information contained in strands of DNA. In the context of the HGP, this information (available to interested researchers over the Internet) becomes the foundation for the much-hailed "library" of the genetic makeup of the human species being.

Among other uses of this rapidly generated, sequenced and databased information, it can be compared with similar genes—in other species— whose function is known, to discern whether the new sequence is part of a gene that might "do" something marketable. (The gene may create a protein that combats anemia, or perhaps marks a predisposition to a certain kind of cancer). The potential value of this information has sparked a flurry of patent claims through which laboratories or scientists responsible for generating the information attempt to corner commercial rights on any product later derived from these particular sequences (see Carey et al. 1995). While sequenced information, without knowledge of its function, has yet to be granted the status of legitimate property by the U.S. Patent and Trademark Office, "useful" proteins or genes that create them *have* been designated as patentable inventions.

If, in the mode of cultural analysis at work in this chapter, meanings are constructed in part by the process of bringing different domains together, then the patenting of human gene sequences and pharmaceutical products made from the extracts of plants and insects suggests particularly rich fields of intersection. The construction of these forms of "life"—always a volatile category—as patentable property is part of a rich history of negotiation within U.S. patent law itself around the nature of nature (as raw material and/or patentable invention), on the one hand, and of human innovation, on the other hand. In the next section, I want to trace, in preliminary but I hope suggestive fashion, some of the negotiations through which genes and living organisms have recently become constituted as patentable property. These negotiations within patent law have everything to do with the always messy boundary between nature and culture: I want to suggest that they are themselves domaining activities, inasmuch as they are materially implicated in the creation and legitimation of new forms of property and new permutations of the analogies through which certain forms of nature and culture become mutually intelligible.

Patently Natural

The patent was codified in the U.S. Constitution as a temporary monopoly granted to a person for his or her invention in exchange for public disclosure of the invention. As articulated by founding father (and ardent seed collector) Thomas Jefferson, patent law is a quintessentially modern, market-driven engine of knowledge production, fueled by the generative tension between private reward and public knowledge/benefit. Ideas and inventions become available for public consumption faster if inventors are rewarded with temporary commercial rights (or monopolies) in those ideas, and without the promise of financial reward through rights in property, capital investment in innovation would be harder to attract, to the serious detriment of Progress (Chon 1993).

The key criteria for issuing a patent—novelty, nonobviousness, and utility—clearly institutionalize this commitment to innovation. Based in Locke's Enlightenment notions of property in the self and a specifically gendered configuration of authorship and creativity, the kind of innovation rewarded by a patent is figured as the mixing of [man]'s labor with something taken out of the state of nature (Rose 1993: 114; Rose 1995). This world-building, gendered distinction between nature and innovation receives a formal boost through the "products of nature" doctrine, which excludes extant "life" from the realm of ownable innovation. Not surprisingly, the historical trajectory of U.S. patenting practices is in many ways a story of the ongoing renegotiation of this distinction between nature and human labor.

A quick look at some of the key decisions on patenting nature (successful or not) in the United States clearly suggests that the scope of nature that has become imaginable as property has moved significantly across (up?) several taxonomic orders, with particularly important leaps in the last fifteen years. An alarmist's reading of this chart (Table 8.1) would point out the unnerving expansion of the kinds of nature that become imaginable as property, from a purified form of an existing microorganism (granted to Louis Pasteur) and purified chemical compounds, to "new," genetically engineered microorganisms, to multicellular animals, and now to bits of DNA, the code that ostensibly resides in all of us. The 1980 Supreme Court decision, *Diamond v. Chakrabarty*, was a major catalyst in this broadening of the realm of nature subject to manipulation and ownership. In this decision, the Court ruled that a genetically engineered microorganism useful in cleaning up oil spills could indeed be patented as if it were an inanimate invention (overturning the Patent and Trademark Office's ruling). The Court justified this particular construction of commensurability with a remarkably broad interpretation

TABLE 8.1. Suggestive Moments in U.S. Patent History.

1873	Pure culture of a microorganism
1911	Purified adrenaline
1930	Asexually reproducing plants (patent-like protection)
1970	Sexually reproducing plants (patent-like protection)
1980	Genetically engineered microorganism (*Diamond v. Chakrabarty*)
1984	Human cell line (John Moore)
1988	Transgenic animal (OncoMouse)
1989	Gene for protein used to treat blood disorders
1991	Human brain DNA sequences (*denied* on utility)
1991	Guaymi cell line (*withdrawn* after protest)
Pending:	Breast cancer gene (filed by Myriad Genetics Inc. and the University of Utah)

TABLE 8.2. The Nature of Innovation.

Not patentable	*Patentable*
Discovery	Invention
Products of nature	Products of human intervention
Natural nature	Manmade nature
Impure nature	Purified nature
Wild nature	Stabilized nature

of patentable subject matter as "anything under the sun that is made by man" (*Diamond v. Chakrabarty*, 447 U.S. at 303).

While *Diamond v. Chakrabarty* is precedent-setting insofar as it carves out a new domain of property, it also does so within a long-recognized refinement of the boundary between nature and labor (Table 8.2). From Louis Pasteur's purified microorganism to DuPont's OncoMouse, the products of nature exclusion has been reworked periodically into a distinction between "things of nature that occur naturally" and "things of nature that occur by man's handiwork" (Sherwood 1990: 47, gender appreciated). This distinction has long been crucial for the pharmaceutical industry, in which drug development is often a matter of using human/scientific enterprise to make "imperfect" nature fit for human consumption. Natural compounds such as enzymes are thus made "novel"—that is, stable, reliable, and marketable—through such enterprising activities as purification, distillation, or isolation.

While there are other standards by which the patentability of genetic material (as opposed to chemical compounds) could be judged, one commentator notes that U.S. courts have tended to analogize the manipulation of DNA to the patentable interventions undertaken in the pharmaceutical industry (Docherty 1993: 530). Thus purifying, hybridizing, isolating, and cloning DNA (often but not always for pharmaceutical development) have been deemed patentable enterprise. In the analogies being constructed here (genes to chemical compounds, and both to inanimate inventions), the crucial transformative axis is the idea of improvement.[27] Making products of nature suitable for human use and, importantly, for mass (re)production turns them into legitimate forms of innovation.

Along these instrumental lines, another key element of patentability is the utility requirement. A patent claim is rarely denied on the grounds of utility; as one legal scholar notes, people do not ordinarily try to patent something that has no known use in the first place (Docherty 1993: 530). But, in 1991, the U.S. National Institutes for Health (NIH) filed an application for patents on several hundred gene fragments of undetermined function. The fragments, taken from human brain tissue (source unmarked), had been sequenced in the laboratory of NIH scientist Craig Venter as part of the HGP. The Patent and Trademark Office rejected the request, ruling that sequencing gene fragments—determining the order of their nucleotide bases—without knowing what they do does *not* get to count as a patentable contribution to humanity.[28]

Despite its failure, a rather marked amount of controversy has followed the NIH patent attempt. Internationally, scientists have decried the "gold-rush" mentality in the U.S. government's perceived attempt to cordon off sections of the genome, citing this domaining move as an affront to scientific decorum and the "conventional" understanding that the genome is common "genetic patrimony" (Dausset and Cann 1994). Others within and outside the scientific community, including a coalition of leaders of virtually every major religion in the United States and an international coalition of indigenous, consumer, and nongovernmental organizations, have issued statements decrying the commodification of "life" inherent in such patent claims.[29] And, calling up a not-too-distant past in which (certain) humans were indeed considered property, some legal scholars have explored whether patenting human genes violates the Thirteenth Amendment to the U.S. Constitution, which abolished slavery and forbids the granting of property rights over human beings.[30] Much like the equation of genetic material with cultural identity, the nature of the homologous relationship between "the gene" and "the person" is key to untangling this thorny constitutional issue. But it also brings U.S. racial politics of labor, property, and reproductive control to the front line in discussions about the reproduction and ownership of (certain kinds of) life. Along with fears about the possibilities of governments cloning and owning an entire "class" of bioengineered slaves,[31] this seemingly fantastic invocation of the traffic in human capital is also a powerful reminder of the connections among race, reproduction, kinship, and property in the history of U.S. reproductive politics (see Spillers 1987). The speculative power of genes to stand for (ownable) persons, and for cultures or ethnic groups in the HGDP more broadly, suggests ways in which race, ethnicity, and culture continue to be meaningfully reproduced through genetic idioms, despite all earnest claims to the contrary by HGDP defenders.

Darwin's Loan, Revisited

I began this discussion with a reference to an analogy that Darwin posed in 1859, that between genealogy, as a metaphor for tracing specific family lineages, and the idea of a genealogical connection unifying all living creatures. Darwin's use of human kinship metaphors to make sense of a grid of vast, cross-species relatedness had the eventual effect of naturalizing human kinship, insofar as genealogy and notions of human reproduction became newly intelligible as biological facts. Yanagisako and Delaney note that this articulation of the relationship between biology and the production of human lineages, solidly materialized as it is now, was not seen as particularly "natural" at the time: " 'Reproduction' as the term to refer to the process of coming into being came into use in the nineteenth century and was at first considered a quaint *metaphor*, hardly a description of fact. The metaphor consisted of analogizing human reproduction to that of plants and animals" (1995: 7, original emphasis). As suggested by the complex traffic within and between the HGDP and the Merck/INBio agreement, Darwin's loan is still generating interest at a dizzying rate. I have highlighted a number of streams of this traffic, such as HGDP proponents' uneasy conflation of genetic (biological?) diversity with cultural and ethnic diversity; the contestation of the patenting of human cell lines under the United Nations Convention on (floral/faunal) Biological Diversity; the construction of human, floral, and faunal chemical compounds as commensurate in pharmaceutical value; and (some) scientists' construction of both human and nonhuman diversity as collectable, commodifiable informational code.

It has been my goal here to illuminate the historical, discursive, material thickness of these commensurabilities. That is, I want to avoid the temptation to celebrate some kind of biotechnology-mediated "collapse" of certain ideas about nature and culture and instead attend to the materiality and generative effects of these particular instances of ricochet. In this light, Darwin's loan does multiple service for me here: it illuminates the historical and generative discursive connections between ideas about social facts and natural facts, and, in a wider methodological sense, it also illuminates the materializing effects of metaphors and analogies. Thus, we might say that the loan is being extended insofar as the metaphors and analogies that courts, scientists, and activists mobilize to make sense of human DNA fragments have serious (though not equally weighty) implications for the domaining of new kinds of property; insofar as catchy "Northern" rhetoric about "our" common genetic past and future also produce new fodder for, and articulations of, international power struggles between the North and the South (or the gene-rich and the gene-poor); and enterprising visions of biologized diversity as information help generate new and contested constructions of both extinction and salvage.

These strategic reinscriptions of nature and culture, of the biological and/as the human,[32] thus offer pointed examples of the materiality of new discursive permutations and combinations. More specifically, I would suggest another level of thickness or ricochet, insofar as the HGDP and biodiversity prospecting are also implicated in refiguring the meanings of reproductive process itself. That is, they can be seen as cultural negotiations of the shape of, and proper relationship among, nature, culture, property, and reproduction.[33] What counts as a natural fact or a social fact, as life or property, as legitimate reproduction or unauthorized transgression, as the reproduction of persons and lineages or merely the replication of cell-lines, as natural nature or instrumentalized, enterprised-up nature? These contested determinations weave through and around the HGDP, biodiversity prospecting, wary nongovernmental organizations, and patent offices. And in a different but related story line, they also ricochet across and through U.S. and European debates over human reproductive technologies, which have occasioned much discussion of the nature of natural relatedness and social facts, the place of technological intervention in the domain of reproductive nature, the legal and ontological status of new kinship entities (such as frozen embryos), and, more generally, the proper sites at which reproduction and property rights can legitimately hybridize. I do not mean to argue that debates over human reproductive technologies index precisely the same issues as do the HGDP and bioprospecting. Rather, as my invocation of Darwin's loan is meant to suggest, these different arenas form part of a rich narrative field in which ideas about kinship, nature, and culture are woven together in complex and historically dense ways. That these discursive ricochets continue to be elaborated is not a matter of epistemological self-replication, but a result of concrete instances of cross-pollination through which biologized constructions of "our" reproductive pasts and futures are powerfully articulated and refigured.

Many thanks are due to Sarah Franklin and Helena Ragoné, as well as to Anna Tsing, Stefan Helmreich, and the members of Donna Haraway's Spring 1995 writing seminar at UC Santa Cruz (Julian Bleecker, Brendan Brisker, Beth Drexler, Rae Fry, Melinda Harris, Karen Hoffman, Mimi Ito, Sarah Jain, and Barbara Ley).

Notes

1. Arturo Escobar (1994), Kathy McAfee (1995) and David Takacs (1996) note the emergence of biodiversity as the symbol of nature itself, and as an exceedingly expansive term. Beth Drexler is also charting the concept and term "biodiversity" as it is translated across cultural and institutional contexts (unpublished manuscript, Department of Anthropology, University of California, Santa Cruz). Also see Simon Cole's article, "Do Androids Pulverize Tiger Bones to Use as Aphrodesiacs?" (1995) for a great reading of the traffic between biodiversity discourses and science fiction.

2. On the potent multivalence of "nature," see, among other things, Raymond Williams' "Ideas of Nature" (1980) and Anna Tsing's article, "Empowering Nature: Or, Some Gleanings in Bee Culture" (1995).

3. Steinberg, personal communication, May 1995.

4. *Human Biodiversity* is the title of molecular anthropologist Jonathan Marks' 1995 book on human genetic variation.

5. My interest in analogy is also tied to the fact that many of the negotiations I chart here have their referents in the realms of U.S. and international law. Legal reasoning is, formally, based on the model of precedent and analogy—decisions are based on a given question's literal similarity to past cases, or, in the absence of such precedent, on the construction of similarities and analogous situations. Legal negotiations about the kinds of biotechnologically engineered nature that can be considered patentable, for instance, constitute fruitful cultural terrain for identifying points of possible conjuncture and disjuncture—that is, for identifying what can and cannot be thought together.

6. See also Collier and Yanagisako (1987); Strathern (1992a,b); Weston (1991); Haraway (1995).

7. Frankel and Soulé (1981). See Tsing (1995) for an exploration of the racialized, gendered, and nationalized implications of such species definitions in discourses about bees.

8. See Charis Cussins' fictional but not fabricated essay, "Confessions of a Bioterrorist" (forthcoming) for a wonderful account of the dizzying overlaps between the management of human and nonhuman reproduction. On the frozen zoo, see also the U.S. Congress's Office of Technology Assessment's 1987 report, *Technologies to Maintain Biological Diversity*.

9. In addition to essays in this volume, there is a wide range of literature on the negotiation of natural facts and social facts in the context of reproductive technologies, and within reproductive politics on a wider scale. A partial but indicative list might include Ginsburg and Tsing (1990); Ginsburg and Rapp (1995); Strathern 1992a,b; Ragoné (1994); Rapp (1995); Dolgin (1995); Franklin (1995a); Squier and Kaplan (forthcoming); Hayden (1992).

10. See the Human Genome Diversity Project, North American Committee's statement, "Answers to Frequently Asked Questions About the Human Genome Diversity Project," 1994.

11. See King 1993a and 1993b, and articles such as Leslie Roberts' "A Genetic Survey of Vanishing Peoples," in *Science* (1991), and Roger Lewin's "Genes from a Disappearing World," in *New Scientist* (1993).

12. Draft report of the HGDP, quoted in the *RAFI Communique* (Rural Advancement Foundation International 1993: 3). Meanwhile, in an ironic display of concern about the ethics of "sampling" indigenous people, the U.S. leaders of the HGP have testified to the U.S. Congress that the federal government should withhold support for the HGDP until its leaders adequately address the concerns of indigenous organizations. Arguably, the HGP leaders' concern about ethics is not far removed from anxieties over their own material resources. The HGDP is seeking funding from the same set of institutions that funds the HGP—the Human Genome Organization (HUGO), internationally, and the National Institutes for Health, Department of Energy, and National Science Foundation, within the United States. It is thus perhaps not surprising that an epistemic/ethical confrontation over the proper cartography of "the" human species being has its accompanying financial turf battles. Francis Collins, director of the NIH's genome initiative, argued in a 1993 Senate hearing that the HGP should indeed be understood as a crucial tool-building project that will undoubtedly benefit the researchers engaged in the HGDP, but the HGP's funding should not be used to fund research on genetic variation (Collins 1993: 10–14). Donna Haraway has pointed out the complex ironies of the HGDP's troubles with difference: "It has proved easier to slow down or stop the HGDP, itself a kind of oppositional effort, than to question the powerful HGP. . . . That makes the trouble with 'difference' built into this potentially positive scientific project all the more disturbing—and important" (1995: 29).

13. See also Goodman 1994 and Marks 1995a for trenchant critiques of the biologized and geneticized notions of race that continue to circulate through biological anthropology, particularly in the context of the Human Genome Diversity Project.

14. Greely, personal communication, June 1994; see also the HGDP's North American Committee statement (1994), distributed by Greely.

15. In the 1970s, an international movement emerged to establish legal frameworks for granting collective rights to indigenous peoples, rather than relying on the individualist construction inherent in the concept of human rights (see Chapman 1994 and Suagee 1994). Among the multilateral conventions established in this vein was UNESCO's 1970 Convention on the Means of Prohibiting and Preventing the Illicit Import, Export, and Transfer of Ownership of Cultural Property, which was designed to cover material artifacts of "religious" or "cultural" significance.

16. For critiques of botanical imperialism in the context of "North-South" relations, see Juma 1989; Kloppenburg (1988, 1991); and Shiva et al. (1991).

17. For explorations of colonialist science and the role and history of botanical gardens, see Grove 1991; Headrick 1988; and Brockway 1988.

18. See Mark Rose's paper, "From Paternity to Property: The Remetaphorization of Writing," (1995) and Carol Delaney (1986) for discussions of the links between notions of paternity, generativity, and authorship in both Judeo-Christian cosmology and British-derived intellectual property conventions.

19. That "prospecting" calls up not very positive images of mining, plunder, and exploitation seems not to bother many of those who are involved in such projects—rather, the term is often glossed in the sense of encouraging so-called developing nations to explore and make the best possible use of their own resources.

20. The San Francisco-based company Shaman Pharmaceuticals is a well-known proponent of ethnobotanically based drug discovery.

21. In the wake of the 1992 Convention and the shift within a certain element of the international conservation community towards industry-friendly modes of conservation, the U.S. government has established a program for funding "international cooperative

biodiversity groups." Under the stewardship of a triad of federal agencies—the National Institutes for Health, the National Science Foundation, and the U.S. Agency for International Development—the ICBG program awards funding to U.S. researchers who establish prospecting collaborations with pharmaceutical companies, universities, collection agencies, and indigenous people. The ICBG program actually requires that its projects involve indigenous people, setting it apart from the model suggested by the Merck/INBio agreement. The first round of five-year grants under this program was awarded in 1993; five teams of researchers received $2.5 million each to establish networks for collection, screening, and compensation in both tropical and desert settings (Carrizosa and Shaw 1995).

22. Eisner and Beiring argue that private chemical prospecting agreements do the work the Convention is meant to do without having to rely on "government coercion of private parties" (1994: 97).

23. See McAfee (1995) for an excellent account of the institutional genealogy of this trend.

24. Along these lines, it is perhaps no surprise that one of Merck's hyperbolic goals is to screen all the plants in the world. Lest such a goal seem a bit far-fetched, Merck biochemist Lynn Caporale notes, "We are doing it in a taxonomically logical way" (quoted in Joyce 1992: 400).

25. Writing of early twentieth-century taxidermic enterprises, Haraway notes, "Scientific knowledge canceled death; only death before knowledge was final, an abortive act in the natural history of progress" (1989: 34). In the 1990s, knowledge also, sometimes, does literally cancel death. While the Body Shop exhorts consumers to patronize "green" businesses because "Extinct is Forever!" Jurassic Park and the real-life bacteria-revival with which I began this paper offer evidence that technoscientific mastery of genetic processes can indeed take the sting out of extinction (see also Bleecker 1995).

26. When ethnobotanical knowledge of useful species is involved, this knowledge is similarly coded as labor that deserves proper compensation.

27. Miranda Paton's unpublished manuscript, "Breaking the Code: The Building and Burying of an Analogy" (1995) provides a fascinating account of how U.S. courts actually went through "a moment of copyright," from 1982 to 1985, in which the copyright, rather than the patent, was seen as the most appropriate form of intellectual property rights for genetic material. This determination was made in large part by comparing DNA to text in the same way that computer software was seen as copyrightable text. Paton argues that this move was defeated in part by the dismantling of the molecule-software-text analogy by legal scholars, but that current crises in patent law over the patenting of DNA arise in large part because the biotechnology industry has continued to materialize the metaphor of DNA as text.

28. Meanwhile, Venter has gone on to form his own nonprofit research institute, The Institute for Genomic Research (TIGR), in partnership with Human Genome Sciences (HGS), which in turn has ties to the pharmaceutical company SmithKline Beecham. HGS finances Venter with high-powered sequencing machines in return for rights to commercialize TIGR's findings, which are then licensed to SmithKline Beecham. Ironically, this particular alliance has been at the heart of yet another maelstrom about public knowledge and private gain, along quite similar lines. Venter reportedly has sequenced fragments of 85 to 90 percent of "all" human genes. Given his earlier experience with NIH and the U.S. Patent Office, he has decided not to attempt to patent the sequences. Rather, in what some see as yet another breach of scientific communal ethics, TIGR/HGS have not made their findings public. The database that they command, meanwhile, is seen to have enormous value. As a 1995 article in *BusinessWeek* notes, ". . . a database of all human genes must be laden with clues to previously unknown biochemical pathways that could be ma-

nipulated to treat or prevent disease" (Carey et al. 1995: 77). To complete the circle nicely, for my purposes at least, Merck and Co. (not only an INBio collaborator but a SmithKline competitor) recently funded a large-scale sequencing operation at Washington University in St. Louis, designed to duplicate the TIGR database and to make its sequence information public. By feeding roughly 4,000 sequences a week into a public database, Merck executives hope to give their own scientists and others with whom they have licensing agreements a fair start on the drug discovery process, and, it has been implied, to undermine the TIGR/HGS/SmithKline Beecham effort.

29. See the *New York Times*, May 12, 1995 (Andrews 1995), on the religious coalition's statement against patenting human genetic material.

30. See, for example, Kevin deBre's 1989 article, "Patents on People and the U.S. Constitution: Creating Slaves or Enslaving Science?"

31. Again see the *RAFI Communique* (Rural Advancement Foundation International 1994) and the *Abya Yala News* (Spiwak 1993).

32. The semantic messiness here is significant. "Human" is not always synonymous with culture or the social; biology does not always mean nature to the exclusion of culture; genetic can index culture as often as it indexes the biological; human vs. natural diversity is not (necessarily) an effective distinction, though it can be; nature does not necessarily preclude human intervention. As the history of patenting "life" suggests, such a proliferation of qualifications of the nature/culture split is not itself "novel," but what is notable is the particular shape of the commensurabilities that are generated in the conceptual traffic evident between the HGDP and biodiversity prospecting.

33. As the invocation of slavery by those objecting to granting property rights for human DNA suggests, the mixing of kinship and property is not a new issue on the discursive scene here. In fact, Brackette Williams has argued that kinship ideologies are less about the regulation of any particular kind of shared substance (such as blood or genes), than they are means of regulating the distribution of rights and resources, and the flow of property and persons (1995). Raymond Williams, too, has noted that property has long been the terrain in which "crucial questions about man and nature" are worked out (1980: 76).

References

Andrews, Edmund L. 1995. "Religious Leaders Prepare to Fight Patents on Genes." *New York Times*, May 13, pp. 1, 35.

Bleecker, Julian. 1995. "Building a Better Dinosaur: The Special Effects of Technoscience." Work in progress, presented to the University of California, Santa Cruz, History of Consciousness Board, May 15.

Blum, Elissa. 1993. "Making Biodiversity Conservation Profitable: A Case Study of the Merck/INBio Agreement." *Environment* 35, 4: 17–20, 38–45.

Bouquet, Mary. 1994. "Displaying Knowledge: The Trees of Haeckel, Dubois, Jesse and Rivers at the *Pithecanthropus* Centennial Exhibition." Paper presented at the conference, What's Blood Got to Do With It? University of California, Santa Cruz, 29 April–1 May.

Brockway, Lucille. (1979) 1988. *Science and Colonial Expansion: The Role of the British Royal Botanic Gardens.* New York: Academic Press.

Browne, Malcolm W. 1995. "30-Million-Year Sleep: Germ Is Declared Alive." *New York Times*, May 19, pp. A1, A9.

Brush, Stephen R. 1993. "Indigenous Knowledge of Biological Resources and Intellectual Property Rights: The Role of Anthropology." *American Anthropologist* 95, 3: 653–86.

Carey, John, Joan O'C. Hamilton, Julia Flynn, and Geoffrey Smith. 1995. "The Gene Kings." *BusinessWeek*, May 8, pp. 72–78.

Carrizosa, Santiago and William W. Shaw. 1995. "Intellectual Property Rights and the Convention on Biological Diversity: An International Biodiversity Group Involving the United States, Chile, and Argentina." Paper presented at the 1995 Annual Meetings of the Society for Applied Anthropology, Albuquerque, N.M., April 1.

Cavalli-Sforza, Luca L., A. C. Wilson, C. R. Cantor, R. M. Cook-Deegan, and M.-C. King. 1991. "Call for a Worldwide Survey of Human Genetic Diversity: A Vanishing Opportunity for the Human Genome Project." *Genomics* 11: 490–91.

Chapman, Audrey R. 1994. "Human Rights Implications of Indigenous Peoples' Intellectual Property Rights." In *Intellectual Property Rights for Indigenous Peoples: A Sourcebook*, ed. Tom Greaves. Oklahoma City: Society for Applied Anthropology, pp. 211–22.

Chon, Margaret. 1993. "Postmodern Progress: Reconsidering the Copyright and Patent Power." *DePaul Law Review* 43: 97–146.

Cole, Simon. 1995. "Do Androids Pulverize Tiger Bones to Use as Aphrodisiacs?" *Social Text* 42 (Spring): 173–93.

Collier, Jane and Sylvia Yanagisako, eds. 1987. *Gender and Kinship: Essays Toward a Unified Analysis*. Stanford, Calif.: Stanford University Press.

Collins, Francis. 1993. Congressional Hearing on the Human Genome Diversity Project, before the Committee on Governmental Affairs, United States Senate, April 26. Washington, D.C.: U.S. Government Printing Office.

Coombe, Rosemary J. 1993. "The Properties of Culture and the Politics of Possessing an Identity: Native Claims in the Cultural Appropriation Controversy." *Canadian Journal of Law and Jurisprudence* 6, 2 (July): 249–85.

Cussins, Charis. Forthcoming. "Confessions of a Bioterrorist: Subject Position and Reproductive Technologies." In *Reproductive Technologies: Narratives, Gender, Culture*, ed. Susan Squier and E. Ann Kaplan, Rutgers, N.J.: Rutgers University Press.

Darwin, Charles. (1859) 1936. *The Origin of Species*. New York: Modern Library.

Dausset, Jean and Howard Cann. 1994. "Our Genetic Patrimony." *Science* 264 (30 September): 1.

deBre, Kevin D. 1989. "Patents on People and the U.S. Constitution: Creating Slaves or Enslaving Science?" *Hastings Constitutional Law Quarterly* 16:221–59.

Delaney, Carol. 1986. "The Meaning of Paternity and the Virgin Birth Debate." *Man* 21, 3: 494–513.

Docherty, Pamela A. 1993. "The Human Genome: A Patenting Dilemma?" *Akron Law Review* 26 (3–4): 525–55.

Dolgin, Janet L. 1995. "Family Law and the Facts of Life." In *Naturalizing Power: Essays in Feminist Cultural Analysis*, ed. Sylvia J. Yanagisako and Carol Delaney. New York: Routledge, pp. 47–68.

Eisner, Thomas. 1989–1990. "Prospecting for Nature's Chemical Riches." *Issues in Science and Technology* 6, 2 (Winter): 31–34.

Eisner, Thomas and Elizabeth A. Beiring. 1994. "Biotic Exploration Fund—Protecting Biodiversity Through Chemical Prospecting." *BioScience* 44, 2: 95–98.

Elisabetsky, Elaine. 1991. "Folklore, Tradition, or Knowledge?" *Cultural Survival Quarterly* 13, 3: 9–14.

Escobar, Arturo. 1994a. "Cultural Politics and Biological Diversity: State, Capital, and Social Movements in the Pacific Coast of Colombia." Paper presented at the Guggenheim Foundation Conference on Dissent and Direct Action in the Late Twentieth Century, Otavalo, Ecuador, June 15–19.

———. 1994b. "Notes on Science and Biodiversity." Paper presented at the 93rd Annual Meetings of the American Anthropological Association, Atlanta, Georgia, November 30–December 4.

———. 1995. *Encountering Development: The Making and Unmaking of the Third World.* Princeton, N.J.: Princeton University Press.

Frankel, O. H. and Michael E. Soulé, eds. 1981. *Conservation and Evolution.* Cambridge: Cambridge University Press.

Franklin, Sarah. 1995a. "Postmodern Procreation: A Cultural Account of Assisted Reproduction." In *Conceiving the New World Order: The Global Politics of Reproduction,* ed. Faye D. Ginsburg and Rayna Rapp. Berkeley: University of California Press.

———. 1995b. "Science as Culture, Cultures of Science." *Annual Reviews of Anthropology* 24: 163–84.

geneWATCH. 1994. "Following Protest, Patent Claim Withdrawn on Guaymi Indian Cell Line." *geneWATCH* 19 (January): 6–7.

Gillis, Anna Maria. 1994. "Getting a Picture of Human Diversity." *BioScience* 44, 1: 8–11.

Ginsburg, Faye and Rayna Rapp, eds. 1995. *Conceiving the New World Order: The Global Politics of Reproduction.* Berkeley: University of California Press.

Ginsburg, Faye and Anna Lowenhaupt Tsing, eds. 1990. *Uncertain Terms: Negotiating Gender in American Culture.* Boston: Beacon Press.

Goodman, Alan. 1994. "The Problematics of 'Race' in Contemporary Biological Anthropology." Paper presented at the Biological Anthropology "State-of-the-Science" Summer Institute, George Washington University, Washington, D.C., June 6–11.

Greaves, Tom, ed. 1994. *Intellectual Property Rights for Indigenous Peoples: A Sourcebook.* Oklahoma City: Society for Applied Anthropology.

Grove, Richard H. 1991. "The Transfer of Botanical Knowledge Between Asia and Europe, 1498–1800." *Journal of the Japan-Netherlands Institute* 3: 160–76.

Haraway, Donna. 1989. *Primate Visions: Gender, Race, and Nature in the World of Modern Science.* New York: Routledge.

———. 1995. "Universal Donors in a Vampire Culture: Biological Kinship Factors in the Twentieth-Century United States." In *Uncommon Ground: Toward Reinventing Nature,* ed. William Cronon. New York and London: Norton, pp. 321–78.

———. Forthcoming. "Mice into Wormholes: A Technoscience Fugue in Two Parts." In *Cyborgs and Citadels: Interventions in the Anthropology of Technohumanism,* ed. Gary Downey, Sharon Traweek, and Joseph Dumit. School of American Research. Seattle: University of Washington Press.

Hayden, Corinne P. 1995. "Gender, Genetics, and Generation: Reformulating Biology in Lesbian Kinship." *Cultural Anthropology* 10, 1 (February): 41–63.

Headrick, Daniel R. 1988. *The Tentacles of Progress: Technology Transfer in the Age of Imperialism, 1850–1940.* New York: Oxford University Press.

Human Genome Diversity Project, North American Committee. 1994. "Answers to Frequently Asked Questions About the Human Genome Diversity Project." Contact person: Henry Greely, Stanford University School of Law, Stanford, Calif.

International Union for the Conservation of Nature, United Nations Environmental Programme, and World Wildlife Fund. 1990. *World Conservation*

Strategy: Living Resource Conservation for Sustainable Development. Gland, Switzerland: World Conservation Union.

Joyce, Christopher. 1991. "Prospectors for Tropical Medicines." *New Scientist* 132: 36–40.

———. 1992. "Western Medicine Men Return to the Field." *BioScience* 42, 6: 399–403.

Juma, Calestous. 1989. *The Gene Hunters: Biotechnology and the Scramble for Seeds.* Princeton, N.J.: Princeton University Press.

King, Mary-Claire. 1993a. Congressional Hearing on the Human Genome Diversity Project, before the Committee on Governmental Affairs, United States Senate, April 26. Washington, DC: U.S. Government Printing Office.

———. 1993b. Interview. *Omni* 15, 9 (July): 68–74.

Kloppenburg, Jack. 1988. *First the Seed: The Political Economy of Plant Biotechnology.* Cambridge: Cambridge University Press.

———. 1991. "No Hunting! Biodiversity, Indigenous Rights, and Scientific Poaching." *Cultural Survival Quarterly* (Summer): 14–18.

———. 1992. "Conservationists or Corsairs?" *Seedlings* (June/July): 12–17.

Krasny, Michael. 1995. Commentary at forum on "Myths and Promises of the Human Genome Project." Part of the lecture series, Diving into the Gene Pool, at the Exploratorium, San Francisco, April 19.

Lévi-Strauss, Claude. 1969. *The Elementary Structures of Kinship*, trans. James Harle Bell, John Richard von Sturmer, and Rodney Needham; ed. Rodney Needham. Boston: Beacon Press.

Lewin, Roger. 1993. "Genes from a Disappearing World." *New Scientist* 138 (29 May): 25–29.

Marks, Jonathan. 1995a. *Human Biodiversity: Genes, Race, and History.* New York: Aldine de Gruyter.

———. 1995b. "The Human Genome Diversity Project: Good *for* If Not Good *as* Anthropology?" *Anthropology Newsletter* 36, 4: 72.

McAfee, Kathy. 1995. "Biodiversity in the Market-World." Unpublished manuscript, Department of Geography, University of California at Berkeley.

McNeely, Jeffrey A., Kenton R. Miller, Walter V. Reid, Russell Mittermeier, and Timothy B. Werner. 1990. *Conserving the World's Biological Diversity.* Washington, D.C.: World Resources Institute, World Conservation Union, Conservation International, World Wildlife Fund, and World Bank.

Morgan, Lewis H. (1871) 1970. *Systems of Consanguinity and Affinity of the Human Family.* Smithsonian Contributions to Knowledge 17. New York: Humanities Press.

Office of Technology Assessment. 1987. *Technologies to Maintain Biological Diversity.* Washington, D.C.: Congress of the United States, Office of Technology Assessment.

Paton, Miranda. 1995. "Breaking the Code: The Building and Burying of an Analogy." Unpublished manuscript, Department of Science and Technology Studies, Cornell University.

Ragoné, Helena. 1994. *Surrogate Motherhood: Conception in the Heart.* Boulder, Colo. and London: Westview Press.

Rapp, Rayna. 1995. "Heredity; or Revising the Facts of Life." In *Naturalizing Power: Essays in Feminist Cultural Analysis*, ed. Sylvia J. Yanagisako and Carol Delaney. New York: Routledge, pp. 69–86.

Reid, Walter V., Sarah A. Laird, Carrie A. Meyer, Rodrigo Gámez, Ana Sittenfeld, Daniel H. Janzen, Michael A. Gollin, and Calestous Juma, eds. 1993. *Biodiversity Prospecting: Using Genetic Resources for Sustainable Development.* Washington, D.C.: World Resources Institute, with Instituto Nacional de Biodiversidad, Costa Rica; Rainforest Alliance, USA; and African Centre for Technology Studies, Kenya.

Roberts, Leslie. 1991. "A Genetic Survey of Vanishing Peoples." *Science* 252 (21 June): 1614–17.

———. 1992. "Chemical Prospecting: Hope for Vanishing Ecosystems?" *Science* 256 (22 May): 1142–43.

Rose, Mark. 1993. *Authors and Owners: The Invention of Copyright.* Cambridge, Mass.: Harvard University Press.

———. 1995. "From Paternity to Property: The Remetaphorization of Writing." Unpublished manuscript. University of California, Irvine.

Rural Advancement Foundation International. 1994. *RAFI Communique* (January/February).

———. 1993. *RAFI Communique* (May).

Schneider, David M. (1968) 1980. *American Kinship: A Cultural Account.* Chicago: University of Chicago Press.

Sherwood, Robert. 1990. *Intellectual Property and Economic Development.* Boulder, Colo.: Westview Special Studies in Science, Technology, and Public Property.

Shiva, Vandana. 1991. "Biodiversity, Biotechnology and Profits." In Shiva et al., *Biodiversity: Social and Ecological Perspectives.* London: Zed Books, pp. 43–58.

Shiva, Vandana et al. 1991. *Biodiversity: Social and Ecological Perspectives.* London: Zed Books.

Spillers, Hortense. 1987. "Mama's Baby, Papa's Maybe: An American Grammar Book." *Diacritics* 17, 2: 65–81.

Spiwak, Daniela. 1993. "Gene Genie and Science's Thirst for Information with Indigenous Blood." *Abya Yala News* 17, 3–4: 12–14.

Squier, Susan and E. Ann Kaplan, eds. Forthcoming. *Reproductive Technologies: Narratives, Gender, Culture.* Rutgers, N.J.: Rutgers University Press.

Strathern, Marilyn. 1992a. *After Nature: English Kinship in the Late Twentieth Century.* Cambridge: Cambridge University Press.

———. 1992b. *Reproducing the Future: Anthropology, Kinship, and the New Reproductive Technologies.* New York: Routledge.

Suagee, Dean B. 1994. "Human Rights and Cultural Heritage: Developments in the United Nations Working Group on Indigenous Populations." In *Intellectual Property Rights for Indigenous Peoples: A Sourcebook,* ed. Tom Greaves. Oklahoma City: Society for Applied Anthropology, pp. 193–208.

Takacs, David. 1996. *The Idea of Biodiversity: Philosophies of Paradise.* Baltimore: Johns Hopkins University Press.

Tangley, Laura. 1990. "Cataloguing Costa Rica's Diversity." *BioScience* 40, 9: 633–36.

Tsing, Anna Lowenhaupt. 1995. "Empowering Nature: Or, Some Gleanings in Bee Culture." In *Naturalizing Power: Essays in Feminist Cultural Analysis,* ed. Sylvia J. Yanagisako and Carol Delaney. New York: Routledge, pp. 113–43.

Yanagisako, Sylvia and Carol Delaney. 1995. "Naturalizing Power." In *Naturalizing Power: Essays in Feminist Cultural Analysis,* ed. Yanagisako and Delaney. New York: Routledge, pp. 1–24.

Weston, Kath. 1991. *Families We Choose.* New York: Columbia University Press.

Williams, Brackette. 1995. "Classification Systems Revisited: Kinship, Caste,

Race, and Nationality as the Flow of Blood and the Spread of Rights." In *Naturalizing Power: Essays in Feminist Cultural Analysis,* ed. Sylvia Yanagisako and Carol Delaney. New York: Routledge, pp. 201–36.

Williams, Raymond. 1980. "Ideas of Nature." In *Problems in Materialism and Culture.* London: Verso, pp. 67–85.

World Resources Institute, World Conservation Union, and the United Nations Environmental Programme in consultation with Food and Agricultural Organization of the United Nations and United Nations Educational, Scientific, and Cultural Organization. 1992. *Global Biodiversity Strategy: Guidelines for Action to Save, Study, and Use Earth's Biotic Wealth Sustainably and Equitably.* Washington, D.C.: World Resources Institute.

Chapter 9
Replicating Reproduction in Artificial Life: Or, the Essence of Life in the Age of Virtual Electronic Reproduction

Stefan Helmreich

In the beginning, Tierra was an elementary computer model of evolution. Tom Ray, the creator of Tierra, claimed that Tierra was best thought of as a computational "ecosystem" or "artificial world" in which "populations" of "self-replicating" programs "evolved." Ray was happy to extend predicates usually associated with "life" to his "digital organisms" because he defined biological evolution as the story of the differential survival and replication of information structures. For Ray, and for many others in the nascent scientific field of Artificial Life, computer programs that self-replicate—like "computer viruses"—can be considered new forms of life, forms that can be quickened into existence by scientists who view the computer as a new universe ready to be populated with reproducing, mutating, competing, and ultimately unpredictable programs.

On July 7, 1994, some four years after Tierra's nativity, Tom Ray spoke to a large audience of scientists at an MIT conference on Artificial Life. He suggested that the digital organisms in Tierra needed more space to live, to reproduce, and to evolve. He proposed that people using computer networks around the world volunteer to accept a franchise of the system, that they give a portion of their Internet accounts over to running Tierra as a "low-priority background process," that Tierra—Spanish for "Earth"—become coextensive with our planet. Ray's talk was entitled, "A Proposal to Create a Network-Wide Biodiversity Reserve for Digital Organisms," and Ray was evangelical about his cause. His vision of a global version of Tierra was spectacular. He hoped that Tierran organisms could "roam freely" in a cyberspace reserve, "evolving" into new, unexpected, and potentially useful software forms. At one point in his talk, Ray supplemented his petition with a candid and personal pronouncement, declaring, "I think of these things as alive, and I'm just trying to figure out a place where they can live." As he finished up, he condensed his plea into a mantric phrase, asking the audience repeatedly to "give life a chance" (Ray 1994b).

How has it become possible for people to see computer programs as life forms? What is Artificial Life? What do Artificial Life scientists mean when they say that their computer programs can reproduce? Whose definitions of reproduction are being reproduced in Artificial Life simulations? Given that most Artificial Life scientists are men who participate in white, Euro-American, heterosexual, middle-class culture, what might their attempts to make explicit what they mean by reproduction tell us about dominant conceptions of procreation, kinship, and relatedness? And how might working with Artificial Life systems both stabilize and trouble these conceptions?

From May 1993 to July 1994, I conducted ethnographic fieldwork at the Santa Fe Institute for the Sciences of Complexity, in Santa Fe, New Mexico, a major locus of Artificial Life research and a center for computer simulation-based investigation of complex systems.[1] During my time at the Institute, I examined how culturally particular stories about life were being packed into computer simulations that were said to capture something of the "essence" of vitality. In this piece, I discuss how Euro-American ideas about reproduction and kinship were transplanted into computer models of evolutionary process. Sarah Franklin and Helena Ragoné have argued that with new reproductive technologies such as IVF and surrogacy we witness the "incorporation of new technologies into established idioms." Here, I show how in Artificial Life simulations, themselves species of new reproductive technologies for the formulations of evolutionary biology, we can see the "incorporation of established idioms into new technologies."

Artificial Life is a field devoted to the computer simulation—and, some would ambitiously add, synthesis in virtual space—of biological systems. It coalesced in the late 1980s, growing out of interdisciplinary conversations among a small set of biologists, computer scientists, economists, and physicists. Today, the community numbers in the high hundreds. Artificial Life researchers see their project as a reinvigorated theoretical biology and as an initially more modest but eventually more ambitious endeavor than Artificial Intelligence. Where Artificial Intelligence attempted to model the mind, Artificial Life workers plan to simulate the life processes that support the development and evolution of such things as minds. They hope to capture on computers the formal properties of organisms, populations, and ecosystems. A mission statement on Artificial Life generated by the Santa Fe Institute summarizes the approach:

Artificial Life studies "natural" life by attempting to recreate biological phenomena from first principles within computers and other "artificial" media. ALife complements the analytic approach of traditional biology with a synthetic approach in which, rather than studying biological phenomena by taking apart living organisms to see how they work, researchers attempt to put together systems that behave like living organisms. Artificial Life amounts to the practice of "synthetic biology." (Santa Fe Institute 1993: 38)

The intellectual and ideological warrant for this practice is captured by Artificial Life scientist Christopher Langton's declaration that life "is a property of the organization of matter, rather than a property of matter itself" (Langton 1988: 74). Many have found this figuring of life as a formal process so compelling that they maintain that alternative, real, artificial life forms can exist in the informatic medium of the computer. For these people, Artificial Life is not only a tool for modeling biology, but also an engine for constructing new biologies.

At the heart of many researchers' beliefs about vitality is the idea that reproduction is a defining characteristic of life (see, for instance, Farmer and Belin 1992). This conviction motivates individual and team efforts to write evolutionary simulations in which programs, understood as virtual organisms in a virtual universe, can "reproduce." Self-reproducing programs are crafted so as to reproduce imperfectly, with "mutations," so that they can proliferate in a diversity of forms that can then be sorted by a computational surrogate of natural selection. The histories of these proliferations are carefully recorded in a host of scientific papers on Artificial Life (see such collections as Langton 1989; Langton et al. 1992; Varela and Bourgine 1992; Langton 1994; and Brooks and Maes 1994).

What is often omitted in descriptions of the "evolution" of virtual creatures is the fact that self-reproducing programs must initially be produced by human programmers. It is this production, this writing of code into virtual life, with which I begin.

Creation Stories for Virtual Worlds and the Masculine Monogenesis of Artificial Life

I inaugurate this examination of "reproduction" in Artificial Life with Tom Ray's Tierra, narrating the creation in Tierra as it appeared to me when I used the system myself. While I was in residence at the Santa Fe Institute, I obtained over the Internet a version of Tierra that I could run on the Institute's UNIX workstations. I spent many late nights at

TABLE 9.1. The STATS and PLAN Area in the Tierra Display

InstExec = 0,005911	Cells = 7		Genotypes = 1	Sizes = 1
Extracted =				
InstExeC =	0	Generations = 0	Mon May 9 21:08:29	1994
NumCells =	1	NumGenotypes = 1	NumSizes =	1
AvgSize =	80	NumGenDG = 1	NumGenRQ =	1
RateMut =	3191	RateMovMut = 640	RateFlaw = 9600	
tsetup: soup gotten				

the Institute fastened to the light emanating from my Sun Sparcstation, gazing at the tables of statistics and graphs of data generated by the Tierra program. The visuals that accompany Tierra are unspectacular. There are no little creatures that flit about on the screen; there are only windows of buzzing textual and numerical data from which the user is supposed to follow and construct the histories of generations of self-reproducing computer programs.

To use the Tierra simulator, one types "tierra" at the user prompt. As soon as one types in this word of creation, one is presented with a display like the one in Table 9.1, which includes information about the history of the world as it unfolds. When Tierra runs on a screen, these numbers are constantly updating, showing us how many instructions have been executed, how many generations have been cycled through, how many creatures exist in the system, what the average size of a Tierran organism is, and so on.

The screen display I reproduce in Table 9.1 is taken from the very beginning of a run and reports information sampled from the dawn of a Tierran history. We can see that we are at generation zero, and we can note that at this time there is only one digital organism in existence, indicated by NumCells = 1. This is a self-replicating program that Ray created from scratch, the program he used and provides to start up the system. Ray explains what we are seeing: "Evolutionary runs of the simulator are begun by inoculating the soup of 60,000 instructions with a single individual of the 80 instruction ancestral genotype" (1992a: 382).

Ray calls this single individual the "ancestor" and describes it as a "'seed' self-replicating program" (1992b: 37). "Seed" is a common word in computer science, usually used in the phrase "random number seed," which refers to a pseudo-random number used as a starting point for a set of computational processes. Ray's use of the word echoes this usage, but also evokes the common meaning of seed as a germinal entity that has latent within it the potential to develop into a living thing capable of producing more seeds. At the instant of Tierran creation, then, the programmer/experimenter provides the "seed" that vivifies the system, the seed that will be replicated down digital generations. The choice of the word "seed"—and of the word "ancestor"—is important, for it plants the idea that from the word go (or rather, "tierra") we are witnessing nothing less than life forms in motion and realized potential.

But the use of the word "seed" does more than this. Carol Delaney has argued that in cultures influenced by Judeo-Christian narratives of creation and procreation, using the word "seed" to speak of the impetus of creation summons forth gendered images. In Judeo-Christian tales of creation, God, imagined as masculine, sparks the formless void of the earth to life with a kind of divine seed: the Word of creation or *logos spermatikos*. In Judeo-Christian tales of procreation, males, made in the image of a masculine god, are empowered to plant their active "seed" in the passive, receptive, yielding, and nutritive "soil" of females, thereby "fertilizing" them (see Delaney 1991). Creation and procreation in these narratives are "monogenetic," generated from one source, symbolically masculine. "Man" and "God" take after one another. I suggest that the creation in Tierra—and note that Tierra means "soil" as well as "Earth" in Spanish—symbolically mimics the story of creation in the Bible. The programmer is akin to a masculine god who sets life in motion with a word, a word that plants a "seed" in a receptive computational matrix, a "seed" that, in its search for nourishment, organizes an initially undifferentiated "soup." Following N. Katherine Hayles's discussion of Artificial Life programs, we might see in Tierra images of a symbolically "male programmer mating with a female program to create progeny whose biomorphic diversity surpasses the father's imagination" (1994: 125).

Christopher Langton has claimed in a programmatic statement that Artificial Life is about "the attempt to abstract the logical form of life in different material forms" (quoted in Kelly 1991: 1), a definition that holds that formal and material properties of entities can be usefully partitioned, and that what really matters is form. We might be reminded of the fact that form and material, like seed and soil, also have gendered valences for those of us swimming down the stream of Western natural philosophy and life sciences. Aristotle proclaimed in his *Generation of Animals* that in procreation "The male provides the 'form' and the 'principle of movement', the female provides the body, in other words, the material" (I.XX: 729a). Judith Butler notes that "The classical association of femininity with materiality can be traced to a set of etymologies which link matter with *mater* and *matrix* (or the womb)" (1993: 31). This gendering of form and material works hand in glove with the seed and soil metaphor unpacked above,[2] and one could argue that images of "form" and "seed" easily overlap in Artificial Life when practitioners make analogies between computer code (information) and genetic code. When Tom Ray writes of single-handedly creating digital life in

Tierra with a seed, when he remarks that this "digital life exists in a logical, not material, informational universe" (1994a: 183), and when he asserts, as he often does, that he is the god of Tierra, it is hard not to hear the echoes of a masculine monogenetic creation.

Like God and Adam, Tierran creatures are enabled to create in their own image. When one attends closely to the language in the Tierra model, however, one notices that Ray refers to the ancestor he created as a "mother," and to its descendants as "daughters." There is an interesting twist here, but it remains the case that reproduction is about the transmission of form, though this has now been democratized to "females." Parentage has become generically defined as an informational relation, just as "real" parents in the age of IVF have become synonymous with "genetic" parents, a move that ensures that mothers and fathers are "equal" on terms set by a masculine model.[3] And interestingly, for all the "femininity" of the Tierran "seeds," they still engage in the practice of "begetting"—in Tierra, the user has access to a tool called the genebanker, which, as Ray stated at one conference, "keeps track of who begat whom." "Begetting" is a word used in chapter 5 of the Book of Genesis to chronicle the passage of "seed" down generations of men. Webster's Ninth Collegiate Dictionary defines "beget" as "to procreate as the father: SIRE."

According to Ray, the designation of the Tierran creatures as mothers and daughters had no deep motivation. We might recall, though, that the words "mother" and "daughter" immediately suggest terms from cell biology, and hence something of the primitive, primordial, primeval, and primary[4] (not to mention something of the legitimacy of "real" cell biology). The terms are also effective because of a cultural assumption that what women do "naturally" is "reproduce." So, although reproduction in Tierra is modeled after a masculine monogenetic transmission of form and seed, the "primitivity" of the process is indexed through the terms "mothers" and "daughters," terms that also trade on popular cultural and scientific understandings of females as a preliminary developmental stage towards the more advanced and complex male form (see Fausto-Sterling [1985] 1992).

The generative image of "seeds" is used by several others in the field of Artificial Life. Larry Yaeger, in his discussion of his PolyWorld program, writes, ". . . the term *created* is applied to organisms spontaneously generated by the system (like the initial seed population)" (1994: 269). And Jeffrey Putnam writes that his simulator, Stew, sparks up when "The world is created and seeded" (1993: 948). When one prominent Artificial Life researcher reported on an ecological simulation at the Santa Fe Institute, he opened his talk by saying, "This system is seeded with a population of hand-crafted ancestors." Christopher Langton has said

of a simple instantiation of a self-reproducing automaton, "These embedded self-replicating loops are the result of the recursive application
of a rule to a seed structure" (1989: 30).

An incredible computer-animated short called "Panspermia," included in the video proceedings of the second Artificial Life workshop,
makes some of the masculine imagery that guides the seed concept
blisteringly clear. In this film by researcher Karl Sims (1992), we see
an enormous seed fly through outer space, crash on a barren planet,
and then explode like a piñata into a plethora of bizarre botanical life
forms that ultimately give rise to phallic plants that shoot more seeds
into space, in cannon-like explosions that can only be seen as violent
ejaculations. In many Artificial Life simulations, programmers make
the symbolically masculine principle behind the seed explicit when
they name ancestral programs "Adam." The original "seed structure" in
Christopher Langton's loop is dubbed "Adam" (Farmer and Belin 1992:
824), and an ancestral agent referred to as a "seed" in Dave Ackley and
Michael Littman's "AL" artificial world is also called "Adam" (1992a: 498,
1992b). In a speculative discussion of self-reproducing lunar factories,
Richard Laing tells of a " 'seed' perhaps weighing one hundred metric
tons delivered to an extraterrestrial planetary surface" (1989: 58). And
he reminds us of the masculine principle encased in the seed concept
with his discussion of an automaton offspring receiving "its patrimony"
(1989: 54).

I want to return to how the creator of Artificial Life worlds is symbolically imagined as a masculine god. The possibility that the program-
mer/experimenter in Ray's Tierra system has some resemblance to a
god who monogenetically creates life ex nihilo is suggested directly in
the annotated assembly code file for the ancestor. This code is understood as the "genetic code" of the ancestor. On the second line of the
ancestor's genome file is a data field that reads "parent genotype." In
most digital organisms, this field indicates the program's immediate ancestor, the program from which it descends. For the ancestor, there is
no ancestral program, since it was created by Tom Ray. So, where most
creatures have a parent genotype like "00045aab," the ancestor has the
rather peculiar "0666god," a designation that plays on the idea that
the programmer is a kind of Faustian figure—a devilish digital divinity.[5]
Because Tierra cannot be understood without knowing that it was intentionally written by a human creator, *both* evolutionary and theological
language have become necessary to make sense of the system. Ray is
clearly being playful here, but his jokes in fact perform crucial work in
constructing the programs in Tierra as created life.

Themes of monogentic masculine creation are not idiosyncratic to
Tierra. They appear in a few other programs as well, and they also per-

Figure 9.1. Poster for the second Artificial Life workshop. Copyright 1990 Chris Shaw; reproduced with permission.

meate the public image of Artificial Life. We are often told in the popular press that Christopher Langton is "the father of Artificial Life," a phrase that sounds innocent enough—he's merely a man who is founding a new discipline—until one realizes that we hardly hear the word "mother" used in a similar way, and that the phrase "the mother of Artificial Life" would sound odd, probably most readily calling up images of women birthing babies grown from zygotes manufactured in laboratories.[6] Langton has written that Artificial Life is "life made by *man* rather than by nature" (1989: 2, emphasis added), a phrase that depends for its efficacy on the fact that the noun for humanity is not gender-neutral (what would people make of "life made by people rather than by nature"?). The notion that Man replaces God and renders Woman irrelevant in the new creations of Artificial Life is vividly illustrated in Figure 9.1, a reproduction of the poster for the second workshop on Artificial Life, in which a white male programmer touches his finger to a keyboard to meet the waiting fingers of a skeletal, circuit-based artificial creature. This Escheresque quotation of Michelangelo's Sistine Chapel rendering of the creation of man, in which God touches the extended index digit of the first man, Adam, condenses many of the themes of creation I've been trying to pinpoint here.

Imagery of a masculine monogenetic creation is not only present in the texts, programs, and publicity of Artificial Life, it also surfaces in researchers' casual comments, jokes, and, occasionally, their confessions about why they work in Artificial Life at all. The symbolic links between masculinity, heterosexuality, paternity, and the creation of Artificial Life worlds were evoked for me one day when, at a workshop at the Institute, a male researcher claimed to have a certain "grandfatherly pride" in a program he had had the inspiration for but had not himself programmed. The symbolically masculine creation of silicon life is a theme that some men in Artificial Life explicitly play with; some joke that their wives take care of the kids while they take care of the virtual creatures. Tom Ray quotes his wife, Isabel Ray, in an epigraph to a recent article: "I'm glad they're not real, because if they were, I would have to feed them and they would be all over the house" (Ray 1994a: 202). Craig Reynolds, in the acknowledgements for his article in *Artificial Life IV*, writes, "Special thanks to my wife Lisa and to our first child Eric, who was born at just about the same time as individual 15653 of run C" (1994: 68).[7] One female scientist I interviewed was suspicious that Artificial Life was an expression of male researchers' birth envy. She said:

Women create things, right? We have babies and we certainly know the role of males in that, but it's not clear how much men feel that role, and maybe that's what ALife is. Maybe men would like to give birth to something and here it is, this is it. They're saying to us, "We're going to beat you guys. We're going to create entire worlds."

One male scientist did in fact tell me that he created his artificial worlds in part because he felt frustrated that he wasn't a woman and couldn't create "naturally" (by which he meant birthing). Another suggested that if he were pressed to account for the fact that there were more men in Artificial Life than women, he would "propose the theory that men are more frustrated in the urge to create life than women, and [that] ALife gives an outlet to this frustration."[8] In these statements, male creation is imagined to be fundamentally artificial, and female creation fundamentally natural. Men create artificial life, while women create natural life.[9]

There is, of course, an interesting contradiction bundled up in this way of looking at things. Females are imagined to create "naturally," virtually without any meaningful contribution from the male. At the same time, as the images I've been excavating here suggest, males are imagined to be the sole creative force in creation and procreation, with feminine contributions figured as simply supportive. Female birthing is everything at one moment and becomes nothing in the next,[10] so *much* nothing that reproduction can proceed without women, can even be pristinely transferred to a different vessel, the computer. Some people believe that the pure and uncorrupted virgin Mary was the perfect vessel for the seed of God, birthing a child who was not half-God, half-Mary, but all God. Computers might well be seen as capable of the same kind of pregnancy as Mary, bearing faithfully those formal self-reproducing seed programs that are the conceptions of Artificial Life scientists.

Stories about masculine creation usurping or bettering female creation can be found in many scientific narratives. Brian Easlea (1983) has written of how male nuclear weapons scientists often speak of the bombs they produce as babies, and he has interpreted this as bespeaking the desires of a masculine science to appropriate and transcend female reproductive capacities. But whether the use of such birth metaphors necessarily points to deep psychological motivations is perhaps not so important. More consequential is how this language, by drawing on shared cultural imagery, shapes the way projects are framed and completed. This is not to say that the language is only utilitarian; it often does reproduce problematic structures of feeling and reasoning about relations between women and men.

Though it would be a stretch to argue that Artificial Life is ultimately driven by a masculine envy of women's "ability" to birth (as if such an "ability" were not itself already culturally construed), I think the fact that Artificial Life is predominantly the work of men *is* crucial to how frequently and easily images of a masculine god are used. My suspicion is that men feel comfortable comparing themselves to God because the dominant images of God they reference figure God as a man. There are several Artificial Life scientists who are women, and none, to my knowledge, have ever publicly used God imagery to talk about their relationships to their programs. I would wager that the reference wouldn't work without a certain amount of dissonance, since God is imagined as a father. I would guess that women would feel uncomfortable claiming that they occupied the position of Goddess of their artificial worlds, especially in a scientific culture in which women are often very careful and are even instructed not to "highlight" their gender. And God and Goddess are not structurally equivalent terms. Goddesses are rarely imagined as creatrices of entire universes.

While masculine God imagery in Artificial Life tells us something about who participates in the discipline, the whole affair is not as simple as lining up masculine imagery with masculine science or male-dominated science. It's perfectly possible for women to use masculinist imagery of creation and even to refigure what this refers to. And many men have argued that Artificial Life can actually be seen as countering a historically masculine aesthetic in computer programming. Some men who have recognized that controlling and creating computer worlds can be a very stereotypically masculine practice have argued that creating Artificial Life worlds is different. In an interview with two heterosexual men about how their gendered subjectivity might be implicated in the ways they did their science, the men told me that Artificial Life work allowed them to express and work with a side of themselves that they felt was more intuitive, perhaps more stereotypically "feminine." They suggested that if Artificial Intelligence had expressed typically masculine imperatives for control, Artificial Life was about seeing oneself as a surprised participant in the creation of decentralized virtual worlds. Others have asserted that Artificial Life is in line with a more Gaian view of things, that Artificial Life can lead in an almost ecofeminist way to a view of ourselves as part of an ongoing creation in which nature and humanity mutually produce the conditions of each others' possibility.

Whether this change of optic really means that Artificial Life is helping people erode gender stereotypes, however, is unclear at best. It seems to me that this way of putting things shores up essentialized categories of gender even as it purports to erode them, keeping "femininity" stable as a resource that men can mine to "broaden" their intellectual work. Bill Maurer (1991) has argued that refigurations of masculinity that cannibalize previously stereotypic constructions of femininity in fact serve to solidify gendered boundaries by taking the category of gender for granted in the first place and by reinscribing the traditional masculine subject who incorporates all that is generically human. As we examine how gender is rewritten in the practice of Artificial Life, we might do well to join Teresa de Lauretis in asking, "If the deconstruction of gender inevitably effects its (re)construction, the question is, in which terms and in whose interest is the de-reconstruction being effected?" (1987: 24).

Usages of masculine god imagery are made possible by a particular cultural history, and they situate Artificial Life as a science imagined by people who are predominantly men. Such images are not mere window dressing for ultimately transparently sensible programs. In a very effective way, masculine god imagery allows researchers to imagine that they are really creating life in fertile but empty worlds. Of course, if this imagery were all there was to it, Artificial Life worlds could not function without it. As it turns out, there are a number of other metaphors and analogies that enable computer programs to be described as alive.[11] The next I examine manufactures "program" and "organism" as synonyms.

Organism as Information

In Tierra, and in most Artificial Life models, an organism is simply a string of information. Ray writes that "the 'body' of a digital organism is the information pattern in memory that constitutes its machine language program" (1994a: 184). This information pattern is considered the "genotype" of a digital organism, an idea made thinkable by the fact that contemporary life science already understands genetic material as a "code" of sorts—a metaphor that is itself indebted to computer science and informatics.[12] The belief that organisms can be thought of as programs makes it plausible to think of programs as varieties of organisms. Once organismic identity is flattened out like this, so is the definition of life, such that digital organisms suddenly come alive. The frequent slide of the term "reproduction" into "replication" also makes possible a folding of full-bodied organisms into simple flatland facsimile machines.

There are many sites in Artificial Life discourses where life process is imagined as fundamentally informatic. In their discussion of the RAM simulator, Taylor et al. write that "RAM is based on the observation that the life of an organism is in many ways similar to the execution of a program, and that the global (emergent) behavior of a population of interacting organisms is best emulated by the behavior of a corresponding population of co-executing programs" (1989: 275; see also Hogeweg 1989).[13] One researcher summarized to me the informatic view of organisms:

After a while the analogy between self-replicating programs and living organisms becomes so perfect that it becomes perverse to call it merely an analogy. It becomes simpler just to redefine the word "organism" to apply to both chemical and software creatures. What they have in common is much more important than how they differ.

The collapse of the organism into its genetic code[14] is everywhere in Artificial Life.

This identification of organisms with programs not only references a commitment to form over matter, but plays on the popular and mainstream scientific conceit that organisms are ultimately nothing more than the unfolding of a genetic plan and that genes are finally nothing more than information structures analogous to computer programs. The idea that organisms can be usefully identified with their genes motivates Ray's contention that "the bit pattern that makes up the program is the body of the organism and at the same time its complete genetic material" (1994a: 185). Ray has argued that his organisms are analogous to hypothesized early life forms made entirely of RNA, and this may indeed be so, but there are many cultural histories and social beliefs that make possible a preference for identifying organisms with genes, genes with information, and information processes with organisms.

The idea that genes make the organism is a philosophy known to evolutionary biologists as genetic determinism. Genetic determinism has its roots in beliefs that there are essential, inborn differences between organisms, and that these can be traced to hereditary material. There are deep roots for genetic determinism even in pre-Mendelian biology. In the seventeenth and eighteenth centuries, spermist preformationists held that each human and animal sperm contained a miniature person that simply grew in size as it was nourished by an egg (see Tuana 1989). In the early twentieth century, the discovery of the fact that mammalian gametes (sperm and eggs) were "sequestered" from the rest of the body —that is, that they were not subject to change in an organism's lifetime except through mutations—led some people to posit that differences between groups must be grounded in heredity. All species of genetic determinism embody metaphysical commitments to essential and inborn difference. Social fetishes of the "hereditary material" have shaped an intense focus on genes in evolutionary and population biology.

In mid-twentieth-century molecular biology, scientists likened the hereditary material to a sort of code. Modern molecular genetics developed heavily in dialogue with computer science; many of the people using computers during World War II (for physics problems, decryption projects) were the same who later turned their attention to problems in molecular biology. Physicist Erwin Schrödinger's contention that "chromosomes . . . contain in some kind of code-script the entire pattern of the individual's future development and of its functioning in the mature state" (1994: 20) was an important image for the development of molecular biology. After this time, it became commonplace to speak of a "genetic code," and problems of embryogenesis and development took a back seat to "cracking" the genetic code, commonly understood to contain the "secret" of life (see Keller 1992a). One developmental biologist I interviewed, skeptical of the grand claims of Artificial Life and unhappy with the compression of organisms into programs, said to me, "In modern biology, organisms have disappeared. They've been replaced by genes and their products."

Ideologies of genetic determinism and images of DNA as a code have combined to make possible the thinking of programs as life forms, but they also continue and mutate more profound metaphysical traditions. Susan Oyama, in *The Ontogeny of Information*, locates the idea that genes are a "blueprint" for an organism in a Western metaphysical tradition of separating form from matter, of assuming that ontogeny is merely the playing out of a developmental "program," and that "information . . . exists before the interactions in which it appears" (1985: 27).[15] Richard

Doyle (1993) writes that twentieth-century biology has, under the spell of understanding DNA as a code-script, conflated vitality and textuality, and that Artificial Life is a recent symptom of this. The "implosion of life and information" has rendered it possible to interpret information processes as living processes.

While the vivification of computer programs in Artificial Life is enabled by the inheritance of a science that compacts organisms into reproducing genetic programs, it is also made possible by the infiltration of genetic definitions of life into everyday discourse. Artificial Life researchers encounter and think through these notions not only in science, but in other domains as well. Consider how my informants responded to questions about abortion and the U.S. American debate about "when life begins." All the people I spoke with felt strongly that women had a political right to choose whether to follow a pregnancy to term, but all of them also believed that "life" began at conception. One researcher said, "I think abortion is really a horrible thing. I think life has started there, and it's analogous to squashing a little tiny seedling. . . . I think life has started the moment after conception." Another said to me that a zygote is alive because of its genetic potential, a genetic potential he understood as a program: "You start out with a fertilized egg, and yes, it's alive. It is definitely alive. It's a living cell, and it's programmed to develop into this fabulous complicated thing you call a baby. So there's no doubt that this is alive." It is this view of life as genetic potential, as many feminist critics point out, that allows people to say that "life" begins at conception (the genetic fusion of the gametes); see Franklin 1993). When Tom Ray pleads for an Internet-wide version of his Tierra system by saying that we've got to "give life a chance," he, like people in the "pro-life" movement, identifies "life" with genetic potential. Life, genetics, and information processing are melted into synonyms in the alchemical recombinations of Artificial Life.

In his book, *The Selfish Gene*, evolutionary biologist Richard Dawkins provides the sociobiological precedent and parallel for the view of organisms as gene machines: "We [humans] are the survival machines—robot vehicles blindly programmed to preserve the selfish molecules known as genes" (1976: ix). Dawkins's phrasing of the issue itself relies on a computational metaphor, illustrating the self-referential character of an Artificial Life that borrows ideas from a biology already filled with computational analogies. Many people in Artificial Life are trained in computer science, and some of their only biological reading has been of Dawkins' popular books. The ways the "robot vehicle" proposition lumbers into the way people talk can be astounding. At a Santa Fe Institute workshop on computation and evolutionary biology, one man remarked, "Here we are sitting around the table talking, when all we're about is replicating." The conceit that our "genes" express purposes that go beyond those of our own lives is given spiritual torque in Tom Ray's "An Evolutionary Approach to Synthetic Biology: Zen and the Art of Creating Life":

I prefer to achieve immortality in the old-fashioned organic evolutionary way, through my children. I hope to die in my patch of Costa Rican rain forest, surrounded by many thousands of wet and squishy species, and leave it all to my daughter. Let them set my body out in the jungle to be recycled into the ecosystem by the scavengers and decomposers. I will live on through the rain forest I preserved, the ongoing life in the ecosystem into which my material self is recycled, the memes spawned by my scientific works, and the genes in the daughter that my wife and I created. (1994a: 204)[16]

The image of genes as repositories for "life"—indeed, as tokens for personal immortality—expresses a Mendelian and neo-Darwinian worldview, one that in the present day motivates people to seek technological assistance to have children of "their own," and one that shapes Artificial Life scientists' efforts to ensure that their digital organisms can reproduce without hindrance.

Newly Reproductive Technologies: Genetic Algorithms and Assisting Artificial Life Couples to Have Children of Their Own

In many Artificial Life simulations, virtual organisms can "mate." Because Artificial Life organisms are made of information, "mating" in this context refers to the mutual exchange of computer code or bit strings.

"Mating" is usually accomplished through a "genetic algorithm," a computational procedure that can "evolve" solutions to complex problems by generating populations of possible solutions and by treating these solutions metaphorically as individuals that can "mate," "mutate," and "compete" to "survive" and "reproduce."[17] In Artificial Life systems, "solutions" would stand for different variants of a kind of program organism. Individuals in the genetic algorithm are represented ultimately as strings of zeroes and ones, and they can produce "offspring" using a procedure called crossover, thought of as analogous to "sexual recombination." As the inventor of the genetic algorithm puts it, "Biological chromosomes cross over one another when the two gametes meet to form a zygote, and so the process of crossover in genetic algorithms does in fact closely mimic its biological model" (Holland 1992: 68).[18] Algorithmist Lawrence Davis writes, "In nature, crossover occurs when two parents exchange parts of their corresponding chromosomes. In a genetic algorithm, crossover recombines the genetic material in two parent chromosomes to make two children" (1991: 16). The terms "parents" and "children" are routinely used to refer to genetic algorithm bit strings' "generational" relation to one another: "In reproduction, we use the parent selection technique to pick two *parent* chromosomes. The Reproduction Module applies the one-point crossover and mutate operator to those two parents to generate two new chromosomes, called *children*" (Davis 1991: 12).

There are a number of ways one might understand the exchange of bits between strings, but the metaphor of productive heterosexual coupling is gleefully emphasized by most researchers. David Goldberg writes, "With an active pool of strings looking for mates, simple crossover happens in two steps: (1) strings are mated randomly, using coin tosses to pair off the happy couples, and (2) mated string couples cross over, using coin tosses to select the crossing sites" (1989: 16). And John Holland writes, "As the genetic algorithm proceeds, strong rules mate and form offspring rules that combine their parents' building blocks" (1992: 71). In a popular account in Steven Levy's *Artificial Life*, we hear, "Next, the strings mated. In a mass marriage ceremony worthy of Rev. Moon, each string was randomly paired with another" (Levy 1992: 163). A notable algorithmist once said at the Santa Fe Institute that he thought intuitively about "crossover" in the genetic algorithm by "thinking about what it means to recombine my genes and my wife's genes." In these descriptions, monogamous heterosexual marriage (even if pairs are randomly selected) is considered a realistic template for natural processes of sexual coupling for reproduction. The common-sensicality of male-female procreative couplings is a resource for thinking about how crossover works in the genetic algorithm.

But there is something fishy (bacterial?) about the way genetic algorithm bit strings "reproduce." Although people routinely invoke human heterosexual coupling to talk about what goes on in the genetic algorithm, there is no "sexual" difference between genetic algorithm bit strings. Artificial organisms never ovulate or menstruate and are never pregnant.[19] The idea that mating can happen between structurally identical entities recalls what Evelyn Fox Keller has called the masculine bias of mathematical population genetics. In this discourse, all individuals are structurally equal, all just bags of genes. Keller writes:

Effectively bypassed with this representation were all the problems entailed by sexual difference, by the contingencies of mating and fertilization that resulted from the finitude of actual populations and also, simultaneously, all the ambiguities of the term reproduction as applied to organisms that neither make copies of themselves nor reproduce by themselves (1992b: 132).

"Sex" becomes an informational affair; no disorderly bodies intervene, and all is reduced to the all-important "seed." That this definition of sex has purchase on the popular imagination is evidenced by the practice of IVF, in which the "essence" of reproduction (as genetic) has been distilled into an out-of-body experience. Or, as one male Artificial Life researcher put it to me, in a sentence that is iconic of the ways genetic relatedness has been culturally isolated as the essential connection between organisms, "It doesn't make any difference whether people make babies in a test tube or by fucking."

When virtual organisms reproduce, they do so in artificial worlds that have been provided with a sort of computational imitation of natural selection; in this way, they "evolve." Under this regime, parent programs are understood to be eugenically fit and productive of offspring that are different from and fitter than they. Computer scientist John Koza writes, "The crossover operation produces two offspring. The two offspring are usually different from their two parents and different from each other. Each offspring contains some genetic material from each of its parents" (1992: 23). Holland writes, "The algorithm favors the fittest strings as parents, and so above-average strings will have more offspring in the next generation" (1992: 68). Eshelman et al. state that "two parents are selected according to fitness and material between them is exchanged to produce two children which replace them" (1989: 11). And Koza says, "The genetic process of sexual reproduction between two parental computer programs is used to create new offspring computer programs from two parental programs selected in proportion to fitness" (1992: 74–75). (See Figure 9.2 for a picture of two parental computer programs from Koza 1992; see also Figure 9.3 from Zhang and Mühlenbein 1993). This commitment to the proposition that children should be better off than their parents is premised on an understanding of kinship as a system that continually generates future possibilities. Marilyn Strathern describes this English and Euro-American cultural view of the future: "Increased variation and differentiation invariably lie ahead, a fragmented future as compared with a communal past. To be new is to be different. Time increases complexity." (Strathern 1992a: 21). Strathern maintains that for Euro-Americans, "Kinship delineated a developmental process that guaranteed diversity, the individuality of persons and the generation of future possibilities" (Strathern 1992a: 39). In this kin system, children are "new" "individuals" that emerge from parental relations.

Strathern argues that the Euro-American reproductive model is an algorithm for the generation of future possibilities—something of great use to those who would write programs that produce new programs. She writes of children what one might equally well write of the brave new organisms of Artificial Life and genetic algorithms:

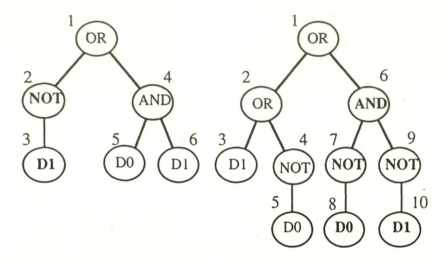

Figure 9.2. Two parental computer programs. From John Koza, *Genetic Programming: On the Programming of Computers by Means of Natural Selection* (Cambridge, Mass.: MIT Press, 1992), p. 101. Copyright 1992 Massachusetts Institute of Technology; reproduced with permission.

> The child's guarantee of individuality lies in genetic origin: its characteristics are the outcome of a chance combination from a range of possibilities. . . . Genetic potential . . . maintains an array of possible characteristics from which an entity might emerge; the future is known . . . by its unpredictability, and one would not necessarily wish to anticipate it. (Strathern 1992b: 172)

In the hegemonic folk kinship constructs of white, middle-class Euro-America, the act of heterosexual intercourse that "produces" children is thought to be the generative knot that produces "families" and makes people "related" (Schneider 1968). In Artificial Life, the relatedness of digital organisms is produced through couplings fashioned after this model. The people I interviewed were overwhelmingly white Euro-Americans, and David Schneider's reflections on white U.S. American kinship are directly relevant here: "In American cultural conception, kinship is defined as biogenetic. This definition says that kinship is whatever the biogenetic relationship is. If science discovers new facts about biogenetic relationship, then this is what kinship is and was all along" (1968: 23). For Artificial Lifers, who inhabit a world in which genetics has become an information science, kinship is becoming fundamentally informatic. It should be no surprise that Artificial Life researchers can speak of the relatedness of the information structures they think of as organisms.

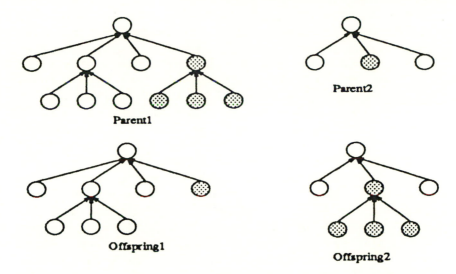

Figure 9.3. Crossover operation. From Byoung-Tak Zhang and Heinz Mühlenbein, "Genetic Programming of Neural Nets Using Occam's Razor," *Proceedings of the Fifth International Conference on Genetic Algorithms*, ed. Stephanie Forrest (San Mateo, Calif.: Morgan Kaufmann), pp. 342–49. Copyright 1993 Heinz Mühlenbein; reproduced with permission.

Genetic algorithm techniques, modeled after evolution, are quite instructive for understanding how Euro-Americans think about reproduction and kinship, since many Euro-Americans understand kinship to be a simple cultural recognition of biological "facts." Stories about reproduction, relatedness, and kinship are all made explicit in this Artificial Life formulation. What is most striking are the ways that, even in this heterosexual model, organisms are considered normatively masculine. There are both age-old and novel constructions of sex, gender, and reproduction here, and they combine in ways reminiscent of their mixings in the practices surrounding new reproductive technologies in the United States.

Reproducing Reproduction in Artificial Life

> Every day the urge grows stronger to get hold of an object at very close range by way of its likeness, its reproduction.
> —Walter Benjamin, *The Work of Art in the Age of Mechanical Reproduction*

That object that Artificial Life researchers want to get hold of is *life*, understood as reproducible in its essence, since its essence is considered to be a replicating information structure. For Artificial Life scientists who adhere to the idea that computers are alternative universes, replicating reproduction in computers will confirm for them that their ideas about how reproduction works are correct. It will also put them on the trail of the grail of Artificial Life: a self-reproducing program that mimics life so well that it transubstantiates into an instance of life itself.

How is it that programs ultimately presented as visual data on computer screens can be said to "live," "die," "evolve," and "reproduce"? Richard Doyle has noted that "what makes possible the substitution of the signs of life for life is the reproducibility of 'life-like behavior,' a reproducibility that ultimately points to the fact that ALife organisms are themselves reproductions, simulations and performances cut off from any 'essence' of life" (1993: 226). Artificial Life organisms can "reproduce" precisely because it is possible to reproduce behaviors in a computer that fulfill particular cultural definitions of "life" and biological reproduction, definitions that these days conflate the two and envision them as processes of copying information.

In "The Work of Art in the Age of Mechanical Reproduction," Walter Benjamin argues that when a work of art is mass-reproduced, it enters into a sphere of existence that robs it of its uniqueness, its authenticity, its "aura" ([1936] 1968). Following Benjamin's romantic impulse, we might say that when "life" is reproduced *in silico*, it enters into a sphere of existence that robs it of its authenticity and essence. Parting company with the nostalgia of Benjamin and the empiricism of Artificial Life scientists, though, we might also say that it enters into contexts that reveal that there never was an "essence" of life.[20] Continuing this curve of thinking, we could say that when reproduction is reproduced in computers, we learn that what we call reproduction emerges out of a cluster of cultural and scientific definitions and practices. We learn too that calling it "reproduction" itself indexes a set of commitments that make thinkable its duplication in computers.

Artificial Life scientists see themselves as ushering in a new stage of evolution, one in which new life forms will be birthed through scientific conceptions that lead to self-reproducing computer programs. They view biological reproduction and the machinic reproduction they are engineering as parts of a larger evolutionary story, and they see themselves as "in the employ" of evolution, creating new life forms that will unchain themselves from carbon chemistry, perhaps traveling off-planet in the silicon splendor of robot bodies. Artificial Life researchers can claim that organic biological reproduction can be subsumed, transcended, and devoured by new technobiological reproduction because they participate in a culture that uses the word "reproduction" to refer to both the perpetuation of practices and ideas and the generation of new organic beings (see Harris and Young 1981). This is how Artificial Life has become thinkable.

Marilyn Strathern has commented that the Euro-American reproductive model "makes us greedy for both change and continuity, as though one could bring about momentous (episodic) change while still being regarded as the continuous (evolutionary) originators of it" (1992b:177). These words illuminate the cultural logic beneath Artificial Life researchers' contentions that the manufacture of Artificial Life is both novel and evolutionarily inevitable.[21] When Langton writes, "The creation of life is not an act to be undertaken lightly. We must do what we can to ensure that the future is equally bright for both our technological and our biological offspring" (1992: 22), we learn that reproduction is the real fuel for Euro-American time travel into the future.

Langton has suggested that Artificial Life will expand biology's purview to include not just *life-as-we-know-it*, but also *life-as-it-could-be* (1989: 2). Given this extraordinary charter, it is perhaps surprising that Artificial Life stories about generation are so commonplace, that they reiterate all-too-familiar stories about monogenetic masculine creations of life, that they are stories about "reproduction" or about a kind of "recombination" that makes all parents into clones of a naked and masculine "seed."

But Artificial Life is certainly the child of Western life science, and so inherits assumptions from mainstream evolutionary biology and its sociobiological cousins. Artificial Life scientists' imitations of nature often tend to be recreational vehicles into dominant nostalgias for the natural, into places populated with *life-as-it-should-be.* These constructions matter for those of us who do not do the science, because Artificial Life practitioners hope to produce knowledges that will count as legitimate biology and because they also hope to use their techniques to manufacture new ways of thinking about and fashioning computer programs that can be used by engineers, business people, social planners, and others.[22]

I've focused on a narrow but influential band of Artificial Life research, a band associated primarily with Santa Fe Institute computationalists, but there are those in Artificial Life who see the discipline as fixing attention on the artifactual character of our visions of "nature." As one organismic biologist involved with the field said to me, "We are participants in making nature what it is. . . . The things we understand as life . . . actually have the status of the artificial. They are artifacts of our own thinking . . . [Artificial Life] will force upon us the realization that science is our construct." If we think on this possibility, we might see Artificial Life alongside new reproductive technologies as a practice in which fragments and foundations of the "natural" are both solidified and liquefied, in which ideas about the given and the inevitable become newly contestable. Artificial Life resurrects old ideas in new computer codes, but, as Strathern reminds us, novel twists on received texts are always possible: "The ideas that reproduce themselves in our communications *never reproduce themselves exactly.* They are always found in environments or contexts that have their own properties or characteristics" (1992b: 6). Following Sarah Franklin, who has written that "reproduction in the context of the new genetic sciences is not so much 'enterprised-up' as it is 'camped-up', in a mocking representation of 'the real thing' it simulates" (Franklin 1995: 71–72), we might see in Artificial Life a practice in which programs cross-dress as organisms and in the process force us to question what we mean by categories—such as "reproduction," "gender," and "life"—that we have assumed to be "natural." Seeing things this way may open paths toward considering Artificial Life practice as potentially subversive in epistemologically and politically progressive ways. These are paths, of course, that can be blazed only in the contexts of power, and the constellations of patriarchy, masculinity, and heterosexuality within which Artificial Life presently exists should make us careful about thinking about whether Artificial Life can deliver in any radical way on its promise of showing us *life-as-it-could-be.*

Many thanks to Sarah Franklin and Helena Ragoné for inviting me to think through my material on Artificial Life through the optic of NRTs and for pressing me through various drafts of my argument. This essay has also benefited from conversations with Jane Collier, Carol Delaney, Richard Doyle, Helen Gremillion, Heather Paxson, Kiersten Johnson, Dmitry Portnoy, and Jennifer Reardon, as well as from comments from two anonymous reviewers. My gratitude also goes to the many Artificial Life researchers I interviewed, who allowed me to do fieldwork among them even as they knew that they would find peculiar the contexts in which I would reproduce their words.

Notes

1. This category encompasses assemblages ranging from the immune system to the global economy.

2. Some biologists have argued that gendered notions of information and material, seed and soil, blocked the recognition of the role of the ovum in conception until 1826 and contributed to views of nucleic acid as active and cytoplasm as passive (see Fausto-Sterling [1985] 1992). It is still true today that in stories about mammalian conception, the sperm is often said to "activate" a passive egg and set its cytoplasmic machinery into motion (see Martin 1991). The active role of the egg's cytoplasm in regulating the DNA of both egg and sperm is overlooked.

3. I mean here to reference the fact that in U.S. American society, "genetic" mothers have often been legally constructed as "real" mothers—more "real" than the "birth mothers" who contract to gestate zygotes produced with other women's eggs.

4. Thanks to Kiersten Johnson for putting me on the path toward this parade of primal puns.

5. Note that the three letter suffix could as easily reference "tom" or "ray."

6. Webster's Ninth Collegiate Dictionary defines "to father" as "to beget" or "to make oneself the founder, producer, or author of." Note that "the idea of fathering invention refers to thought or knowledge as much as it does progeny in a more familiar sense" (Sarah Franklin, personal correspondence).

7. Jane Collier suggested to me that masculine notions of parenting in Western culture seemed to inform how Artificial Life researchers described their relationships to their systems. Artificial Life researchers fashion themselves as creators/fathers who can inseminate virtual worlds and then continue about other business. Their creatures do not need any feeding or nurturing and are supposed to grow up quickly and become independent.

8. This man did not think the fact that there were more men than women in the field was significant, because this kind of gender skew is present in many other fields. To me, this would suggest that we look for the traces of gender in the knowledge produced by those other disciplines.

9. The symbolic association of men with "culture" and of women with "nature" has been a recurring theme in Western sexual politics and epistemology. In "Is Female to Male as Nature Is to Culture?" Sherry Ortner (1974) maintained that this association exists cross-culturally. Many feminist anthropologists have since argued that Ortner universalized this association when she should have been questioning it and examining how it has been historically constituted in Western political and social theory.

10. Thanks to Kiersten Johnson for this turn of phrase.

11. That the science of Artificial Life proceeds largely through trying to materialize metaphors in computer technologies does not mean that it could or should do otherwise. Science is fundamentally enabled by practices of analogy. Attending to how this is so does not diminish our understanding of scientific activity as scientific. It does, however, allow us to understand how science is always already located in the cultural, social, and political environment in which it is crafted. It also allows us to meditate on how our sciences might be otherwise, in other contexts. For an introduction to the literature on science and metaphor, see Hesse 1966 and Stepan 1993.

12. The analogy is clear in Ray's writings: "The organic genetic language is written with an alphabet consisting of four different nucleotides. Groups of three nucleotides form sixty-four 'words' (codons), which are translated into twenty amino acids by the molecular machinery of the cell. The machine language is written with sequences of two voltages (bits) which we conceptually represent as ones and zeros. The number of bits that form a 'word' (machine instruction) varies." (1994a: 185–86).

13. It is not simply the identification of information with life that vivifies digital organisms; it is the claim that they exhibit "life-like" dynamics, that they *behave* as if they were alive. If one has defined this behavior as "informatic replication with modification," however, then Artificial Life simulations can come to life rather easily.

14. Thanks to Richard Doyle for this image.

15. I would argue that the prevalent description of DNA as a text that is translated and transcribed secularizes the Judeo-Christian idea that the Word determines the form of matter in Creation. Genetic determinism replaces a doctrine of predestination when the divine and unquestionable authority of the biblical text is replaced by the unquestionable authority of the genetic text. "It is genetic" becomes the equivalent of "It is written."

16. By "memes," Ray means ideas. "Meme" is a coinage of Dawkins's, used to refer to units of "cultural inheritance" analytically akin to genes.

In this passage, Ray's list of the multiple ways that he might gain immortality actually troubles a simple story about genes. And his sentiments about genes only partially resonate with his rhetoric around Tierra. Monogenesis, for example, does not frame his account of the procreation of his human daughter. But the model of bilateral inheritance Ray deploys does preserve a focus on genes, a focus that continues a masculinist fixation on form over matter, as I argue in the next section.

17. The genetic algorithm is used by many engineers and computer scientists who see it as a tool for generating solutions to difficult problems. Most of these people are not concerned with the question whether bit strings in the genetic algorithm are alive.

18. For computer scientist John Koza it mimics biology so closely that it might be considered "real" crossover, or even "real" sex:

> The *crossover* (sexual recombination) operation for genetic programming creates variation in the population by producing new offspring that consist of parts taken from each parent. The crossover operation starts with two parental S-expressions and produces two offspring S-expressions. That is, it is a sexual operation. (1992: 101)

Considering evolution as an abstract process implementable in different media allows sex to be similarly reified, even to the point that computer programs can "really" have sex. This conflation of "sex" with recombination is enabled by a relentlessly heterosexist view of what counts as sex.

19. There are some efforts to introduce sexual differentiation into genetic algorithms and into some Artificial Life simulations, by adding parameters for fertility and so on. David Goldberg has outlined a diploidic reproductive scheme for the genetic algorithm which, in the course of reproducing diploid bit strings, activates program procedures named "gametogenesis" and "fertilization" (1989: 162–65). I do not include much about these efforts here because they are very preliminary. It goes without saying that it will be informative to track their development.

20. Benjamin argues that films achieve effects of naturalness only through the greatest artifice: the artifice that erases its own presence. "The equipment-free aspect of reality here has become the height of artifice; the sight of immediate reality has become an orchid in the land of technology" ([1936] 1968: 233). Following Benjamin, I would argue that artificial life is seen as real when people can be persuaded to ignore the technology of the computer and look only at the life-like shapes and behaviors dancing on the screen.

Because the Tierra system and most genetic algorithm programs are not very visually compelling, I have left to one side the ways that Artificial Life creatures in many more aesthetically rich systems are manufactured as "living" for scientists through technologies of visualization. There are suggestive similarities here with recent practices of imaging blastocysts, zygotes, embryos, and fetuses inside women's bodies through technologies such as electron microscopy and ultrasound (see Duden 1993, Haraway 1995). What is remarkable about these sorts of imagings is that they assume the existence of the entities they purport to represent, and so, in a very material sense, end up *producing* embryos and fetuses as real, as already existing, as "individuals," and even as "lives" (see Duden 1993). Images of artificial life forms on the screens of computers accomplish the vivification of entities through a similar activity of visualizing entities presumed to be real but invisible. Here are entities, some researchers say, that are hidden from the spectator's view because they ultimately exist as patterns of voltage in the computer, but that, with suitable technology, can be rendered visible as patterns on a computer screen. We might say of these Artificial Life organisms what Donna Haraway has said for images of the fetus: "The visual image of the fetus is like the DNA double helix—not just a signifier of life, but also offered as the thing-in-itself. The visual fetus, like the gene, is a technoscientific sacrament. The sign becomes the thing itself in ordinary magico-secular transubstantiation" (1997: 178).

In "Lesbian Bodies in the Age of (Post)mechanical Reproduction," Cathy Griggers writes about how the "authenticity" of (in her argument, specifically lesbian) social identities erodes as the signs of those identities are reproduced in a variety of cultural contexts (movies, videos, advertisements, etc.):

> The cultural reproduction of lesbian bodies in the age of (post)mechanical reproduction, that is, in an economy of simulacral repetition, has more than ever destroyed any aura of an "original" lesbian identity, while exposing the cultural sites through which lesbianism is appropriated by the political economy of postmodernity. (1993: 180)

Walter Benjamin reproduces a useful quote on silent film from Italian playwright Luigi Pirandello:

> "The film actor," wrote Pirandello, "feels as if in exile—exiled not only from the stage but also from himself. With a vague sense of discomfort he feels inexplicable emptiness: his body loses its corporeality, it evaporates, it is deprived of reality, life, voice, and the noises caused by his moving about, in order to be changed into a mute image, flickering an instant on the screen, then vanishing into silence. (Benjamin 1936: 229, reproducing a quote from Léon Pierre-Quint 1927)

The actor is presented to us without his aura, without that which makes him "real." A critic sympathetic to Benjamin's nostalgia might argue that Artificial Life forms are exiles from the organic world, exiles that cannot share in the aura of the original living things after which they are modeled. I find this thought useful, but would argue that if people come to believe—as many Artificial Life people actually do—that the essence of life can be discerned in the fidgeting of information structures, then computational organisms can indeed share in the "aura" of the living. Artificial Life flags the possibility that identifying life has become a question of socially and politically located aesthetics.

Sarah Franklin suggested to me that the "aura" that might eventually stick to Artificial Life organisms may not grow so much from the "lost attraction of mystery" as from a "palpable sense of command control" (personal correspondence, 17 April 1995).

21. And like new reproductive technologies, Artificial Life technology is seen as a technology that is the byproduct of the "natural" condition of humans as "cultural" beings (see Franklin 1993: 540). In a talk at MIT in July 1994, Christopher Langton argued that since artificial life is made by humans, who are made by nature, artificial life should be seen as a natural phenomenon. He argued that "Technology is the current state of nature," that we now inhabit what might be called "techno-nature," and that human technological participation in the order of nature should be modeled after "how ecology would want to behave" (1994a).

22. Artificial Life, pursued mostly in universities and in research establishments like the Santa Fe Institute, is funded by such agencies as the National Science Foundation and the Department of Energy, and by a variety of private companies like Apple and Citicorp. People working for these entities hope that "naturalistic" modes of computation can be used for such activities as managing just-in-time manufacturing regimes and for building simulation tools for ecological modeling, social forecasting, military strategizing, and urban planning.

References

Ackley, David and Michael Littman. 1992a. "Interactions Between Learning and Evolution." In *Artificial Life II*, ed. Christopher Langton, Charles Taylor,

Doyne Farmer, and Steen Rasmussen. Redwood City, Calif.: Addison-Wesley, pp. 487–509.

——. 1992b. "Learning from Natural Selection in an Artificial Environment." In *Artificial Life II Video Proceedings*, ed. Christopher Langton. Redwood City, Calif.: Addison-Wesley.

Aristotle. (1979). *Generation of Animals.* Trans. A. L. Peck. Loeb Classical Library. Cambridge, Mass.: Harvard University Press.

Benjamin, Walter. (1936) 1968. "The Work of Art in the Age of Mechanical Reproduction," trans. Harry Zohn. In *Illuminations*, ed. Hannah Arendt. New York: Shocken Books, pp. 217–51.

Brooks, Rodney and Pattie Maes, eds. 1994. *Artificial Life IV.* Cambridge, Mass.: MIT Press.

Butler, Judith. 1993. *Bodies That Matter: On the Discursive Limits of "Sex."* New York: Routledge.

Davis, Lawrence, ed. 1991. *Handbook of Genetic Algorithms.* New York: Van Nostrand Reinhold.

Dawkins, Richard. 1976. *The Selfish Gene.* Oxford: Oxford University Press.

Delaney, Carol. 1991. *The Seed and the Soil: Gender and Cosmology in Turkish Village Society.* Berkeley: University of California Press.

de Lauretis, Teresa. 1987. "The Technology of Gender." In *Technologies of Gender: Essays on Theory, Film, and Fiction.* Bloomington: Indiana University Press, pp. 1–30.

Doyle, Richard. 1993. "On Beyond Living: Rhetorics of Vitality and Post-Vitality in Molecular Biology." Doctoral dissertation, University of California, Berkeley.

Duden, Barbara. 1993. "Visualizing Life." *Science as Culture* 3, 4: 562–600.

Easlea, Brian. 1983. *Fathering the Unthinkable: Masculinity, Scientists, and the Arms Race.* London: Pluto Press.

Eshelman, Larry J., Richard A. Caruana, and J. David Schaffer. 1989. "Biases in the Crossover Landscape." In *Proceedings of the Third International Conference on Genetic Algorithms*, ed. J. David Schaffer. San Mateo, Calif.: Morgan Kaufmann, pp. 10–19.

Farmer, Doyne and Alletta d'A. Belin. 1992. "Artificial Life: The Coming Evolution." In *Artificial Life II*, ed. Christopher Langton, Charles Taylor, Doyne Farmer, and Steen Rasmussen. Redwood City, Calif.: Addison-Wesley, pp. 815–40.

Fausto-Sterling, Anne. (1985) 1992. *Myths of Gender: Biological Theories About Men and Women*, rev. ed. New York: Basic Books.

Franklin, Sarah. 1993. "Postmodern Procreation: Representing Reproductive Practice." *Science as Culture* 3, 4: 522–61.

——. 1995. "Romancing the Helix: Nature and Scientific Discovery." In *Romance Revisited*, ed. Lynne Pearce and Jackie Stacey. London: Lawrence and Wishart, pp. 63–77.

Goldberg, David E. 1989. *Genetic Algorithms in Search, Optimization, and Machine Learning.* Reading, Mass.: Addison-Wesley.

Griggers, Cathy. 1993. "Lesbian Bodies in the Age of (Post)mechanical Reproduction." In *Fear of a Queer Planet: Queer Politics and Social Theory*, ed. Michael Warner. Minneapolis: University of Minnesota Press, pp. 178–93.

Haraway, Donna J. 1997. *Modest Witness@Second Millennium—FemaleMan© Inc. Meets Oncomouse™: Feminism and Technoscience.* New York: Routledge.

Harris, Olivia and Kate Young. 1981. "Engendered Structures: Some Problems in the Analysis of Reproduction." In *The Anthropology of Pre-Capitalist Societies*, ed. Joel S. Kahn and Josep R. Llobera. London: Macmillan, pp. 109–47.

Hayles, N. Katherine. 1994. "Narratives of Evolution and the Evolution of Narratives." In *Cooperation and Conflict in General Evolutionary Processes*, ed. John L. Casti and Anders Karlqvist. New York: John Wiley, pp. 113–32.

Hesse, Mary. 1966. *Models and Analogies in Science.* Notre Dame, Ind.: University of Notre Dame Press.

Hogeweg, Paulien. 1989. "Mirror Beyond Mirror: Puddles of Life." In *Artificial cial Life*, ed. Christopher Langton. Redwood City, Calif.: Addison-Wesley, pp. 297–316.

Holland, John H. 1992. "Genetic Algorithms." *Scientific American* 267, 1: 66–72.

Keller, Evelyn Fox. 1992a. "From Secrets of Life to Secrets of Death." In *Secrets of Life, Secrets of Death: Essays on Language, Gender, and Science.* New York: Routledge, pp. 39–55.

———. 1992b. "Language and Ideology in Evolutionary Theory, Part II: The Language of Reproductive Autonomy." In *Secrets of Life, Secrets of Death: Essays on Language, Gender and Science.* New York: Routledge, pp. 128–43.

Kelly, Kevin. 1991. "Designing Perpetual Novelty: Selected Notes from the Second Artificial Life Conference." In *Doing Science*, ed. John Brockman. Englewood Cliffs, N.J.: Prentice-Hall, pp. 1–44.

Koza, John. 1992. *Genetic Programming: On the Programming of Computers by Means of Natural Selection.* Cambridge, Mass.: MIT Press.

Laing, Richard. 1989. "Artificial Organisms: History, Problems, Directions." In *Artificial Life*, ed. Christopher Langton. Redwood City, Calif.: Addison-Wesley, pp. 49–62.

Langton, Christopher. 1988. "Toward Artificial Life." *Whole Earth Review* 58: 74–79.

———. 1989a. "Artificial Life." In *Artificial Life*, ed. Christopher Langton. Redwood City, Calif.: Addison-Wesley, pp. 1–47.

———, ed. 1989b. *Artificial Life.* Redwood City, Calif.: Addison-Wesley.

———. 1992. "Introduction to Artificial Life II." In *Artificial Life II*, ed. Christopher Langton, Charles Taylor, Doyne Farmer, and Steen Rasmussen. Redwood City, Calif.: Addison-Wesley, pp. 3–38.

———. 1994a. Paper presented at Massachusetts Institute of Technology.

———, ed. 1994b. *Artificial Life III.* Redwood City, Calif.: Addison-Wesley.

Langton, Christopher G., Charles Taylor, J. Doyne Farmer, and Steen Rasmussen, eds. 1992. *Artificial Life II.* Redwood City, Calif.: Addison-Wesley.

Levy, Steven. 1992. *Artificial Life: The Quest for a New Creation.* New York: Pantheon.

Martin, Emily. 1991. "The Egg and the Sperm: How Science Has Constructed a Romance Based on Stereotypical Male-Female Roles." *Signs* 16, 31: 485–501.

Maurer, Bill. 1991. "Warriors of the Gulf: New Technologies, New Masculinities?" Manuscript.

Ortner, Sherry. 1974. "Is Female to Male as Nature Is to Culture?" In *Woman, Culture, and Society*, ed. Michelle Zimbalist Rosaldo and Louise Lamphere. Stanford, Calif.: Stanford University Press, pp. 67–87.

Oyama, Susan. 1985. *The Ontogeny of Information: Developmental Systems and Evolution.* Cambridge: Cambridge University Press.

Pierre-Quint, Leon. 1927. "Signification du cinéma." *L'Art Cinématographique*, 2.

Putnam, Jeffrey. 1993. "A Primordial Soup Environment." In *ECAL 93: Self Organisation and Life: From Simple Rules to Global Complexity*, ed. J. L. Deneubourg,

S. Goss, G. Nicolis, H. Bersini, and R. Dagonnier. Photocopied proceedings from the Second European Conference on Artificial Life, pp. 943–61.

Ray, Thomas. 1992a. "An Approach to the Synthesis of Life." In *Artificial Life II*, ed. Christopher Langton, Charles Taylor, Doyne Farmer, and Steen Rasmussen. Redwood City, Calif.: Addison-Wesley, pp. 371–408.

———. 1992b. "Natural Evolution of Machine Codes: Digital Organisms." In *Santa Fe Institute Proposal for a Research Program in Adaptive Computation*. Santa Fe, N.M.: Santa Fe Institute.

———. 1994a. "An Evolutionary Approach to Synthetic Biology: Zen and the Art of Creating Life." *Artificial Life* 1, 1–2: 179–210.

———. 1994b. "A Proposal to Create a Network-Wide Biodiversity Reserve for Digital Organisms." Paper presented at Artificial Life IV, MIT, Cambridge, Mass., July 6–8.

Reynolds, Craig. 1994. "Competition, Coevolution, and the Game of Tag." In *Artificial Life IV*, ed. Rodney Brooks and Pattie Maes. Cambridge, Mass.: MIT Press, pp. 59–69.

Santa Fe Institute. 1993. *Annual Report on Scientific Programs*. Santa Fe, N.M.: Santa Fe Institute.

Schneider, David. 1968. *American Kinship: A Cultural Account*. Chicago: University of Chicago Press.

Schrödinger, Erwin. 1944. *What Is Life?* Cambridge: Cambridge University Press.

Sims, Karl. 1992. "Panspermia." *Artificial Life II Video Proceedings*, ed. Christopher Langton. Redwood City, Calif.: Addison-Wesley.

Stepan, Nancy Leys. 1993. "Race and Gender: The Role of Analogy in Science." In *The "Racial" Economy of Science: Toward a Democratic Future*, ed. Sandra Harding. Bloomington: Indiana University Press, pp. 359–76.

Strathern, Marilyn. 1992a. *After Nature: English Kinship in the Late Twentieth Century*. Cambridge: Cambridge University Press.

———. 1992b. *Reproducing the Future: Anthropology, Kinship, and the New Reproductive Technologies*. New York: Routledge.

Taylor, Charles, David Jefferson, Scott Turner, and Seth Goldman. 1989. "RAM: Artificial Life for the Exploration of Complex Biological Systems." In *Artificial Life*, ed. Christopher Langton. Redwood City, Calif: Addison-Wesley, pp. 275–96.

Tuana, Nancy. 1989. "The Weaker Seed: The Sexist Bias of Reproductive Theory." In *Feminism and Science*, ed. Nancy Tuana. Bloomington: Indiana University Press, pp. 147–71.

Varela, Francisco J. and Paul Bourgine, eds. 1992. *Toward a Practice of Autonomous Systems: Proceedings of the First European Conference on Artificial Life*. Cambridge, Mass.: MIT Press/Bradford Books.

Yaeger, Larry. 1994. "PolyWorld: Life in a New Context." In *Artificial Life III*, ed. Christopher Langton. Redwood City, Calif.: Addison-Wesley, pp. 263–98.

Zhang, Byoung-Tak and Heinz Mühlenbein. 1993. "Genetic Programming of Minimal Neural Nets Using Occam's Razor." In *Proceedings of the Fifth International Conference on Genetic Algorithms*, ed. Stephanie Forrest. San Mateo, Calif.: Morgan Kaufmann, pp. 342–49.

Contributors

Carole H. Browner is a professor in the Department of Psychiatry and Biobehavioral Sciences, and in the Department of Anthropology at UCLA. She is a social anthropologist whose research interests lie at the intersection of gender, health, and social change. She has worked in urban Colombia on unwanted pregnancy and illegal abortion, in rural Mexico on the impact of local political relations on the gendered politics of reproduction, and in the United States on the growing role that medicalization, particularly information derived from medical testing, is playing in the experience and management of low risk pregnancies. Her current work focuses on how Mexican-origin couples living in the United States interpret the concept of risk in pregnancy and use it in their decisions about fetal diagnostic testing. She is also investigating homeless women's access to and use of reproductive health care services in Los Angeles and obstacles to cervical cancer screening among Latinas on both sides of the U.S.-Mexican border.

Charis Cussins is a NSF postdoctoral research fellow in the department of Science and Technology Studies at Cornell University. She has recently completed a dissertation entitled *Technologies of Personhood: Human Reproductive Technologies*. She has published papers on human and non-human reproduction, focusing on infertility medicine and on wildlife conservation.

Sarah Franklin is a lecturer in the Department of Sociology at Lancaster University. She is also a member of the Lancaster University Institute for Women's Studies. She is the editor of *The Sociology of Gender* (1996) and the author of *Embodied Progress; a Cultural Account of Assisted Conception* (1996).

Corinne P. Hayden is a doctoral candidate in cultural anthropology at the University of California, Santa Cruz. She has written previously on kinship and lesbian motherhood in the United States, and her doctoral research explores constructions of property, (bio)diversity, and

conservation in the context of a biodiversity prospecting agreement
between Mexico and the United States.

Stefan Helmreich is an external faculty fellow at the Center for the
Critical Analysis of Contemporary Culture at Rutgers. He is writing
an ethnography of Artificial Life scientists at the Santa Fe Institute
for the Sciences of Complexity, where he conducted anthropological fieldwork in 1993–94. He completed his Ph.D. in anthropology at
Stanford in 1995 and finished his article for this volume while working
as a postdoctoral associate in the Department of Science and Technology Studies at Cornell.

Judith Modell received her Ph.D. in Anthropology from the University of Minnesota in 1978. She is currently an Associate Professor of
Anthropology, History, and Art at Carnegie Mellon University. Publications include *Ruth Benedict: Patterns of a Life* (University of Pennsylvania Press, 1983); *Kinship with Strangers: Adoption and Interpretations
of Kinship in American Culture* (1994). A book on Homestead, Pennsylvania in collaboration with a documentary photographer is currently
under review. Her new research projects include work on adoption,
foster care, and family policy in Hawai'i; a book on open adoption in
the United States; a life-history of a Hawaiian man. Her interests are
in kinship, family, and the links between interpretations of those concepts and the policies imposed by national and state institutions.

Laury Oaks is a Ph.D. candidate in Anthropology and Population Dynamics at Johns Hopkins University. In addition to her research in
the Republic of Ireland, she has published on the cultural politics of
reproductive rights in Japan. Her dissertation analyzes the politics of
pregnant women's lifestyles, fetal care, and public health warnings on
prenatal risks in the United States.

Nancy Press is Associate Research Anthropologist in the Department of
Psychiatry and Biobehavioral Sciences of the UCLA School of Medicine. Her areas of interest are women's health and genetics, including issues in bioethics and the cultural construction of risk. Past research focused on the use of the noninvasive, maternal serum alpha
fetoprotein screening test, in the context of a California mandate to
offer testing to every pregnant woman. She is currently co-Principal
Investigator on an NIH grant to study women's and health care providers' attitudes toward genetic susceptibility testing for breast cancer.
Dr. Press is a collaborator as well on a Hastings Center project to examine the societal tensions inherent in the co-existence of wide-scale
prenatal testing and the growing disability rights movement. Dr. Press
is the sole social scientist on the Task Force on Genetic Testing of the
National Center for Human Genome Research.

Helena Ragoné teaches anthropology at the University of Massachusetts-Boston. She is the author of *Surrogate Motherhood: Conception in the Heart* (1994) and co-editor of *Situated Lives: Gender and Culture in Everyday Life* (1997). Her current writing projects include *Distant Kin: Gestational Surrogacy and Egg Donation* and an ethnography tentatively entitled *Riding Danger: Women in Horse Culture.* She is co-editor of an upcoming volume, *Ideologies and Technologies of Motherhood: Race, Class, Religion, and Nationalism.*

Janelle S. Taylor is currently completing her dissertation in anthropology at the University of Chicago, on the topic of obstetrical ultrasound. Her work has also appeared in *Public Culture, Science as Culture, Techniques et culture,* and *Journal of Diagnostic Medical Sonography.* The present essay was selected for the 1996 Nicholas C. Mullins Award of the Society for Social Studies of Science.

Index